HANNIBAL

Sir Gavin de Beer

HANNIBAL

*Challenging
Rome's Supremacy*

A Studio Book
THE VIKING PRESS
New York

Published in 1969 by The Viking Press, Inc.
625 Madison Avenue, New York, N. Y. 10022
SBN 670–36048–1
Library of Congress catalog card number: 75–80030
Second printing February 1970
Printed and bound in West Germany by
Mohndruck Reinhard Mohn OHG Gütersloh

CONTENTS

A witch, by fear, not force, like Hannibal,
Drives back our troops

(1 *Hen. VI.* i. 5. 21, 22)

Preface

THE STORY OF HANNIBAL is a tragedy, the inevitable outcome of conflict between different ideals and customs, built up between different races during the previous thousand years into a situation where rivalry and lust for riches, land, and power, between the two great Mediterranean nations of the day, could only burst into violent explosion.

Seen against the thickness of time, Hannibal's endeavours to save his native city, Carthage, were doomed to failure before he ever started, and there is some reason to think that he knew it. He risked everything on one last long throw, and lost, and could not begin again because his tools were not only worn out but taken from him. If there had been a major female figure in his life or background, Shakespeare might have used him as a theme. But apart from the shadowy figure of his wife Imilce, the ephemeral and equivocal role of Sophonisba, and the ghost of Dido (the last two of whom did provide characters for dramatic art), Hannibal's story is one long struggle between men, the result of which decided the pattern of subsequent European history for two thousand years.

It is necessary, in order to understand the moves of the chief pieces on the chessboard, to glance at the other pieces, where they came from, the squares that they stood in, and the ways in which they moved. This is why a preliminary look must be cast at the cradle of western civilization, and its chief inhabitants three thousand years ago. Ligurians and Gauls, Minoans and Greeks, Phoenicians and Carthaginians, Etruscans and Romans all play their parts. For long, it was Carthaginians against Greeks, with infant Rome on the side-lines. Then it was Rome against her own neighbours, Etruscans, Gauls, and Samnites. Finally it was Rome against Carthage, with all that that meant.

The curtain-raiser for the big clash was the First Punic War, as a result of which Rome for the first time became an imperial power with sea-power, and Hamilcar prepared for the second round by building a personal empire in Spain. This round was started by his son Hannibal, who then performed his astounding feat of moving an army from Spain to Italy by land over the Alps. This subject has occupied me for nearly forty years, and for details of the argument and references, I must refer the reader to my previous books (see Bibliography). This is not a text-book of ancient history, or of military or naval strategy or tactics. The only aim has been to provide a text which is readable and as accurate as possible, without subjecting the reader to digressions on textual criticism, source-criticism, critical apparatus, or exhaustive bibliographical references. One difficulty is that on the chief actor in the drama, Hannibal, nothing whatever has come down to posterity written by him or by his own people. Everything that is known about him has come from, or through the hands of, his deadly enemies the Romans. It is as if a history of Napoleon were written solely from British sources.

The main feature in Hannibal's history was, undoubtedly, his passage of the Alps, which has not failed to fascinate for two thousand years. It was, however, only one dramatic feature in a much larger series of events, and it must be led up to, and led away from, and that is why this book starts with the Stage and its Players.

Valuable new research has come to light as a result of the Symposium on Hannibalic Studies, published in the *Annuario* of the *Accademia Etrusca di Cortona*, to which reference is made in the Bibliography. Here, I should like to express my thanks to Professore Celestina Bruschetti, Secretary of that Academy, to Professore Giancarlo Susini for sending to me the results of his remarkable researches, and to Mr I. de Courcy Lyons for kindly putting me in touch with the Academy.

G. de B.

North entrance to the Palace of Minos at Knossos, Crete. Mastery in the Mediterranean has always depended on sea-power, and Minoans had it until the cataclysm of Santorin destroyed their empire. Sea-power was next exercised by Mycenaean Greeks, and then by Phoenicians and Carthaginians

I The Stage and the Players

LIGURIANS AND GAULS, MINOANS AND GREEKS

THE EARLIEST INHABITANTS of western Europe of which history speaks were the Ligurians, dark-haired people who covered the country stretching from the Mediterranean to the Ocean, which means the Bay of Biscay and the English Channel. When the Celts came from eastern Europe in the second millennium BC, fair-haired Gauls with their knowledge of metals and battle-axes, they subdued the Ligurians who were then able to maintain an independent existence only in the south of present-day France, the southern Alps between France and Italy, and the chain of hills which follows the curve of the Riviera behind Genoa, the province of Liguria extending into Apuania with its marble town of Carrara.

The Ligurians also continued, for a time, to live independently in the southern part of Provence, east of the Rhône and south of the Durance, until in 121 BC it was incorporated in the Roman Province; but their mountain tribes in the Alps and the Apennines were not subdued until the reign of Augustus, who commemorated the victory in the triumphal monument of La Turbie, near Monaco. The Ligurians therefore occupied the Alpine regions, on both the west and east sides of the watershed, when Hannibal crossed the Alps in 218 BC.

As the Ligurians were certainly pre-Indo-European and are related to the Basques, it means that the Basques are also pre-Indo-European, and together they formed the Neolithic Mediterranean race of western Europe, which the Indo-Europeans in the form of Celts or Gauls overran.

The invaders, in Gaul as well as in Britain, were Indo-European Celts. In Caesar's *Commentaries on the Gallic War*, the seven words which open the first chapter are well known, but often misunderstood. When he wrote that all Gaul is divided into three parts, he meant the rough subdivisions between the country north-east of the line of the Seine and the Marne, the country between that line and the Garonne, and

The triumphal monument of Augustus at La Turbie near Monaco, built in 6 BC to commemorate the Roman victory over the Ligurian tribes who lived along the Riviera and in the Western Alps

the country south-west of the Garonne. But Caesar went on to say that the inhabitants of these three parts of Gaul differed in their customs and their language. North-east of the Seine-Marne line, the Belgae, germanized Celts; between Seine-Marne and Garonne the Gauls, true Celts; south-west of the Garonne the Aquitani, Basques and Iberians, among whom the Gauls had not penetrated in Roman times. What this means is that the inhabitants of all Gaul were not all Gauls. The importance of this is that the so-called 'Gauls' who misled Hannibal in the Alps, were not Gauls at all, but Ligurians.

The eruption of Santorin in 1925. The eruption of the fifteenth century BC is believed to have annihilated Minoan sea-power and was the origin of the story of Atlantis

Gauls never penetrated into the south of Provence, south of the Durance where the Ligurians lived; and they did not break through to the Mediterranean until the fourth century BC, when the Volcae came and drove a wedge between the Iberians and Basques on the west and the Ligurians on the east, and founded the towns later known as Narbonne and Toulouse. That was why Hannibal had to deal with them when he was on his way from Spain through the south of Gaul and crossed the Rhône.

The prehistoric inhabitants of Crete, the Minoans, come into the present story only to go out of it again. This is neither a solecism nor a paradox, for their importance to their successors in time, in the Mediterranean, was the collapse of their great sea-power, after which other people could and did take to the sea. About their origin, nothing is known, but a few things are suspected. Homer attributed to king Minos a 'Phoenician' mother, and there are indications that the

Tablets written in Minoan Linear A script (above) and in Minoan Linear B

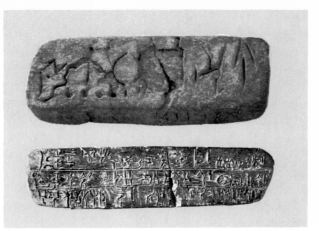

language of Minoan Linear A had a Syrian origin, and also possibly the Minoans themselves, which would make them distantly connected with the Phoenicians. Hannibal may have been a distant relative of king Minos.

The eruption of Santorin about 1450 BC could not have avoided wrecking the entire Minoan fleet, and this would provide an adequate explanation of the sudden collapse of Minoan sea-power. While the Minoans ruled the seas, no other peoples·could aspire to sea-power, but with the Minoan empire ruined, their place was taken, first by the Mycenaean Greeks, and next by the Phoenicians.

The Greeks were an Indo-European people who came south from the Danube basin, down the valley of the Vardar, in more than one wave; of which the earliest, that of the Achaeans, is believed to have arrived in Greece about the beginning of the second millennium B C. In Greece the Achaeans superimposed themselves on most of the pre-existing Mediterranean population, but the original inhabitants whom the Greeks called Pelasgians maintained themselves in some regions, such as Arcadia, the inaccessible centre of the Peloponnese, and in Attica itself, where Athena the tutelary goddess of Athens, and the fact that she was a goddess, are pre-Greek.

Some idea of the pattern of events may be derived from a study of the evolution of Greek myths, to which attention has been drawn by Robert Graves and C. Kerényi. The Mediterranean peoples were originally matrilinear and worshipped female deities, whereas the Indo-Europeans were patrilinear and their gods were very masculine. To Hera, Athena, and Demeter, of the original pantheon there were then added the Indo-European Zeus, Poseidon, and Hades. But Zeus

13

and his male colleagues gradually established their absolute supremacy in Olympus, and this may represent the subjugation of the original Mediterranean peoples in Greece by the Indo-European newcomers from the north. Homer referred to Achaeans as 'yellow-haired', and this must have been because the original inhabitants of Greece were dark-haired, like the Basques, Iberians, Ligurians, and pre-Celtic inhabitants of Britain.

From the middle of the second millennium BC, the Greeks produced the Mycenaean civilization, of which the palace of Mycenae, first excavated by Heinrich Schliemann, with its wonderful works of art, is an example. In addition, as soon as Minoan sea-power had disappeared, the Mycenaeans established their own. Although when they came to Greece the Greeks had no word for 'sea', since it is clear that *thalassa* is a pre-Greek form, nevertheless their life was soon deeply influenced by the sea, and their mastery over it was shown not only by evidence of their sea-borne trade, and the expedition to the siege of Troy, but by the epics of the Greek legends which showed that they ventured far into the western Mediterranean, as well as into the eastern waters of that sea and of the Black Sea.

Next, it was the Mycenaeans' turn to suffer disaster, for about the beginning of the eleventh century BC another wave of Greeks, hard, uncultured, and savage, the Dorians, came down from the north and put the Mycenaean centres to fire and sword. Greece entered a Dark Age lasting for three centuries, during which the command of the sea passed to the Phoenicians. Meanwhile, the Greeks gradually worked out a civilization of their own, in their city-states, where their individualism, love of freedom, originality, and powers of speculative thought eventually blossomed out into the most inspiring way of life that the world had yet seen.

There was constant strife, both in Greece itself, and on the islands and the western coast of Asia Minor where the Greek cities very soon founded daughter-cities as famous as themselves. Presently, the pressures, from over-population and from hostile influences in Asia Minor, led the Greeks to found other daughter-cities farther afield. It would be misleading to call them 'colonies', for they were autonomous and not subject to their mother-cities, to which they were connected only by religion and ties of family sentiment. Considering only those founded in the north-western quarter of the Mediterranean,

The Lion Gate of Mycenae. After the collapse of the Minoan empire sea-power in the Mediterranean devolved on the Mycenaean Greeks

14

the most important group of Greek daughter-cities was in the south of Italy and on the east and south coasts of Sicily, which, together, formed what was known as Magna Graecia.

Among the earliest to be settled were Pithecussae (Ischia) and Cumae, about 750 BC. These were followed in 734 BC by Syracuse, birthplace of Archimedes. Also in the eighth century BC came Naxos, and Messana (Messina), both in Sicily; in Italy, Sybaris, Crotona where Pythagoras took refuge and established a school, Rhegium (Reggio), and Parthenope which became known as Neapolis (Naples). In the following century there were founded, in Italy, Taras, Tarentum, Locri, Caulonia, and Metapontum where Pythagoras died in 497 BC. Thurii, where Herodotus was among the colonists, was founded in 445 BC.

According to Thucydides, when the Greeks first arrived in Sicily there were some Phoenician posts in the east of the island, but they all withdrew to the west, leaving the east, south, and north coasts freely available for the Greeks who founded Gela in 689 BC, Selinos (Selinunte) in 628 BC, and Acragas (Agrigentum, Girgenti), described by Pindar as 'the most beautiful city of mortals', and birthplace of Empedocles.

◀ *The Temple of Zeus at Acragas (Agrigentum), Sicily, with the giant figure of Atlas. Acragas was founded by the Greeks from Gela in the seventh century BC*

The island of Ischia, first called Pithecussae, opposite the Bay of Naples. Founded by Greeks from Chalcis, it was among the earliest Greek settlements in the West

All these Greek settlements played a great part in the history of Rome, not only because of the intellectual leaven which they spread in Italy, but also because of the wars in which they constantly became involved, against the Carthaginians, and against the Romans themselves.

At the time when the Greek expansion into the western Mediterranean was taking place, Tuscany was already occupied by the Etruscans. It was therefore further west that the Greeks continued their settlements. In 600 BC Protis and his Phocaeans from Phocis in Asia Minor founded Massalia (Marseilles), in a small inlet in Ligurian territory, now the Old Harbour of Marseilles.

From Massalia there budded other daughter-cities, the names of which read like a child's guide to Greek: Antipolis, 'the other city', Antibes; Heracles Monoikos, 'Heracles alone in the house', Monaco; Nikaia, 'victory', Nice; Agathe, 'good', Agde. Then came others spread along the coast of Iberia: Pyrene, daughter of Cimbrix and paramour of Mars, buried in the mountains that bear her name, perhaps Banyuls; Emporiae, 'market', Ampurias. Zakynthos (Saguntum) is said to have been founded by emigrants from the island of the same name, now Zanthe. Further south along the coasts of Spain, but not long to survive Carthaginian pressure, were Hemeroskopeion near Alicante, and Maenake near Málaga.

There may have been Greek attempts to settle in Corsica, but a combination of Etruscans and Carthaginians, both deadly enemies of the Greeks, defeated a Greek fleet off Alalia in 537 BC. Perhaps the Etruscans were settling an old score with the Greeks, because Henri Rolland found traces of an Etruscan settlement at Massalia, pre-dating that of the Greeks.

The earlier of these Greek cities were not founded for the purpose of opening markets for commerce, but as places for the inhabitants to continue their freedom-loving way of life, tilling the ground, fishing, and thinking. This did not prevent some of the cities from becoming extremely rich as a result of trade, like Massalia. Sybaris, on the 'instep' of Italy, benefited greatly from being situated where an overland portage route from the Tyrrhenian to the Ionian sea enabled traders to avoid the dangers of the Strait of Messina, and it became so rich that it gave its name to luxurious living. Perhaps that was why it was destroyed by its jealous neighbour Crotona in 510 BC.

The actual foundation of a daughter-city must have been a picturesque ceremony. The founder, in great pomp, went to the acropolis in the mother-city and took a brand from the sacred fire and images of the protector deities. In the new city, there was always a hill on which the

Coin of Crotona-Sybaris. It shows the Tripod of Crotona and the Bull of Sybaris

18

The entrance to the Old Harbour of
Marseilles, the inlet where c. *600* BC
Phocaean Greeks founded the settlement of
Massalia

Drachma from Massalia, c. *350* BC:
reverse showing a lion and the inscription
MASSA

new acropolis was built, and as soon as the citizens arrived, the gods
were installed, the fire was rekindled, and a sacrifice was offered. It
was a religious ceremony, and, indeed, the only tie between the Greek
cities, mother and daughter, and sister, was religious, of that free kind
which nobody was obliged to follow. Wherever they went, there was
one centre with which the daughter-cities, all over the known world,
always retained contact in war and in peace, the temple of Apollo at
Delphi with its famous oracle, which was consulted not only by
Greeks, but, later, even by Romans, as the sequel will show. The

The Temple of Apollo at Delphi at the foot of Mount Parnassus. This shrine, famed throughout the classical world, was referred to by Homer in the 'Odyssey' when, through the Pythis-priestess, Apollo gave an oracle to Agamemnon about the dispute between Odysseus and Achilles

priests of Delphi were so well-informed by their contacts with visitors from every part of the ancient world that their advice was well worth having.

Such were the Greeks, always a people but never a nation organized into a single state, who exerted such an enormous influence on thought and events, both before and after they were absorbed by Rome and acted as a leaven on their conquerors.

> *Graecia capta ferum victorem cepit*
> *et artes intulit agresti Latio*
> (Horace)

PHOENICIANS AND CARTHAGINIANS

IN SPITE OF THE OLD TESTAMENT which makes them out to have been sons of Ham, the Phoenicians were Canaanites, a Semitic people who spoke a Semitic language. They settled in the strip of land between the mountains of Lebanon and the sea which became known as Phoenicia. The name Phoenician, given to them by the Greeks, means dark-skinned. The Romans called them *Poeni* from which has come Punic. The Canaanites as such settled further inland and to the south, in Palestine.

The Phoenicians were certainly not autochthonous, and when they arrived in Phoenicia is unknown; perhaps in the second millennium BC. But the land whence they came must have been on the sea for they were seafarers very early, and probably came from the Persian Gulf. Their narrow strip of settlement in Phoenicia, much too small to support a population by agriculture, implies that they made their living by fetching and carrying in their ships, maritime trade. For this

Assyrian relief depicting river craft propelled by oars carrying timber from the forests of Lebanon, one of the most important export products of the Phoenicians; other logs are shown being towed behind the boats

Ivory plaque from Nimrud showing a priestess wearing the horns and disk of the Egyptian goddess Hathor, while the wings surrounding her body are an attribute of the Phoenician Ashtoreth

Gold belt with Phoenician embossed and granulated decorative motifs, from Aliseda, Spain, evidence of the extent of Phoenician trade in the Mediterranean ▶

Two necklaces and pendants from Tharros, Sardinia, of gold, coloured glass beads, cornelian, agate, and amber, examples of Phoenician manufacture of ornaments, sixth century BC

purpose their home was ideal, for they were half-way between the empires of the Hittites to the north and the Egyptians to the south, on caravan routes from everywhere, and the cedars of Lebanon provided the Phoenicians and their clients with the finest timber for the building of ships.

The Phoenicians organized their trade along caravan routes and shipping lanes. From Arabia came incense, myrrh, and onyx; from India precious stones, spices, ivory, and perfumed wood; from Egypt horses, linen, and cotton; from Africa gold, ebony, ivory, ostrich feathers, and black slaves; from Spain wheat and silver; from the Greek islands copper, tin, marble, and the shell-fish that provided purple dyes; from Assyria precious stuffs, carpets, perfumes and dates; from the Caucasus metals and slaves. Their slave-markets provided servants for all the palaces in the Middle East and Egypt.

In addition to these imports and exports, the Phoenicians manufactured consumer goods by mass-production in factories, particularly vases, jewels, necklaces, bracelets, brooches, earrings, images of gods, and textiles. Their great specialities were transparent glass made from the white sand of their coastline, and Tyrian purple, the dye from the mollusc *Murex* of which the Phoenician species provided a royal purple colour. (A more violet colour is derived from the mollusc of Greek waters, and from the Atlantic variety an almost black tint.)

The Phoenicians also undertook building contracts. Solomon entrusted the construction of the temple in Jerusalem, and also the port

23

Pendant glass heads from Carthage, sixth to fourth century BC. Similar grimacing masks of Phoenician origin, often made of terracotta, have been found in Sardinia and the Balearic Islands, and at Hazor in Israel

of Ezion-Geber on the Red Sea, to Phoenician builders; the Assyrian king Sennacherib invited Phoenician engineers and seamen to build a fleet for him on the Euphrates and the Persian Gulf.

Commerce implies the keeping of records, and in the development of the technique necessary for this operation, the whole of posterity in the western world is indebted to the Phoenicians, on two scores. One relates to the fact that they traded in writing material, papyrus, much more portable and convenient than clay tablets. It was made in Egypt from leaves of the plant *Cyperus papyrus*, now extinct there, by hammering together two leaves with their fibres at right angles. The place where the papyrus trade flourished was the Phoenician port of Byblos, which gave its name to the Greek word for book.

The second, and more important debt, relates to what is written. Writing was invented by the Sumerians in the third millennium BC. Their script, which was in cuneiform on clay tablets, consisted of signs, some of which were ideograms meaning complete words, some syllabic signs conveying the sound of particular syllables, and some determinative signs affixed to words to make their meaning more precise. There were in all between five and six hundred signs.

In Egypt, the same general idea was adopted of using visible signs to convey the meaning of words. The result was hieroglyphics, little pictures or pictograms, but likewise consisting of some ideograms, some syllabic signs, and some determinatives. Around 3000 BC a simpler form of cursive writing, hieratic, was developed for more general use.

For merchants, traders, and recorders of wealth, such systems of writing were cumbersome and expensive. Something simpler was required, which could only be ensured by breaking a script down, not to the number of syllables which can be pronounced, which amount to nearly one hundred, but to the number of simple sounds which the voice can make, under thirty in number.

Obelisks in the enclosure behind the temple at Byblos in Phoenicia. Phoenician sanctuaries often contain such stele, some marking the burial places of votive objects or of funerary urns

Hebrew letter	Hebrew	Phonetic value	Ahiram	Elibaal (Osorkon bust)	Shipitbaal	Mesha	Kara Tepe bilingual	Punic	Neo-punic	Early Greek	Modern Greek	Modern Roman	Greek letter
aleph		ʼ									A	A	alpha
beth		b									B	B	beta
gimel		g									Γ	G	gamma
daleth		d									Δ	D	delta
he		h									E	E	epsilon
waw		w										V	digamma
zayin		z									I	Z	zeta
heth		ḥ									B	H	eta
teth		ṭ									Θ		theta
yodh		y									I	I	iota
kaph		k									K	K	kappa
lamedh		l									Λ	L	lambda
mem		m									M	M	mu
nun		n									N	N	nu
samekh		s									Ξ		xi
ayin		ʻ									O	O	omicron
pe		p									π	P	pi
tsade		ṣ											
qoph		q									Φ	Q	
resh		r									P	R	rho
shin		š									Σ	S	sigma
tau		t									T	T	tau
Probable dates of inscriptions			early 10th cent.	c.915	end of 10th cent.	c.830	8th cent. B.C.	5th cent. & later	2nd cent. & later	8th cent. B.C.			

The alphabet from the tenth century BC; all 22 Phoenician letters were consonants

26

Gradually these scripts lost their pictorial signs, and these became transformed into non-pictorial signs, or letters. This is the system which in the tenth century BC the Phoenicians developed, out of originally Egyptian pictograms, through the Sinaitic script, into their alphabet of twenty-two letters; all of these were consonants, vowels being commonly omitted in Semitic languages, since the reader knew from the context which vowel sounds were to be intercalated. This Phoenician alphabet was the basis of the Hebrew, Greek, Etruscan, Latin, and later, Cyrillic alphabets, and therefore of literacy throughout the western world. An instrument had been invented in which it was possible not only to record quantities of goods bought and sold, but to express thoughts and emotions. The debt owed to the Phoenicians is no less than this.

The Phoenician language, as we have said, was Semitic, related to the Hebrew of the Israelites, Aramaic, Syrian, and Arabic. With the exception of some inscriptions, all Phoenician and Punic literature is lost, although the language was still spoken in North Africa in the days of Saint Augustine, whose native land it was. It is said that the Maltese language today preserves some traces of Phoenician. It is

Tyre, mother city of Carthage. Originally an island, it was connected with the mainland by a causeway built by Alexander the Great when he captured Tyre in 332 BC. Since then the causeway has widened to form a peninsula

Repoussé bronze band from the Assyrian gates of Balawat built by Shalmaneser III of Assyria (858–825 BC) to commemorate his victories. It shows (from the left) tribute shipped from Tyre to the mainland and carried to Assyria by a line of bearers under guard

28

ironical and unfortunate that those who invented the alphabet should be the only important people in the antiquity of the western world not to have benefited from it by leaving to posterity their own account of their history. This is particularly regrettable for the history of Hannibal. Although there was a Phoenician people, there was no Phoenician State. Instead, along the two hundred miles of coast of Phoenicia, a string of little towns had been established, all worshipping similar gods, speaking the same language, and engaged in the same occupations, but all more or less independent. These towns illustrate one of the characteristics of Phoenician settlements. If possible, they were situated on small islands close to the coast, with good anchorages for shipping, like Aradus (Ruad) and Tyre (Sur). Otherwise they tended to be sited on headlands and promontories easy to defend against attacks from the landward side, with good anchorages beside them, like Byblos (Gebeil) and Sidon (Saida).

The Egyptian expansion of the sixteenth century BC brought the Phoenician cities under its sway, but the tide flowed back again, and after the Hittite empire had been destroyed and the Egyptians had fallen into decline, the power vacuum left between them was filled by the Assyrians, who about 1100 BC temporarily occupied the Phoenician town of Aradus. For many centuries more, pressure bore increasingly from the east on Phoenicia, from Nineveh, Babylon, and Persia. In 586 BC Nebuchadnezzar broke the power of Tyre, and Alexander the Great shattered it with its capture in 332 BC.

Reverse of a shekel of Sidon showing the fortified city from the sea with warships before the walls, and lions in the exergue; and (right) obverse of a coin of Adramalek of Byblos showing a warship with ram manned by armed soldiers, and beneath it a hippocamp. Both mid-fifth century BC

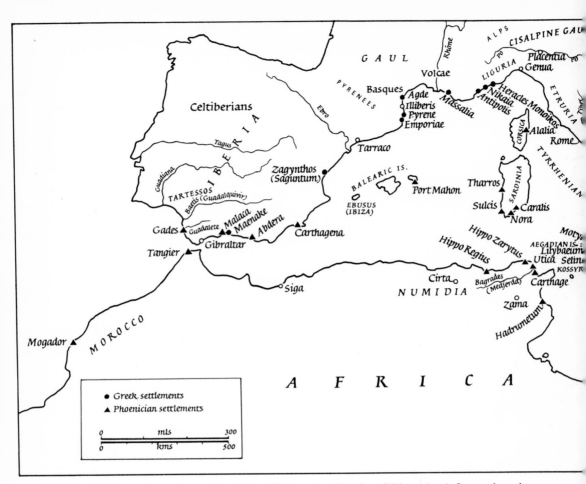

Map of the Mediterranean, showing the spread of Greek and Phoenician influence throughout the ancient world, and other principal sites

From the eleventh century BC onwards, after the Mycenaeans had lost their command of the sea, the inhabitants of the Phoenician cities lessened their risks and increased their business by founding settlements overseas. Of these there were three kinds: in civilized states like Egypt, they established agencies or concessions, as at Memphis. Elsewhere they founded trading stations, the purpose of which was to open up markets. Ultimately some of these, and notably Carthage, were able to colonize the land behind them and exploit it for their own enrichment, in the form of a subject colony worked by slaves.
Phoenicians must have reached Cyprus early, and settlements have been found at Kition (Larnaka), while staging-posts were placed along

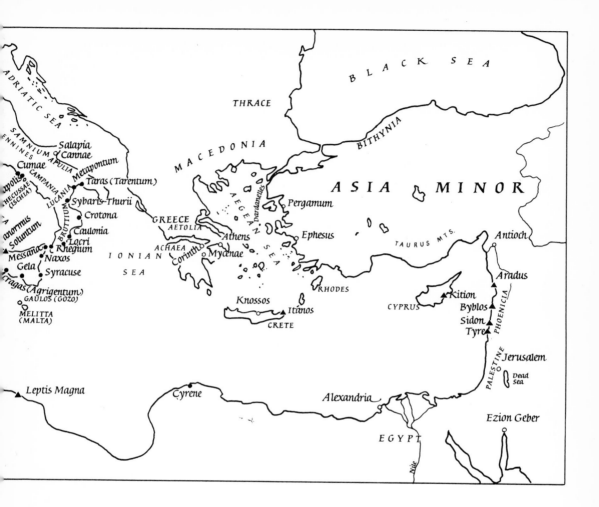

the southern coast of Asia Minor. In Crete, Itanos is believed to have been a Phoenician foundation; but the most sensational expansion from Tyre was the establishment of a trade post at Gades (Cadiz), then an island such as the Phoenicians loved, near the mouth of the river Baetis (Guadalquivir) and the rich country of Tartessos (Tarshish), on the Iberian Peninsula. The traditional date for the foundation of Gades was 1110 BC, and the temple of Melqart (Phoenician equivalent of Heracles whose worship had been introduced into Tyre by Hiram) which they built there enjoyed enormous prestige.

The next in order of traditional date of the Phoenician stations to be founded was Utica, in 1100 BC, near the mouth of the river Bagrades

Coloured limestone sarcophagus from Amathus, Cyprus, seventh century BC, showing a procession with a royal chariot preceded by an advance guard of horsemen. The style of the sarcophagus is Cypriote but it shows Phoenician influence. Mixtures of style were common in Phoenician decoration

Terracotta statuette of the head and bust of a woman, from Idalion, Cyprus. The features, decoration, and style show Syriac and Asiatic influences

I Inlaid ivory plaque from Nimrud in Assyria, eighth century BC, showing Phoenician influence; it depicts a lioness attacking a Negro boy

(Medjerda) in Tunisia, followed in 950 BC by Hippo Zarytus (Bizerta) with its wonderful harbour. Then, in 814 BC, came Carthage.

The traditional foundress of Carthage was Dido-Elissa, sister of king Pygmalion of Tyre, and grand-niece of queen Jezebel, the wife of king Ahab. Dido married her uncle Sychaeus whom Pygmalion, her brother, murdered. With a band of friends, Dido left Tyre, called at Cyprus, and sailed on to the coast of north Africa, near Utica, where the local king, Iarbas, granted her as much land as could be covered by an ox-hide. By cutting the hide into strips as thin as possible, a substantial piece of land was secured (as, many centuries later, was done in England by Hengist and Horsa) on which was founded *Qart Hadasht*, 'New Town', Carthage.

The same pattern of establishment of trading stations by Phoenicians is found in Sardinia where, reputedly in the eighth century BC, Nora on the Cape Pula Peninsula, Tharros (San Giovanni di Sinis) on the San Marco Peninsula, Sulcis (San Antioco) on the island of San Antioco, and Caralis (Cagliari) on the promontory of Sant'Elia were founded. These were soon followed by many more, on the coast at Bithia (near Cape Spartivento), Othoca (Oristano), Bosa, and, inland, Macopsis (Macomer) where African slaves were imported to work the land as a colony.

Melitta (Malta), Gaulos (Gozo), and Kossyra (Pantellaria), islands in the channel between Sicily and north Africa, and midway between Phoenicia and Gades, provided useful relay stations and were occupied at about the same time. An ideal site for a Phoenician settlement was the island of Motya, close to the shore at the western end of Sicily. Another island on the seaward side afforded protection and provided a splendid roadstead. Motya served as the main Carthaginian base until Dionysius I destroyed it in 398 BC, after which it was replaced by Lilybaeum (Marsala). Other settlements in Sicily were Panormus (Palermo) and Soluntum.

In the Balearic Islands, Carthage planted a station at Ebusus (Ibiza) in 654 BC; with eventful consequences, for the inhabitants of the Balearic Islands were expert slingers, an art which gave its name to the islands, from the Greek *ballein*, to throw. Balearic slingers formed important contingents of Carthaginian armies, including Hannibal's. Through the Strait of Gibraltar and on the Atlantic coast of Morocco

II   Phoenician glass scent bottle from Cyprus, fifth to fourth century BC, in the shape of an eastern Greek amphora

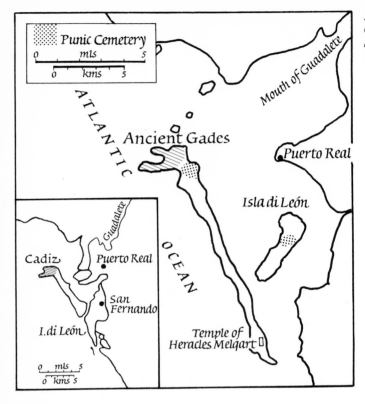

Site of the Phoenician settlement of Gades (modern Cadiz), showing the change of coastline since ancient times (after Harden)

Punic tombs excavated at Punta de la Vaca, Gades (Cadiz) in 1912. The Phoenicians paid great attention to their tombs which to some extent were influenced by Egyptian patterns

Within img_2 (map labels):

Punic Cemetery
0   mls   5
0   kms   5

ATLANTIC

Ancient Gades

Mouth of Guadalete

Puerto Real

Isla di León

OCEAN

Guadalete

Cadiz   Puerto Real

San
Fernando

I. di León

Temple of
Heracles Melqart

0   mls   5
0   kms 5

Askos, or small jug, in the shape of the head of a Negro, from Lilybaeum (Marsala), Sicily, fourth to third century BC

Staircase at the entrance to the Punic town on the island of Motya, off the western coast of Sicily, a fine example of Phoenician masonry of the sixth century BC

Remains of the citadel of the Punic settlement of Soluntum, on the north coast of Sicily, near Palermo. To the right of the columns of the temple is a precinct in which has been found an open-air altar on which animals were sacrificed

a station was founded on the island of Mogador in 600 B C and another at Tangier. Other stations in Spain just east of Gibraltar were Abdera (Adra) and Malaca (Málaga). In Africa, south of Carthage, stations were founded at Hadrumetum (Sousse), Leptis Magna (Lebda), and elsewhere. The whole south-west quarter of the Mediterranean was thus a Carthaginian preserve.

As Carthage emerged from proto-history into history, its land possessions grew. The territory surrounding the city itself was increased until it represented the northern half of the present State of Tunisia, to which were added coastal strips in Libya and Tripolitania, with Sabratha and Leptis Magna to the east, while in the west Carthage's influence extended over Numidia, the land of nomads, in Algeria and Morocco. The land was farmed, but not by Carthaginians, who preferred to amass fortunes by trade and to employ Berbers and Negroes to work in their fields.

The Bay of Carthage with the sands known as the 'Plage d'Amilcar'. Across the waters of the bay, the mountains in the distance are those of Cap Bon peninsula

To this African homeland, there were added the western parts of Sicily and of Sardinia, the Balearic Islands, Melitta (Malta), and Kossyra (Pantellaria), developed out of the Phoenician colonies established in those islands. In addition to these, there were colonies in Spain at Gades, Malaca, and Abdera, possibly Calpe (Gibraltar), and, in Morocco, Tangier and Mogador.

The government of Carthage was originally a kind of monarchy, under the dynasty of the Magonides. But the disaster of the battle of Himera in Sicily in 480 BC, the defeat of the Persians by the Greeks in the same year, and the decline of the power of the Etruscans, brought about a change, both religious and political at the same time, as was natural in a Semitic state. Tanit became the supreme deity, and a constitution superficially not unlike that of republican Rome was established. Instead of Consuls, it had Suffetes as chief magistrates, a Senate and an Assembly. After an attempt by a general, Malchus, to usurp power in

37

The entrance to the ancient Punic harbour of Carthage, with the mountains of Cap Bon in the distance

the state, a Board of Judges was instituted to control army commanders, who had at their side a deputy from the Senate. It became the policy not to arm the local population, with the exception of the Sacred Band, a kind of Praetorian Guard formed of Carthaginian aristocrats, but to hire mercenary troops in large numbers, which Carthage could easily afford to pay, and then get rid of.

While Carthage became far and away the richest, and by that token the most powerful of the Phoenician cities in the west, dominating them by the strength of her fleet, armies, and commerce, they were not strictly her possessions, and their inhabitants were not her citizens, except of course for the colonies. The other cities had their own governments and struck their own coins, but they were dependent on Carthage for their defence for they had no military forces of their own. There was thus no solidly built political unity or cohesion between them. As for the subject territories, in Africa and in Sardinia, they were made to pay tribute, and their discontent was reflected in the part which they subsequently played in revolts against Carthage.

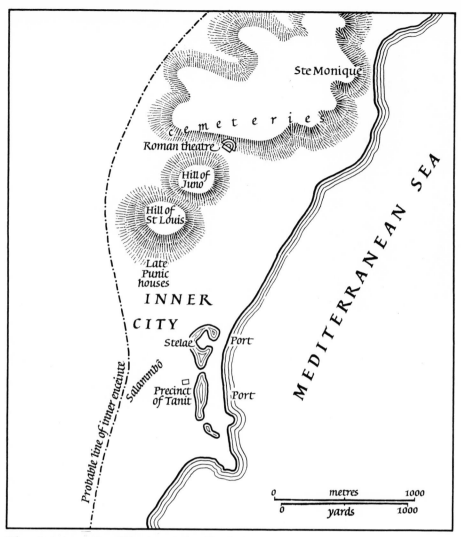

Plan of the inner city of Carthage (after Harden)

Aristotle analyzed the constitution of Carthage as it existed in his time. He noted that choice of a man depended more on eminence than on age, that vacancies in bodies were filled by their own co-option, that those in office enjoyed long terms, and that they looked with favour on pluralism. The most conspicuous feature of the Carthaginian constitution was the principle that candidates for office should be not only the most efficient people available but also the most wealthy, on the grounds that it was impossible for anyone but a rich man to be a

Stele of Baalyaton (left), from Umm el Amad near Tyre, fourth or early third century BC, and the inscribed stele of Baal Hammon, from Lilybaeum (Marsala), Sicily, with Punic religious symbols

good ruler and to have the free time to be one. The result was corruption, for not only were the highest offices available by purchase, but the purchaser looked for a return on his money, and the example spread down to all levels of society. This substitution of wealth for merit could only strike a Greek, or a Roman of the Republican period, with horror, for Aristotle held that in good constitutions provision should be made for persons of merit to have the necessary leisure to enable them to become good rulers.

The religion of Carthage, as of Phoenicians, was the worship of Baal against which the Old Testament thundered so loud. Although Baal was the chief god, he was not the only one. Tyre had its Melqart, *Melek Qart*, Lord of the city, whose name is to be found in those of Hamilcar and Bomilcar.

The name of Mol'k or Moloch has been regarded as that of a terrible god to whom human children were sacrificed in the fire. That the practice existed is only too true, as the remains of children's calcined bones prove, in excavations on many Carthaginian sites, in Africa and Sardinia; but it seems that the word Mol'k means the sacrifice itself rather than the name of the god, or rather, in this case, goddess.

The only female deity in the Phoenician pantheon was Ashtoreth, Astarte, or Tanit as she was known in Carthage where she had a temple in which inscriptions mention, and funeral urns reveal, the

40

The precinct of the goddess Tanit at Carthage, full of funerary urns, and (below) examples of such urns, eighth to fourth century BC, containing ashes of cremated infants and small animals

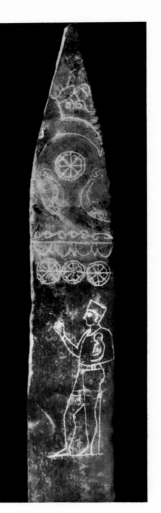

Limestone stele with inlaid slab recording seventeen generations of priests of Tanit, from Carthage, fourth century BC. The lineage may therefore go back to the foundation of Carthage

Limestone obelisk showing a priest holding an infant to be sacrificed, from the precinct of Tanit at Salammbô, Carthage, fourth century BC

practice of infant sacrifice. Sacrifices also involved food, drink, birds, and mammals, as fertility cults. There was even a recognized tariff for sacrifices, and the text of one from the temple of Baal Saphon at Carthage has been found at Marseilles, prescribing that for each ox sacrificed, whether as a peace offering or a sin offering, the priest shall have ten pieces of silver, and, in addition, for a sin offering, three hundred pounds of meat.

From the fact that they included grave goods with the dead, it can be inferred that the Carthaginians believed in some form of after-life; but the quality and quantity of these goods decreased as time went on, which gives rise to the suspicion that they were eventually regarded as a waste of money.

ETRUSCANS AND ROMANS

FOR HALF A MILLENNIUM, the highest level of civilization was reached in central Italy by a mysterious people, the Etruscans, who occupied the region south of the river Arno and west of the Tiber and the Apennines, bordering on the Tyrrhenian sea. They were so different from their neighbours that their origin has been a puzzle and subject for discussion for two thousand five hundred years. Herodotus, writing in the fifth century BC, when the Etruscans were still a great power, said that they came from Lydia in Asia Minor because of famine and emigrated by sea to the west coast of Italy at a date shortly after the fall of Troy, early in the eleventh century BC.

It seems, however, that it was the devastation of Asia Minor by the Cimmerian and Scythian invasions, in the eighth century BC, which determined the significant emigration of the people responsible for the oriental type of civilization that characterizes Etruscan sites from that period onwards. The Phoenicians had occupied north Africa and west Sicily, and eastern Sicily and the south of Italy were being occupied by the Greeks, leaving Tuscany as the next vacant space in the central Mediterranean.

In that part of Italy which they first occupied, and which came to be known as Etruria or Tuscany, the Etruscans founded twelve important city-states. In the south of the area which they covered, between the Arno and the Tiber: Tarquinia (Corneto), Veii and Falerii, close to Rome and long her enemies, Caere (Cerveteri) also close to Rome and soon to become her ally, Volsinii (perhaps on the site of Orvieto, *Urbs vetus*) by the lake of Bolsena. In the north: Vetulonia (Colonna which has since resumed its old name), Rusellae

Bronze figurine of an Etruscan peasant ploughing with yoked oxen, found near Arezzo, sixth century BC

43

Detail of one of the bands of the bronze situla or pail from the Etruscan necropolis of La Certosa near Bologna. The repoussé relief shows a sacrificial procession headed by two robed priests followed by women carrying baskets on their heads; sixth to fifth century BC

(near Grosseto), both near the coast. Inland, Volaterrae (Volterra), Clusium (Chiusi), Arretium (Arezzo), Cortona and Perusia (Perugia). There was also the sea-port of Populonia, a colony of Volaterrae facing the island of Ilva (Elba).

The Etruscan cities soon expanded into prosperous and luxurious communities, under their system of aristocratic rule. There was an Etruscan people, but no Etruscan State, for they were totally lacking in political genius, they never formed a centralized nation, and they were eventually engulfed piecemeal by Rome. Before then, however, expanding as they did both to the south and to the north, they were a power to be reckoned with.

The Etruscan expansion to the south took them through Latium, which, including Rome, they controlled to some extent at that time, and they debouched into the fertile district of Campania. There they founded Vulturnum (old Capua) traditionally in 598 BC, and the towns of Acerra, Pompeii, Nuceria Alfaterna (Nocera), Nola, Marcina on the Gulf of Paestum, also probably Surrentum (Sorrento) and Salernum (Salerno: the word-ending *-erno* is non-Italic), and other towns the location of which has not been discovered, but whose coins have been

Map of Italy and Sicily, showing principal Etruscan settlements and spheres of Etruscan, Greek and Phoenician influence; seventh to sixth century BC (after Bloch)

found elsewhere. Among these were Urina, Velcha, Velsu, and Irnthi, all typically Etruscan names.

The Etruscans attacked the Greek city of Cumae on land in 520 BC without success, and, passing over to the offensive a dozen years later, the Cumaeans under their leader Aristodemos started to drive the

45

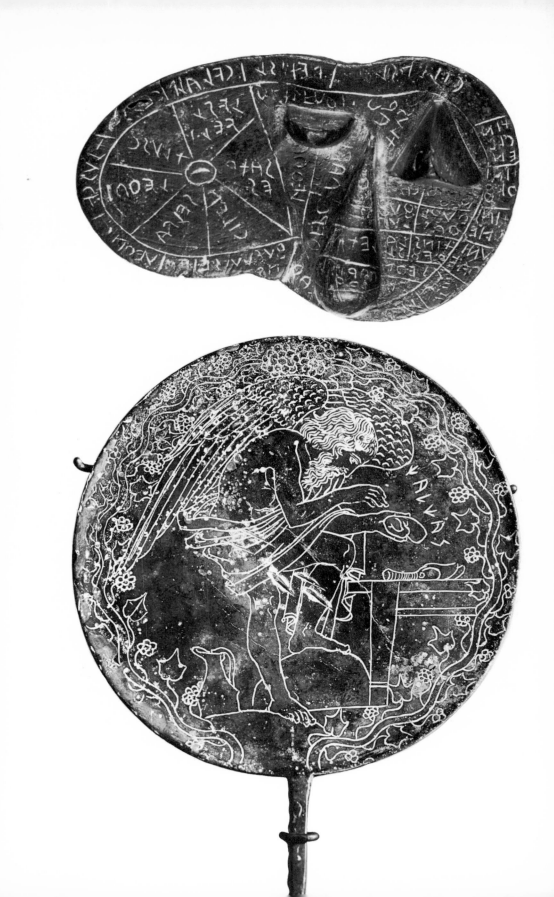

Ivory writing tablet from Marsiliana d'Albegna, c. 700 BC. The letters on the upper border, read from right to left, are the oldest known Etruscan alphabet and preserve the Phoenician sibilants samekh *and* tsade, *which show that the Etruscans got their alphabet from the eastern Mediterranean*

◄ *Etruscan bronze model of a liver, found near Piacenza; it served to instruct apprentice diviner-priests in the art of discovering omens in the entrails of animals; third century BC. Similar models have been found in Asia Minor. (Below) Etruscan engraved bronze mirror from Vulci showing an augur examining a liver for omens; fourth century BC*

Etruscans out of Campania by his victory at the battle of Aricia, and thereby helped the Romans and the Latins to push the Etruscans northwards beyond the Tiber, and to free Rome from the Etruscan kings who until then had ruled there.

After Etruscan sea-power had been crushed by Hiero I of Syracuse, in the battle fought off Cumae in 474 BC, and Hiero's occupation of the island of Ischia, the Etruscans' connexions with Campania having then been severed by sea as well as by land, their hold over Campania melted away. In 424 BC the Samnites captured Capua, Cumae fell to the Sabellians in 420 BC, and so the whole area of Campania fell into Oscan hands. The Etruscan foundations in Campania were thus wrenched away from them by Oscans, Samnites, and also by Greeks, many years before the Romans established their mastery over them.

47

Detail of an Etruscan stele from Felsina (Bologna) of the third century BC, showing Hellenistic influence. The well-armed horseman is attacking a naked warrior, presumably a Gaul, who protects his body with his shield

The Etruscan expansion towards the north, which began about 525 BC, was no more fortunate. It took them from Etruria across the Apennines into Umbrian country where they founded (or occupied) the cities of Felsina (Bologna), Marzabotto, Ariminum (Rimini), and Ravenna (the word-ending *-enna*, as also in Chiavenna, is Etruscan), and entered the plain of the Po. That fertile valley was occupied in its western part by Ligurians, and in its eastern part by Venetii. The Etruscans brushed them aside and founded Melpum (Milan), Parma, Mutina (Modena), and Spina at the mouth of the Po, and also Hadria from which the Adriatic Sea takes its name.

The Etruscan settlements in the Po valley were soon overwhelmed by the Gauls, who came over the Alps in the fifth and fourth centuries BC. They destroyed Melpum, where they established their city of Mediolanum (Milan), traditionally in 396 BC, and drove the Etruscans out. There were five main groups of these Gauls, with whom the Romans subsequently had to deal. The Insubres settled in what was to become Lombardy, round Mediolanum; the Cenomani round Bergamum, Brescia, Cremona, Mantua, and Verona; the Boii round Felsina which became their Bononia (Bologna); the Lingones in the coastal region on the Adriatic between Ariminum and Ravenna; and the Senones,

LATINI   TROIANI   LATINVS

HAECEFFATOSEQVOSNVMEROPATERELLIGITOMNE
STABANTTERCENTVMNITIDIINPRAESEPIBVSALTIS·
OMNIBVSEXTEMPLOTEVCRISIVBETORDINEDVCI·
INSTRATOSOSTROALIPEDESPICTISQVEIATTIIS·
AVREATECTORIBVSDEMISSAMONILIAPENDENT·
TECTIAVROFVLVVMMANDVNTSVBDENTIBVSAVRVM
ABSTIAENTIAECVRVSGEMINOSQVITVCALIS·

last to arrive, between Ravenna and Sena Gallica. In this manner, the north of Italy became Cisalpine Gaul and moulded a political pattern which was of great importance in Hannibal's strategic plans.

Under pressure from all these enemies, in Campania and in the valley of the Po, the star of the Etruscans was setting; but they still retained sufficient powers of resistance to give the Romans trouble for many more years. It is now time to turn attention to these Romans.

It was from the north, across the Alps, that Italy received its quota of Indo-European peoples, of that branch known as Italic. The Italic-speaking peoples were themselves a diversified lot in which, from their languages, a number of groups can be recognized. There were the Latins, who settled in the open country south of the lower reaches of the river Tiber and gave it its name of Latium. The Latins were, however, very far from representing all the Italic peoples who came into Italy. The other great branch was composed of the Osco-Umbrians who also contained a number of tribes speaking different dialects. The Oscans included the Sabines who lived in the mountains bordering on Latium, Samnites who inhabited the mountainous country of the Abruzzi, known as Samnium, and, to mention only the more important, those who lived in Bruttium, Lucania, and Apulia, respectively the 'toe', 'instep' and 'heel' of Italy.

So it happened that when the Etruscans came to Tuscany, the peoples whom they found there were Umbrians; and when the Greek colonists founded their cities of Magna Graecia in the south of Italy, the inhabitants whom they found inland in Bruttium, Lucania, and Apulia, were Oscans, with the exception of those who lived in the extreme tip of the 'heel' of Italy, near Uzentum (Ugento). These were the Messapians, and their inscriptions show that although their language was Indo-European, it was not Italic, but Illyrian, like that of the inhabitants of the eastern shores of the Adriatic; they shared place-names with Croatia. How they came is of course unknown, but it seems that they must have formed part of the stream of Indo-European peoples which flowed down into Italy.

The name 'Italy' itself is believed to have been derived from an Oscan word, *viteliu*, meaning 'country of calves', a name used for Bruttium in the 'toe' of Italy. This word, which is found in Latin *uitellus*, Italian *vitello*, was extended to cover the whole peninsula.

IV   Aeneas received by King Latinus on the Latin shore, from a manuscript copy of Virgil's 'Aeneid', fourth century AD (cf. page 50)

Reconstruction of a hut of the Villanovan period, eighth century BC, characteristic of the Early Iron Age in Etruria. Remains of similar huts, with post-holes and draining channels, have been found on the Palatine in Rome

It is no doubt significant that while the Umbrians had the Etruscans plastered onto them from outside, and the southern Oscans had the Greeks, Latium had no foreigners settled on its seaboard, probably because it had no good harbours.

The Italic peoples were rough and primitive, and the Latins were no exception, as may be seen in the remains of their round Bronze Age huts, with post-holes and rain runways, found on the Palatine Hill in Rome, dating from the eighth century BC, which takes in the traditional date for the foundation of the city in 753 BC.

There are two accounts of the foundation of Rome, one legendary and the other historical. According to the legend, there lived in Latium a king whose daughter Lavinia married a foreigner, Aeneas, son of Venus and of Anchises, who escaped from Troy after it was captured by the Greeks. After perilous navigation in the Mediterranean and heavy losses from storm and shipwreck, the fleet bearing him and his companions put in at Carthage, where Aeneas managed to avoid the

Fragment from the Ara Pietatis *in Rome showing the banquet of the Vestal Virgins, first century* AD. *Vesta, goddess of the hearth, where the fire must always be kept burning, had a shrine from the earliest times in Rome*

amorous snares of Dido; deserting her, he came to the Latin shore, as the Fates had decided that he should, and where he would found a great nation. After his marriage with Lavinia, he built a town which, in honour of his wife, he called Lavinium.

Their son Ascanius left Lavinium and founded a town of his own, Alba Longa, on the Alban Hills, near Castel Gandolfo. His descendants formed a line of twelve kings, of whom the last, Proca, at his death, left two sons, Numitor and Amulius. Numitor succeeded as king, but his jealous brother, Amulius, usurped the throne, killed Numitor's only son and forced his daughter Rhea Silva to become a vestal virgin, so that she should never marry. But the god Mars became enamoured of Rhea Silva, and she bore twin sons whom Amulius ordered to be thrown into the Tiber. The basket which contained them floated on the waters, then in flood, and became caught in the branches of a fig tree, at the foot of the Palatine Hill, where the river deposited it. When the flood subsided, the twins were left high and dry, and a she-wolf,

Reverse of a bronze coin of Antoninus Pius (left), c. AD 150, showing Mars and Rhea Silva who bore the twins Romulus and Remus; (right) reverse of a denarius of Roman Republican times showing Romulus and Remus suckled by the she-wolf and the shepherd Faustulus who succoured them

attracted by their cries, fed them with her milk. They were found by a shepherd, Faustulus, who took them home to his wife Acca Larentia and gave them the names of Romulus and Remus.

When the twins had grown up and had learnt of their own story, they attacked Alba Longa with their companions, killed Amulius, and reinstated their grandfather Numitor on the throne. They then wished to found a new city, but a quarrel sprang up between them, because Romulus wanted it to be on the Palatine Hill where they had been found, while Remus wanted it to be on the Aventine, and to bear his name. They decided to consult the auspices, and Remus, from the Aventine, saw six vultures, but Romulus from the Palatine saw twelve. Romulus therefore won, and offered a sacrifice to the gods. He then proceeded to harness to a plough a bull and a heifer, symbols of strength and fertility, and ploughed a furrow round the Palatine to indicate the boundary of his future city (an Etruscan custom). In scorn, Remus leaped across the furrow, which was an unpardonable insult to the god Terminus, to avenge which Romulus killed Remus. He then called his city Rome, and the date of its foundation is traditionally given as 21 April 753 BC, the feast-day of the shepherds of Latium dedicated to their goddess Pala. The learned Marcus Terentius Varro afterwards calculated that it was in the third year of the sixth Olympiad according to the Greek calendar instituted by Timaeus of Taormina, dating from the first Olympiad in 776 BC.

In this picturesque rigmarole, it is at any rate possible to read that the Latins were a pastoral and agricultural people, who sacrificed to the gods, possessed innate military virtues, believed in divination, respected strength and fertility, and had a profound reverence for property, one of the bases for a sense of law and order. That they were descended from Mars as well as from Venus must have given them a comfortable feeling of self-reliance.

The historical version of the foundation of Rome is no less interesting. It starts with the Latins who preferred to build their towns on heights, either for reasons of defence, or to escape the ravages of malaria which was then (and for long after) endemic on the undrained banks of the Tiber. In this spirit they founded Alba Longa which quickly became the centre of a federation of Latin towns, *foedus Latinum*. It celebrated its political union every year with solemn sacrifices on the Alban Hills, where a temple dedicated to Jupiter Latialis was built. Among the other towns were Aricia, Tusculum (near Frascati), Praeneste (Palestrina), and Tibur (Tivoli).

Some of these Latin peoples noticed the exceptionally favourable position of the seven hills which commanded the crossing-place over the Tiber, and founded small communities on them, bound to one another only by their religion in common. Then, in the eighth century B C, when the Etruscans had begun to expand southwards over the Tiber into the plain of Latium, three of these communities, the Ramnes (Latins), Tities (Sabines), and Luceres (Etruscans), joined to form a larger one, a *civitas* or state, which became Rome. According to Mommsen, the word *tribus*, very early used in law with the sense of 'threeness', gradually lost its meaning of number when it came to designate a tribe.

The importance of Rome grew not only on account of its strategic position as a fortress, but also because of its economic advantages, situated as it was between the sea and the centre of the peninsula, and controlling the crossing of the Tiber. The oldest bridge, the *Pons Sublicius*, by order of the chief priest or Pontifex Maximus who had bridges directly under his care, was built of wood only, without any metal nails or clamps, so that it could easily and quickly be destroyed. It is clear that the Etruscans made an important contribution to the customs, institutions, and language of the Romans. The oldest inscriptions so far found in Rome, beneath the church of S. Omobono —only a fragment dating from the seventh century B C, bearing the portion of a word, . . *uqnus*—is sufficient to show its Etruscan origin. Many of the inventions and innovations commonly attributed to the

Romans were adopted by them directly from the Etruscans who devised the vaulted arch, drains, and the rectangular lay-out of town-planning. So-called Roman numerals are Etruscan numerals; Etruscans introduced the fasces and the double-headed axe as symbols of constituted authority, eagles as standards for the army, the inlaid ivory ceremonial curule chair and the purple toga for the chief magistrates, amphitheatres, gladiatorial fights, and public triumphs. The word *histrio*, actor, is Etruscan, and so is the custom preserved in the western world to this day of giving people a first name and a family name. The oldest Roman family names became those of *gentes*, or clans, among which the Aemilii, Cornelii, Fabii, Horatii, Julii, occur repeatedly throughout Roman history.

The earliest rulers of Rome were kings, of whom the first were probably legendary, but the last three, Tarquin the Elder, Servius Tullius, and Tarquin the Proud, were probably historical and Etruscan. Tarquin the Elder drained the marsh between the foot of the Palatine and the next adjacent hill by means of the *Cloaca maxima*, the main drain, and on it was built the *Forum*. He also built the temple of Jupiter on that next hill, and among its foundations was found the head of a certain *Olus*; from the words *caput oli*, head of Olus, have come Capitol, Capitoline Hill or Campidoglio.

Virgil's story of the arrival of Aeneas from Asia Minor has been generally regarded as a beautiful myth, invented for the purpose of Roman imperial propaganda. But Virgil did not invent it. Stesichorus, a Greek poet from Himera in Sicily in the seventh century BC, made Aeneas come from Troy to Sicily. Hellanicos of Mytilene, contemporary of Herodotus in the fifth century BC, dispersed the Trojans in Italy. Timaeus of Taormina in the following century appears to have been the first to make Aeneas the ancestor of the founder of Rome. True or false, the story was accepted in the third century BC, when the Acarnanians of Aetolia in Greece implored the help of Rome on the grounds that their people was the only one among the Greeks who took no part in the siege of Troy. In the same century, the historian Fabius Pictor and the poets Naevius and Ennius saw nothing to contradict in the story.

Considering that Aeneas is made to come from Asia Minor, and that the Etruscans certainly came from there, Virgil's poem and the writings of his predecessors appear as the reflection in poetry and in legend of a historical fact, the origin of the Etruscans from Asia Minor. It throws light on the part played by the Etruscans in the early history of Rome, and it also explains a number of things, such as the name of

Inscribed stone funerary stele of the Etruscan Avele Feluske, c. 650 BC. He is armed with helmet, shield and the double-headed axe which later became a symbol of authority borne by Roman lictors

The opening into the Tiber of the Cloaca Maxima, main drain, built in the reign of Tarquin the Elder to drain the Forum in Rome. It shows that the Etruscans had mastered the art of construction of the vault

Coin of Antoninus Pius showing Aeneas escaping from Troy carrying his father Anchises and leading his son Ascanius, and (left) terracotta statuette of Aeneas and Anchises from Veii, fifth century BC, showing that Aeneas was also an Etruscan hero

Roman mosaic at Low Ham, Somerset: (above) ▶ Venus, and (below) Dido and Aeneas embracing

the *Ludi Trojanae*, Trojan games which Aeneas celebrated in honour of the death of his father Anchises, and which the Romans continued to celebrate. But it also means that Aeneas was an Etruscan hero before becoming a Roman hero, and this has been proved by statuettes found at Veii.

Before leaving Virgil and his *Aeneid*, there is a further point to notice. Encouraged by Jupiter's promise that he should found Rome, but pursued by the unceasing hatred of Juno because it was to Aeneas's mother Venus and not to her that Paris handed the golden apple as the prize for beauty, Aeneas was buffeted about the Mediterranean, to Thrace, to Crete, to Sicily, and to Carthage. There he had another danger to face, for as Juno had failed to get all his ships sunk, it suited her book that Aeneas should be kept in Carthage by insoluble bonds, than which none is more powerful than love. Juno therefore enlisted Venus's help in making Dido fall in love with him. Rome would then never be founded.

Dido and Aeneas fell in love as intended, but Aeneas was reminded of his divinely appointed fate, and in spite of all entreaties by Dido

and her sister Anna, he insisted on setting sail, on the last lap of his voyage. The love-hate switch then took place in Dido. She requested Anna to build a funeral pyre and to place on it her nuptial bed and all the clothes and other objects which Aeneas had left behind. Anna thought that it was Dido's intention only to burn these, but Dido herself climbed onto the pyre and launched her imprecation and curse on Aeneas and all his descendants: 'From now on, Phoenicians, you shall pursue and detest every one of his offspring as a duty to my shade; there shall be no friendship or understanding between you and his nation. From my remains may there arise an Avenger who shall pursue these fugitives from Troy with fire and sword. May they fight for ever.' She then fell on Aeneas's sword and killed herself. With such consummate artistry did Virgil introduce Hannibal into his epic without naming him.

Aeneas is always referred to as 'Pious Aeneas', and this introduces the subject of Roman religion. Like everything to do with the Romans, it was practical and matter-of-fact, insofar as superstition made this possible. Their thought was as objective as their morality was hard. They had no notion of abstract, transcendental, or idealistic theology at all. They attributed divinity to the principles that protected the family, defended the state, favoured the harvest, guarded the herds and flocks, and in general watched over the manifold activities of their daily life. They were, of course, markedly polytheistic, and as their history unfolded, they adopted all sorts of foreign gods and goddesses, particularly from the Etruscans and the Greeks.

Some of their gods were public, a concern of the State, while others were domestic, regarding the family. Their most primitive gods seem to have been *di indigetes*, peasants' gods, as was fitting for an agricultural people. They included Janus, the god of doors and passages and literally of everything that opens and shuts, and therefore of the beginning and end of all things. Sacred to him were the first day of the month and the first month of the year, January. He was represented as a head with two faces, looking forwards and backwards, and he had a temple of which the doors were always open in time of war, and only closed in times of peace. In 720 years, these doors were shut only three times. There was also Silvanus, the very popular god of forests and fields, who looked after herds, pastures, peasants, shepherds, and country cottages.

The domestic gods included the Genii who guarded every individual from the cradle to the grave, often extending their protection to cover houses and places; Lares who protected the family and its fertility; and

Penates whose province it was to look after the home, everything in it, especially the larder, and the patrimony.

All the gods, and they became very numerous, had appointed feast-days, and they were worshipped in ceremonies regulated with the most minute precision. The slightest negligence in the traditional ceremony invalidated the appeal, and it had to be repeated.

Worship consisted principally in sacrifices, of the fruits of the country-side, such as cakes, milk and wine; or of animals, pigs, sheep and cattle which had to be white for the major gods like Jupiter, black for the

Roman republican bronze coin bearing the double-headed profile of Janus, and (right) sestertius of Nero showing on the reverse the Temple of Janus with its doors closed, a condition which applied only on the infrequent occasions when Rome was not at war

Relief on the altar of the Temple of Neptune in Rome, c. 40 BC, showing a bull, garlanded and decorated, being led forward for sacrifice

minor gods like Terminus, horns gilt and the body of the animal ensheathed in wreaths. Special sacrifices were ordered when calamities occurred, and these were frequent in the war against Hannibal. Great importance was also attached to the taking of auguries and omens, a custom derived from the Etruscans, and in the interpretation of readings from the Sibylline Books, a sort of secret revealed text, bought by Tarquin from the Sibyl of Cumae, which only the appointed priests could consult. They, also, were frequently appealed to during the long confrontation with Hannibal, as even was the oracle at Delphi.

The Romans believed in the immortality of the soul, but as their concept of divine justice was essentially earthly, they did not recognize a heaven or a hell, and considered the after-life as a semblance of idealism or humanitarianism; it served to educate everybody in the exercise of public and private virtue, in morality without mythology, in respect for authority, and in the sense of duty. *Religere* is the opposite of *negligere*, neglect.

CARTHAGE FIGHTS THE GREEKS

IN THE EARLY DAYS in the establishment of their settlements, dotted about sparsely over the shores of the western Mediterranean, Phoenicians and Greeks did not greatly resent one another's presence, there was still generally room for both. Only on this view can it be understood how Greek sailors towards the end of the seventh century BC were able to trade with Tartessos, so near to Gades, and, according to Herodotus, to make a treaty with its king. Homer's *Odyssey* also betrays knowledge of the geography of the western Mediterranean.

Competition between Carthage and the Greek cities became more and more intense after the seventh century BC, and Carthage seems to have attempted to prevent the Phocaeans from settling at Massalia. A fascinating little problem is presented by Cavalaire, between Toulon and St Tropez, east of Massalia. Its ancient name was Heraclea Caccabaria, and to this day it has a beach known as the Plage d'Héraclée, as Greek as anyone could wish. But Caccabaria is clearly derived from Caccabé, a name for Carthage; so the Carthaginians have left a trace there. In their hostility to the Greeks, they combined with an Etruscan fleet to defeat the Massaliots off Alalia in Corsica in 537 BC, and a Carthaginian army under Malchus defeated the Greeks in Sicily, which became a battle-ground between them for three hundred years.

This hardening of Carthage's position with regard to the Greeks seems to have been a reflection in its foreign policy of the events that were taking place in Phoenicia and the mother-city, Tyre. In 539 BC the Babylonian empire was overthrown by the Persians, who thereby extended their sway over the cities of Phoenicia. As a forthcoming contest between the Persians and the Greeks was becoming inevitable, Carthage followed suit by showing a hostile attitude to all Greeks with whom it came into contact.

It may have been the Greeks who precipitated the conflict in Sicily. In view of the impending inevitable struggle, Doreius of Sparta seems to have tried to cut the communications between Phoenicia and Carthage by attacking the Carthaginian ports in west Sicily, but without success.

When Xerxes led the second Persian expedition against Greece, Tyre supplied ships for his fleet. By what appears to have been concerted action to prevent the Greek cities in Sicily from going to the help of Greece, or because of the opportunity to attack those cities when they had no hope of reinforcement from Greece, Carthage landed an army

Fresco found in 1853 in the Via Graziosa, Rome, showing an episode from the 'Odyssey': Odysseus in the land of the Laestrygones. Ernle Bradford's researches suggest that this was Bonifacio in Corsica; whatever the location it can be inferred that the Greeks in Homer's time were not ignorant of the geography of the western Mediterranean

Base of the monument dedicated at Delphi by Gelon of Syracuse after his victory over the Carthaginians at Himera, 480 BC

Votive stele representing the 'Mourning Athena', from the Acropolis, Athens; this may be connected with the ill-fated Athenian expedition to Sicily, 413 BC

at Panormus in 480 BC. It was completely defeated by the Greeks under Gelon of Syracuse at the battle of Himera.

After his victory, Gelon did not insist on the total evacuation of Sicily by the Carthaginians, who were suffered to remain in their towns at the western extremity of the island; but he stipulated by a clause in the peace treaty that there would be no more infant sacrifices in the Carthaginian settlements, the observance of which has been confirmed by archaeological research at Motya, as Vincenzo Tusa has related.

The Carthaginian position in Sicily was for a time saved by the chronic inability of the Greek cities to live in harmony. Segesta, at odds with Selinos, appealed to Carthage for help, but Carthage, mindful of what had happened at Himera, declined. Segesta then appealed to Athens, and the ill-fated Athenian expedition to Sicily was launched. An attempt to capture Syracuse in 413 BC led only to the downfall of Athens. Segesta then appealed again to Carthage, and this time got more than it bargained for. In 409 BC the Carthaginians landed an army which spread terror through the Greek cities in Sicily. Himera, Selinos, and Acragas were taken by storm, and Dionysius I of Syracuse was obliged to make terms with Carthage.

Silver decadrachm of Syracuse, the so-called 'demarateion', 480–479 BC, with obverse showing the head of Arethusa surrounded by dolphins, and reverse showing a quadriga drawing a chariot, with Nike, Victory, flying to crown the horses; in the exergue is a running lion, symbolic of North Africa and Carthage

The unfinished Greek temple at Segesta, late fifth century BC. The building consists of thirty-six unfluted Doric columns; the steps are unfinished, and the cella not begun. The wars in which Segesta was involved at the time doubtless account for the temple's unfinished state

Very soon, however, Dionysius was able to strike a counter-blow, and in 398 BC he laid siege to Motya, stormed and destroyed it, so that it never rose again. It was replaced by a new town, Lilybaeum. The Carthaginians answered by landing another army in Sicily, which laid siege to Syracuse but failed to capture it. A plague which broke out in their army forced them to withdraw in 397 BC.

In 384 BC Dionysius made his raid on the Etruscan port of Pyrgi and captured the treasure of the temple of Astarte, which he used to hire mercenaries to fight the Carthaginians again. At the battle of Cabala he was successful, but at Cronium he was badly defeated and obliged to make terms favourable to Carthage. The indefatigable adventurer tried again a few years later, and almost succeeded in capturing Lilybaeum, but failed because his ships were defeated at sea. A picturesque figure to the end, Dionysius I died in 367 BC from excessive drinking to celebrate his having won the prize in the Olympic competition with his play, 'The Ransom of Hector'.

The astonishing see-saw went on. The Carthaginians succeeded in gaining possession of the town of Syracuse but not of the citadel, and when Syracuse appealed for help to the mother-city Corinth, Corinth sent Timoleon. That remarkable man and expert general defeated the Carthaginians against heavy odds, Sacred Band and all, at the battle of the Crimisus, near Segesta, in 339 BC; the scales were righted again, and the Sicilian Greeks gained a respite.

In 317 BC the demagogue Agathocles made himself master of Syracuse, and became so obnoxious to the other Greek cities that they again called in the help of Carthage. It came, and in 311 BC a Carthaginian army laid siege to Syracuse. Agathocles escaped from the harbour with a small fleet and an army which he landed in Africa, and used to attack Carthage itself. Shades of things to come. He did not succeed in taking Carthage but he caused so much damage and alarm that the Carthaginians raised the siege of Syracuse and made a treaty by which they retreated to the western end of Sicily. Agathocles returned, and died from a poisoned tooth-pick. In a few years Sicily was again to become a theatre of war, in which Agathocles's son-in-law Pyrrhus held the stage.

ROME CONQUERS ITALY

THE FANTASTIC DEGREE of tenacity shown by the Roman people in their earlier troubled history is a forerunner of what to expect during the Hannibalic War when it came.

The rise of Rome was the conquest of Italy, which took half a millennium. The little city by the Tiber had five foes, of which two were her own kith and kin—some closely related in the other cities of Latium, Latins like herself, and others more distantly related in the Oscans, Umbrians, Samnites and others, all Italic peoples whose history had taken them into mountainous regions of Italy instead of to the plains, with consequent disadvantages and advantages to themselves.

The three other foes were intruders on Italian soil. Foremost among these were the Etruscans, Asiatic in origin at any rate as regards their leaders, and foreign in customs. Next in chronological order of hostilities came the Gauls, land-hungry Celtic marauders from the north who deliberately picked a quarrel with Rome, and paid the full price four centuries later. Finally, there were the Greek cities of Magna Graecia, in the south of Italy and in Sicily. As these had been opposed to both Etruscans and Carthaginians, they had usually found themselves fighting the same enemies as Rome; but the whirlwind of events in the end swept them also into hostilities against Rome. It is impossible to treat all these enemies and the wars that involved them in any tidy or even logical or chronological manner, for Rome was frequently embroiled against two or more at a time.

Rome's first task was to establish her supremacy in the immediate surroundings of Latium itself. The senior city was Alba Longa, which made league with the other Latin cities and marched against Rome. This was still in the time of the kings, but the result of the struggle was the assault and destruction by Rome of Alba Longa, whose inhabitants were removed and made to live in Rome on the Coelian Hill. By this means, already in the seventh century BC, Rome took over the leadership from the Latin League. This was, however, far from being the end of the matter, and fighting went on for centuries more, the Latins frequently being assisted by their easterly neighbours, the Sabines.

The Etruscans did not submit passively to the expulsion of their kings from Rome, and after an attempt at a come-back by Tarquin the Proud, Lars Porsenna of Clusium (Chiusi) attacked Rome, on the occasion when Horatius Cocles held the Bridge, the Pons Sublicius, while it was being destroyed to prevent the enemy from entering the city. In this struggle, the Latin cities had helped Rome to defeat Lars Porsenna, but they then decided not to submit to Roman domination any more, and instead to form an independent confederation. This was defeated by Rome at the battle of Lake Regillus, 496 BC, a victory which did not deter the victors from concluding a generous pact with the vanquished, the Cassian Treaty, after the name of Consul Spurius Cassius. It provided for an alliance, offensive and defensive, between Rome and the Latin cities, whose league Rome recognized with equal rights.

The treaty did not have long to wait before being invoked. A new danger had arisen from the incursions into Latium of the Aequi and the Volsci, savage Italic peoples bent on winning fertile land for their increasing populations. Latium was overwhelmed, and only Rome was able to resist successfully and to liberate the other cities. This was the traditional occasion when Cnaeus Martius Coriolanus distinguished himself by capturing the town of Corioli, and disgraced himself by siding with the enemy.

Rome's chief enemies at that time, however, were the Etruscans. The cities of Veii and Fidenae, only a short distance away, were a constant menace, and fighting went on for more than a century. In 426 BC the Romans destroyed Fidenae, and in 396 BC, after a siege said to have

66

One of the Dioscuri (Castor and Pollux), from the pedestal of the Arch of Diocletian in Rome. They were believed to have intervened in the Battle of Lake Regillus and to have appeared in the Forum in Rome on the same day to announce the victory

lasted ten years (suspect as a copy of the traditional length of the siege of Troy), Marcus Furius Camillus captured Veii and destroyed it. The story went that an Etruscan augur from Veii who fell into Roman hands prophesied that the gods would not abandon the walls of Veii until the waters of Lake Albanus found their way to the sea. The Roman Senate ordered a tunnel to be excavated through the lava, five kilometres long, which still exists, and the water from the lake flowed via the river Anio into the Tiber, and so reached the sea.

No sooner had Rome finished the task of reducing Veii, her first enterprise in the grand manner, than a new danger presented itself. The Gauls had crossed the Alps from Gaul into the valley of the Po, where they chased away the Etruscans. It is said that the fall of Melpum to the Gauls took place at the same time as the capture of Veii by the Romans, and that this was the reason why the other Etruscan cities

68

Head of the Apollo of Veii, terracotta, sixth century BC, one of the most striking examples of Etruscan plastic arts yet discovered

did not go to the assistance of Veii. In any case, it spelled the beginning of the decline of the Etruscans, which was hastened by the attacks of Greeks on Etruscan harbours; in 387 BC Dionysius I of Syracuse raided and sacked Pyrgi, the port of Caere (Cerveteri).

In 390 BC, the Senonian Gauls, pursuing their hitherto triumphant progress southwards, crossed the Apennines and laid siege to Clusium. The Romans tried to bring help to the besieged city in order to stop further incursion by the Gauls, whom they had never yet met in battle. Near the river Allia, a tributary of the Tiber, the Roman army was so discomfited by the savage appearance of the Gauls that it was disastrously defeated, and the Gauls continuing on their way entered Rome, in which only a garrison was left on the Capitoline Hill. The city was sacked and burnt, and those inhabitants who had not taken refuge in the friendly city of Caere were massacred. An attempt by the Gauls

to storm the Capitoline Hill was frustrated by the cackling of the Sacred Geese in the temple of Juno, and the garrison, led by Marcus Manlius Capitolinus, repulsed the attackers. But after some months of siege, hunger obliged Manlius to capitulate, and the Gauls under their chief, Brennus, agreed to leave on payment of a large sum of gold, one thousand pounds in weight. The story goes that when it was handed to the Gauls, it was found to be short weight, the weights being false; upon which Brennus thrust his sword into one of the pans of the scales with the famous exclamation 'Woe to the vanquished!'

On two further occasions, the Gauls came south again, in 360 BC, and 348 BC, but on each occasion the Romans stopped them before they approached Rome. Rome was then soon confronted by fresh trouble which came from the Samnites. This warlike Italic people of mountaineers, in its infertile inland region of Samnium (the Abruzzi), coveted the rich plain of Campania with its seaboard. In 343 BC they threatened Capua, and the Capuans appealed to Rome for protection and offered her their own city.

70

◄ *Bronze figurine of a Gaulish warrior, poised to hurl a javelin, late third century BC, found near Rome, naked except for a belt and a Celtic torque round his neck*

Bronze figurine of a Gaulish prisoner, third century AD, from Gaul. He wears tight-fitting quilted trousers and is naked above the waist

Part of the painted Tomb of the Warrior from Paestum showing a procession of Samnite warriors returning home, fourth century BC

Reconstruction (model) of the Temple of Fortuna at Praeneste (Palestrina), second to first century BC; the oracular shrine of Fortuna Primigenia was situated at the top of a palatial temple with terraces, ramps, colonnades, and porticoes

Rome sent one army under Valerius Corvus into Campania where, near Mons Gaurus (between Cumae and Neapolis) he inflicted a heavy defeat on the Samnites. But the other army, under Cornelius Cossus, which marched into Samnium to carry the war into the enemy's country, was surrounded by the Samnites and succeeded in extricating itself only with great difficulty, which was a taste of things to come. Now, however, the two Roman armies, reunited, defeated the Samnites again at Suessula. The Samnites sued for peace, and Capua and Campania were freed from them in 341 BC.

Trouble then came from the Latin cities, for in defiance of the Cassian Treaty, Rome refused to share the conquered territories of Campania with them. It came to war again, and the Consuls Publius Decius Mus and Titus Manlius Torquatus defeated the Latins, first near Mount

Vesuvius, and then at Sinuessa (Mondragone), in 338 BC. This victory had far-reaching political consequences, for Rome was now strong enough to abolish the Latin League and to impose her own hegemony over all the Latin cities. She did this by granting different status and privileges to the various cities, which deprived them of the possibility of ganging-up against her. This was the time-honoured Roman principle of *divide et impera*. Lanuvium, Tusculum, and Aricia were incorporated in Roman territory and received Roman citizenship; others, Tibur (Tivoli) and Praeneste (Palestrina) were deprived of part of their territory but remained relatively independent; others again, Anzio, Cales (Calvi), and Anxur (Terracina) were obliged to receive Roman colonies.

The hegemony of Rome did not, however, mean complete subjection of the Latin cities now directly incorporated in the Roman Confederacy. They mostly enjoyed local self-government, and paid no tribute in money, but were obliged to provide men for the army. Their status was intended to give them a place beside the Romans in battle, it opened up markets for their commerce, and it dangled before their eyes the promise of betterment in the rank of citizenship which Rome might accord to them. The cities that had been conquered by Rome became her allies. The long-term wisdom of this policy was to show itself in no uncertain manner in the confrontation with Hannibal.

Very soon, war against the Samnites broke out again, because Rome established garrisons at Fregellae and at Cales, facing Samnium as if in provocation, and in Neapolis which had placed itself under Samnite protection, but which the Consul Quintus Publius Filo captured after a long siege. The war started in 326 BC, and in the first three years the Romans devastated the countryside of Samnium to such an extent that the Samnites sued for peace. The Roman conditions were so harsh that the Samnites preferred to continue the war, and the Romans then found that the task on their hands was more difficult than they had estimated. This was because the Samnite commander, Caius Pontius, was a military genius and a magnanimous leader. By skilful manœuvring and by propaganda, he lured the Roman army commanded by the Consuls Titus Veturius and Postumius Albinus into a trap, at the Caudine Forks (between Cancello and Beneventum), and inflicted on them the ignominy of unconditional surrender. Caius Pontius retained six hundred knights as hostages but released the rest of the Roman army and the Consuls returned to Rome, where the Senate denounced the surrender and sent the Consuls back to Pontius, who returned them again.

To this vexatious situation, Rome reacted with redoubled energy. She made alliances with the Oscan populations of Lucania and Apulia, and made use of the system of settling colonies of citizens at strategic points, to secure the neighbouring regions. At places on the coast, the colonists usually retained rights of Roman citizenship, but inland the colonies had Latin citizenship, and a Latin colony was established at Luceria, the key to Apulia, in 314 BC. By this means, Rome surrounded Samnium with her allies; but the Samnites then did the same thing against Rome, by rousing the Etruscan and other populations of central Italy. This combination was broken up by a Roman army under Quintus Fabius Rullianus after a battle near Perusia (Perugia) in 311 BC. In the south, another Roman army under Lucius Papirius Cursor (so called from his speed in running) invaded Samnium, defeated the Samnites repeatedly, captured their capital Bovianum (near Campobasso), and obliged them to sue for peace, in 304 BC, by which the Samnites lost all their territories on the Tyrrhenian and Adriatic coasts, in Campania and Apulia.

Six years later, however, Rome was obliged to begin all over again, for the position which she had achieved in Italy was now regarded by many others besides the Samnites as a menace to their own security and independence. A grand coalition was set up, of Samnites, Etruscans, Umbrians, Lucanians, and the Gallic Senones, under the command of another Samnite military genius, Gellius Egnatius. Rome established another Latin colony at Narnia (Narni) in Umbria, in 299 BC, and four years later the allies were routed by the Romans under Rullianus and Mus at the battle of Sentinum (near Gubbio), which put an end to attempts by Rome's enemies in the north and south of Italy to join together to confront her. It was not the end of the war, however, for the Samnites fought on alone until, decisively defeated by Marcus Curius Dentatus, they made peace in 290 BC, recognized the supremacy of Rome, and abandoned their independence.

There followed the subjection of the country of the Sabines, of the Peligni, and of Etruria, and of the territory of the Senones which was converted into the *ager gallicus* in which Rome founded the colony of Sena Gallica (Senigallia). In the south, a strong colony was founded at Venusia (Venosa) in Samnite territory, to keep them in order.

The importance for Rome of this long struggle against the Samnites, and of her victory, lay in the fact that if the Samnites had not been defeated and incorporated in the Roman confederacy, they would have possessed Campania and established their dominion over the Greek cities of Magna Graecia. There would then have been not one

Campanian landscape, with the aqueduct built by the Emperior Claudius in AD 52 to bring water to Rome from the source of the Anio 50 miles away

but two powers in Italy, and Hannibal would have beaten both. As it was, Rome now controlled all central Italy, from Tuscany and Emilia, down almost to the gulf of Tarentum, and the great consular roads, Via Appia to Capua and the south, Via Flaminia to Narnia, Ariminum and the north, Via Valeria to Alba Fucens and the east, spanned the country.

*Bust of Pyrrhus, king of Epirus,
who came to Italy and Sicily
with his army and elephants to
help the Greek cities there, but
was eventually defeated by the
Romans. From Herculaneum*

There remained the Greek cities in the south of Italy, which had
generally been on good terms with Rome, because they had lived at
daggers drawn with the Oscan savage inhabitants of Lucania and
Bruttium. But now that Rome was mistress of Apulia, Lucania, and
Bruttium, Tarentum, richest and most powerful of the Greek cities
over which she exercised a political and economic dominion, looked
with apprehension on the advance of Roman influence on her very
doorstep.

The collision began in 282 B C when the Greek city of Thurii appealed
to Rome for help against the incursions of the Lucanians. Rome sent
a small fleet, but there had been a treaty between Rome and Tarentum
by which it was agreed that Roman ships should not sail eastwards
beyond the Promontorium Lacinium (Cape Colonne). Ten Roman
ships did so; four were sunk and one was captured by the Tarentine
navy. Rome sent envoys to demand satisfaction, but they were
received with the worst insults and indignities from the Tarentines,
upon which Rome declared war, 281 B C.

Although Tarentum had a good army, it was nothing like powerful
enough to stand against the redoubtable Roman legions; so Tarentum

76

Seated statue of a goddess (possibly representing Persephone) of Tarentum (Taranto), which Pyrrhus came to help. The statue dates from the fifth century BC

decided to hire a foreign army. There was one ready to hand, under Pyrrhus, king of Epirus, who wanted nothing better than to unite all the Greeks of southern Italy and Sicily under his rule. He accepted the Tarentine invitation and crossed the Adriatic with an army of thirty thousand foot, three thousand cavalry, and twenty elephants. The Romans confronted it immediately at Heraclea, on the Gulf of Tarentum, with an army under Levinus Valerius. Unfamiliar with the tactics of the Macedonian phalanx, and unnerved by the elephants which they had never seen before (they called them 'Lucanian cows'), the Romans were defeated, and lost their predominance in the south. But Pyrrhus paid a heavy price for his victory, and he is reported to have said, 'Another victory like this one, and I shall have to return to Epirus alone.' The year was 280 BC.

Aware now that the war would be more difficult than he had imagined, Pyrrhus sent an emissary to Rome to negotiate terms of peace, but the Romans insisted that Pyrrhus must evacuate Italy before they would treat with him. Pyrrhus thereupon decided to march on Rome, and having roused the Samnites, Apulians, Lucanians and Bruttians, he reached Praeneste (Palestrina), within sight of Rome, but realized that

77

with two Roman armies in the field against him, to say nothing of the garrison of the city, he could not accomplish anything. He accordingly returned to Tarentum for the winter. Not a single Roman or Latin colony had sided with him.

In the following year, 279 BC, Rome sent another army to Apulia under Publius Decius Mus, but it also was beaten by Pyrrhus at Ausculum (Ascoli) near Foggia, after a furious battle that lasted for two days. Pyrrhus again proposed to discuss peace, but meanwhile Rome had received an offer of help from Carthage who feared that Pyrrhus might intervene in Sicily in support of the Greek cities there. Rome therefore refused to discuss peace.

Pyrrhus received an invitation from Syracuse in 278 BC to fight in Sicily, and he succeeded in driving the Carthaginians from all their positions in the island except Lilybaeum, but was unable to make further progress. In addition, the Greek cities failed to support him, for their characteristic individualism and love of freedom and independence made united action between them impossible. Meanwhile, the Romans had re-established their position in the south of Italy, and in face of this new menace Tarentum appealed to Pyrrhus to come back to Italy. This he did, in 275 BC, saying prophetically, as he left Sicily, 'What a splendid battlefield we are leaving to the Romans and the Carthaginians.'

For the new campaign, Rome had put two armies in the field, one in Samnium under Marcus Curius Dentatus, and the other in Lucania under Lucius Cornelius Lentulus. To prevent them from linking up, Pyrrhus marched against the former, and battle was joined near Maleventum in 274 BC. The Romans had by now developed tactics against elephants, and the light troops waved torches of burning straw in front of the animals which panicked and broke the ranks of their own army. After this victory the name of the town was changed from Maleventum to Beneventum, and Pyrrhus disconsolately made his way back to Epirus.

The Romans then pounced on all those who had received help from or given help to Pyrrhus, annexed their territories, and planted Latin colonies in them. Tarentum opened its gates to the Romans in 272 BC, Rhegium (Reggio) two years later. The whole of Italy from the Arno and the Rubicon down to the Gulf of Tarentum and the Strait of Messina was in the hands of Rome. At last recognized as a power of world importance, Rome made a treaty with Egypt, and what had begun as a tiny Roman people had now become a great Roman State.

II The Rivals: Carthage and Rome

Part of a relief from the Temple of Fortuna at Praeneste (cf. page 72) showing a Roman warship with prow, ram, foc'sle, two tiers of oars and a fighting crew of fully armed legionaries. It is representative of the ships built by Rome to establish sea-power over Carthage

THE FIRST PUNIC WAR

IN VIEW OF the calamitous manner in which relations between Rome and Carthage ended, it is ironical but in no way contrary to the pattern of human affairs that for some centuries these relations were good, even if not cordial. The Carthaginians, as the senior and greater power, continued with respect to Rome the policy which they had long followed with the Etruscans; with them they had combined to oppose the Greeks of Massalia against whom, off Alalia in Corsica, they won a naval victory in 537 BC which prevented the establishment of Greek colonies in Corsica and in Sardinia, areas respectively of Etruscan and Carthaginian influence.

The relations between Carthage and the Etruscans were closer than is imagined. At Pyrgi (Santa Severa), port of the Etruscan town of Caere (Cerveteri), some fifty kilometres north-west of Rome, there are the remains of two temples dating from the end of the sixth century BC. Between the temples there have recently been found three tablets inscribed on gold, two written in Etruscan and one in Punic, containing a dedication to the chief goddess of Carthage. It runs, 'To the Lady Astarte. This is the sacred place made and given by Thefarie king of Caere in the month of the sacrifice of the Sun in gift within the temple and sanctuary, because Astarte has raised him with her hand, in the third year of his reign, in the month of Krr, on the day of the Burial of the Divinity. And the years of the statue of the goddess in her temple are as many as these stars.' These were the temples which Dionysius I of Syracuse raided in 384 BC.

Punic text invoking Ashtoreth on a gold tablet from the Etruscan temple at Pyrgi (Santa Severa); sixth century BC

V   Terracotta figure of a man and his wife, from the lid of an Etruscan sarcophagus from Caere, c. 500 BC

Etruscan bronze helmet captured by the fleet of Hiero I of Syracuse off Cumae in 474 BC; the Greek inscription shows that it was dedicated by him at the Temple of Zeus at Olympia

From the moment when, in 509 BC, Rome turned out the kings and established the Republic, the power of the Etruscans began to wane. Already in 524 BC they had tried and failed to capture the Greek city of Cumae, and half a century later (474 BC), in the sea battle off that town, their fleet had been routed by that of Hiero I of Syracuse, who in gratitude dedicated the spoils of victory to the temple of Zeus at Olympia, including an Etruscan helmet now in the British Museum. But Carthage had not waited until then to make treaties with Rome, the first of these dating from 508 BC. The next was made in 348 BC, recognizing Carthage's sphere of influence in Africa and in Spain, and safeguarding Rome's trade with Sicily and guaranteeing the immunity of the Italian coast from raids. In 306 BC another treaty was made, less favourable to Rome for it limited Roman shipping in southern

VI   Handle of an Etruscan bronze cista depicting two armed warriors carrying the body of a dead comrade, probably fourth century BC, from Praeneste

81

Mediterranean waters; Rome was paying the economic price for the difficulties which she was having in pursuing her wars against the Samnites.

In 277 BC Rome and Carthage were brought closer together by their common enemy, Pyrrhus, whose prophetic words about Sicily being the imminent battlefield between Rome and Carthage were not long in being verified. That triangular-shaped island was almost designed by nature to invite trouble between the three political powers to which its corners pointed; its western extremity only two hundred kilometres from Carthage; its north-east corner only five kilometres from the mainland of Italy, and therefore, Rome; its eastern and southern coasts inviting the Greeks. It had good harbours, was fertile, and served as a granary for supplies of wheat, more than enough to make it a Naboth's vineyard. For centuries an uneasy balance had been maintained in it between the Greeks and Carthage, and it was only a matter of time before a new armed conflict broke out between these powers; and as Rome increased in strength and influence, she became involved herself.

The fire that had been slowly smouldering for some time was kindled into flame in an unexpected manner. Some Campanian freebooters, the Mamertines (called after Mamers, the Oscan name for Mars), had fought in Sicily as mercenaries for Agathocles against the Carthaginians, and then occupied the Greek town of Messana (Messina) where

Bronze coin of the Mamertini of Messana (Messina) showing a warrior armed with spear, helmet and shield

The great altar of Hiero II at Syracuse in ▶
the form of a stadium, said to have been
built for the sacrifices commemorating the
expulsion from Syracuse of the tyrant
Thrasybulus

they lived by piracy in the Strait. Hiero II of Syracuse besieged them in 265 BC with the object of ridding Sicily of their presence. But the Mamertines appealed for help to Carthage and to Rome, and Carthaginian troops were admitted into Messana. Rome hesitated at first,

*Bust of Hiero II
of Syracuse
(269–216 BC)*

Roman warship showing the inventions of grappling irons and gang-planks for boarding enemy ships; nineteenth-century engraving

Triumphal column of Caius Duilius in the Forum, Rome, decorated with prows of ships captured from the Carthaginians; eighteenth-century engraving

for intervention in Sicily meant inevitable conflict with Carthage, the largest and richest city in the western world. Eventually, however, Rome decided to intervene. The Tribune Caius Claudius Cadix landed in Sicily, invited the Carthaginian commander to parley, arrested him, and the Carthaginians were turned out of Messana which was then occupied by the Romans. So, in 264 B C, the First Punic War began. Carthage then formed an alliance with Hiero of Syracuse, and their troops besieged Messana. But the Consul Appius Claudius Cadix, with his army, crossed the Strait on rough improvised rafts, fell on Hiero's troops, defeated the Carthaginians on the following day, and raised the siege of Messana.

Hiero then dropped his alliance with the Carthaginians and contracted one with Rome, to which he remained faithful for the remainder of his long life. The facilities which he provided in Syracuse and other cities enabled Rome to mount such an offensive that most of the island was gradually brought under her control. After a siege of seven months, the Carthaginian stronghold of Acragas (Agrigentum) was captured in 261 BC, but Carthage held its fortresses of Lilybaeum (Marsala), Drepanum (Trapani), and Panormus (Palermo), which could be kept supplied by sea.

Rome then realized that in addition to a land army, she must provide herself with a navy and establish supremacy at sea if she was to beat the Carthaginians and capture the whole of Sicily. With surprising rapidity, copying Carthaginian models, including a five-banked ship or quinquereme that had been cast ashore on the coast of Bruttium, Rome built a hundred and twenty ships, adding an invention of her own, in the form of mobile gang-planks over which the legionaries could board Carthaginian ships and fight as on land after the latter had been secured by means of grappling irons. The first efforts were disappointing, and a squadron under Cnaeus Cornelius Scipio was captured near the Lipari Islands. But under Caius Duilius the Romans won their first victory at sea off Mylae (Milazzo) on the north coast of Sicily, and the bronzes from the prows of the Carthaginian ships went to adorn Duilius's triumphal column erected in the Forum in Rome. Thus for the first time, the sea-power of Carthage had been successfully challenged.

This Roman victory failed, however, to bring about the desired results, for the Carthaginians, who were the more experienced seamen, resorted to harassing tactics and avoided general engagements. Rome then adopted the expedient of sending an army to attack Carthage on land in Africa, following the precedent set by Agathocles. In 256 BC the Consuls Marcus Attilius Regulus and Lucius Manlius Vulso; with forty thousand men and over three hundred ships, succeeded in beating a Carthaginian fleet off Cape Ecnomo (Monte Sant'Angelo) on the south coast of Sicily, and landed on African soil. But the Roman Senate then made the mistake of recalling Vulso with half the army. With the help of local populations disaffected towards Carthage, Regulus nevertheless defeated the Carthaginians who asked for peace.

But Regulus's terms were so harsh as to be completely unacceptable, and Carthage steeled herself to continue the war. She hired more mercenaries, and invited Xanthippus, the Spartan general, to command the Carthaginian army. Near Tunis, in 255 BC, he beat the Romans completely and captured Regulus himself. A fleet was sent by Rome to rescue the survivors of the disaster but matters were only made worse when it was completely destroyed in a storm off Cape Passaro. Rome then abandoned hope of securing a decision in Africa, and settled down to the long haul of conquering Carthage in Sicily.

The first step was to rebuild a new fleet, with which in 254 BC the Romans besieged and blockaded Panormus and captured the city. But in the following year, this fleet was also destroyed by a storm. With a large army including one hundred and twenty elephants, the Carthaginians attempted in 250 BC to retake Panormus, but they were heavily defeated by Lucius Cecilius Metellus who captured all the elephants. This was a terrible blow to Carthage, which again tried to negotiate a peace, sending Regulus to Rome to ask for it, on condition that he would return. In Rome, however, Regulus urged the Senate to continue the war, because he knew that Carthage was almost exhausted. He returned to Carthage empty-handed, and was put to death.

Meanwhile, the Carthaginian command in Sicily was entrusted to Hamilcar Barca, an aristocrat whose family claimed descent from Dido herself. His name, Hamilcar, contains that of the god Melqart, and Barca means thunderbolt. Endowed with a high degree of military genius, he perfected his well-trained army with promises of high pay, succeeded in stabilizing the position on land, and maintained a successful resistance in Lilybaeum, Drepanum, and Mount Eryx, the only positions which were still held by Carthage in Sicily, and which could be supplied by sea.

In 249 BC Rome built a third fleet of two hundred ships, and the Consul Appius Claudius Pulcher sailed with it to attack Drepanum. Before engaging in a battle, in accordance with custom the omens were consulted, and Pulcher was informed that they were unfavourable because the Sacred Chickens in their golden cage refused to eat. The Consul said the equivalent of 'if they won't eat they'll damn well

The cliffs of Mount Eryx (Monte San Giuliano), western Sicily. Mount Eryx was one of the last Carthaginian strongholds defended by Hamilcar in the First Punic War

drink', and he threw them overboard into the sea. This act of gross impiety and the unfavourable message of the omen sapped the combative spirit of the Romans, and their fleet was completely destroyed by the Carthaginians.

After a period of inconclusive fighting, Rome resolved to try again, and in 242 BC she ordered the construction of yet another fleet, the fourth. The coastal towns of Italy complained that they were unable to comply as they were ruined by the ship-building efforts that they had already put in, and had no more money. The fleet was built with subscriptions from the richest citizens of Rome, and placed under the command of the Consul, Caius Lutatius Catulus, who came upon the Carthaginian fleet off the Aegadian Islands, at the western tip of Sicily, and destroyed it completely.

In 241 BC peace was concluded with a treaty by which Carthage agreed to the following terms: cession to Rome of the whole of Sicily and of all the islands between Sicily and Africa, prohibition of sailing with quinqueremes in Italian waters, prohibition of fighting against Syracuse or any allies of Rome, and payment within ten years of three thousand two hundred talents of silver. The First Punic War—the earliest struggle in recorded history to last so long and pass through such oscillations of fortune—had come to an end, but it was really only an armistice and not a permanent peace that had been concluded between Rome and Carthage.

HAMILCAR'S PLAN

THE TREATY that ended the First Punic War differed in its effects on the two contenders. On Rome it impressed the necessity of possessing and maintaining sea-power, which increased in importance as Rome ceased to be concerned solely with military operations in Italy, and was drawn more and more frequently into wars in distant lands. Without it, the Roman empire, which came into existence long before the Empire, would never have been possible.

The second effect on Rome was political. While Roman arms were confined to operations in Italy, the conquered town or tribe became incorporated in some capacity into the State system and acquired

VII   Punto Milazzo on the north coast of Sicily, looking towards the island of Vulcano; near here in 260 BC the Romans under Caius Duilius defeated the Carthaginian fleet

a share in the Confederacy, subject to Rome but retaining a certain degree of autonomy, paying no tribute to Rome, but supplying men and services for the army. With the conquest of Sicily, Roman imperialism began. The towns and states of the island (with a few exceptions) were not incorporated in the Roman Confederacy, but treated as subjects, paying tribute in money or in kind, under a Roman Governor with almost absolute powers, appointed for a short term of service, too short to enable him to appreciate the local problems properly, and during which he was only too prone to fall into the temptation to feather his nest. The system was to lead later to dire results. On the other hand, the governed benefited by the Roman peace and the Roman administration of justice, which, although rough and ready, was better than that or the lack of it under which they had suffered before. So Sicily became the first Roman Province.

On Carthage the consequences of the peace were more immediate and more serious. Deprived of the possibility of continuing to fight, Hamilcar resigned his command, and another general, Gisgo, evacuated the troops back to Africa. There, trouble was not slow in breaking out, for the Carthaginian government tried to induce the men to accept less pay than Hamilcar had promised them, and, in any case, it wanted to see the army disbanded as quickly as possible. The result was a mutiny and the Mercenaries' War, which broke out in 241 BC when the mutineers blockaded Carthage.

In the face of this danger, Hamilcar was recalled. The mutineers held all the passages over the Bagrades (Medjerda) river, but Hamilcar knew that when a north-west wind blew over the mouth of the river, it was possible to cross the bar, wading in water. With all the reliable troops that he could raise, ten thousand men and seventy elephants, he crossed the bar, took the enemy in the rear, and raised the blockade of Carthage. He next defeated the mutineers in battle by means of a skilful tactical manoeuvre. He withdrew some of his troops, which made the enemy think that they were retreating, whereas in fact the troops came round on the enemy's flanks and defeated the mutineers with great slaughter.

There were still some mutineers, to the number of about forty thousand, near Tunis. After much marching and counter-marching, Hamilcar lured them after him into a defile which he blocked at both

VIII *Reverse of a gold stater of Ptolemy I of Egypt (366–283 BC) showing a quadriga of elephants drawing a chariot (cf. page 100)*

ends with his troops in ambush, and the mutineers were annihilated. The date was 239 B C. A vivid description of these terrible events was given by Gustave Flaubert in his novel *Salammbô*, named after Hamilcar's daughter, priestess of the goddess Tanit.

During this time, well aware of Carthage's helplessness, Rome took advantage of the opportunity to seize and annex the islands of Sardinia and Corsica, which had not been included in the treaty as due to be ceded to Rome. The pretext was that if Sardinia had continued to be in Carthaginian possession, it would have been a perpetual menace to the coast of Italy. The means was handed to Rome on a dish, for in 238 B C, the Carthaginian mercenaries in Sardinia, no less disaffected towards Carthage than those in Africa, and with the terrible example of their fate before them, invited the Romans to occupy the island. The local inhabitants resisted the Romans and fighting went on for some time, but Rome had now secured possession of her Second Province. What was more, Rome obliged Carthage to recognize the new state of affairs, and increased the amount of the indemnity which Carthage was compelled to pay.

This glaring example of power politics rankled with Hamilcar as much as, if not more than, his enforced retirement from Sicily. The immediate danger to Carthage had been avoided, and a precarious peace had been obtained; but another and even more deadly danger had become obvious. If, by means of her sea-power, Rome had been able to conquer Sicily, there was now nothing to prevent her from landing an army in Africa and conquering disarmed, ruined, and helpless Carthage. To make matters worse, there was the danger of a peace party gaining power in the Carthaginian Senate, and Hamilcar's own position was uncertain. In secret he worked out a plan to redeem Carthage's political and military fortunes, before it was too late.

Carthage had lost Sicily, Sardinia, and sea-power; but there remained Spain. Rich in timber, mines, and man-power, Hamilcar saw that if he developed Spain, he could recoup the lost fortunes of Carthage, and do so under the noses of the Romans on the pretext that it was necessary in order to enable Carthage to pay the war indemnity. But Spain would also supply excellent fighting men for his army. Even more important, Spain was on the mainland of Europe. So was Italy. Even deprived of sea-power, it would be possible to get from Spain to Italy overland. Finally, Spain would serve as a base far enough away from both Carthage and Rome for nobody to know exactly what he was doing. Because of all these factors Hamilcar determined to develop Spain as a sort of personal empire, in which he was helped by an influential Spanish Carthaginian, Hasdrubal the Handsome, who became the husband of Hamilcar's daughter.

Carthage had no navy, and was afraid to build one in case Rome should attack her when she was defenceless. There were therefore no warships to carry Hamilcar and his army from Carthage to Spain. He solved the problem by marching westwards along the north coast of Numidia, accompanied at sea by a few transport ships to carry food and fodder, as far as the Strait of Gibraltar which he crossed by improvised methods, and reached Gades in 236 BC, where he made his base. From there, he advanced eastwards, fighting the native tribes, and making allies of them after he had beaten them, in which way he soon consolidated his hold on the southern part of the Iberian peninsula. On the east coast, near Alicante, he established an advanced base,

Coin minted at Carthagena c.230 BC, showing the bearded head of Melqart, generally regarded as a portrait of Hamilcar Barca

Entrance to the harbour of Carthagena, the principal Carthaginian base in Spain

Map of the western Mediterranean to illustrate the approximate route of Hannibal's march (218 BC) from Spain to Italy, and the early stages of the campaign against Rome

ALPS

CISALPINE
GAUL

Insubres

Cremona

Po

Rhône

Isère

LIGURIA

Clastidium

Placentia

Durance

Massalia

Mutina

Ariminum

Faesolae

Arretium

L.TRASIMENE

ETRURIA

ADRIATIC SEA

Telamon

CORSICA

Alalia

Pyrgi

Caere

Rome

Cannae

SARDINIA

TYRRHENIAN

SEA

CAMPANIA

Crotona

Mt.Eryx

LIPARI IS.

Drepanum

Panormus

AEGADIAN IS.

Lilybaeum

Messana

SICILY

Carthage

Agrigentum

CAPE
ECNOMO

Bagrades (Medjerda)

Tunis

Zama

Hadrumetum (Sousse)

MALTA

Leptis
(Lebda)

CERCINA IS.

I A

at Lucentum, but in the course of these operations Hamilcar died, apparently as a result of drowning while crossing a river, in 228 BC. The leadership fell on his son-in-law, Hasdrubal the Handsome, who continued Hamilcar's policies with such success that he was able to extend the Carthaginian sphere of influence as far north as the river Ebro, and he established a new base, New Carthage, Carthagena, in the best harbour on the Mediterranean coast of Spain, where a thriving capital city soon blossomed, with its fortifications, palaces, mint, docks, and arsenal.

The rapidity of the Carthaginian advance to the Ebro caused apprehension among the Greek colonies along the coast, particularly Massalia, and also in Rome with which Massalia was allied. At that time Rome had no territory in Spain or in Gaul, and Roman opposition to any further expansion of Carthaginian power in Spain was probably based on economic rather than on military considerations. Tin was a strategic material, for without ten per cent of tin to alloy with ninety per cent of copper, it was impossible to make bronze, the essential metal for weapons, that did not rust. Copper was not so difficult to come by, but tin was more rare.

The chief source of tin for Massalia and Rome was Cornwall, where the Cornish streamers transported it in wheeled carts to Iktin, St Michael's Mount. There traders came over from Brittany to fetch it in their ships and bring it to the western coast of Gaul, whence it was conveyed to Massalia after a journey of thirty days overland, as Diodorus of Sicily related. The itinerary of these tin caravans was down the coast of the Bay of Biscay, up the valley of the Garonne, across what is now called the Seuil du Languedoc near Carcassonne, down the river Aude, and so to the Mediterranean coast and Massalia. This route passes a short distance to the north of the range of the Pyrenees, which protected it, but it was in order to make it doubly safe that any advance by the Carthaginians north of the Ebro must be resisted by Massalia and by Rome.

A Roman mission was sent to Hasdrubal the Handsome in 226 BC to negotiate a settlement of this problem, and it was agreed that the Roman sphere of influence should extend down to the northern, and the Carthaginian up to the southern bank of the Ebro. But south of that river, on the coast, was the Greek city of Zakynthos, Saguntum, which, at a date later than the agreement, came under the protection of Rome, a fact which was to have tremendous consequences.

Meanwhile, in 221 BC, Hasdrubal the Handsome was murdered, and Hamilcar's mantle then fell on his eldest son, Hannibal.

94

ENTER HANNIBAL

HANNIBAL, in Punic *Chenu Bechala,* meaning 'Grace of Baal', the eldest of Hamilcar's sons, was born in 247 BC. With his three brothers, Hasdrubal, Hanno, and Mago, they formed what their father called 'The Lion's Brood', and such indeed they proved to be. Hannibal was brought up in Carthage which was then undergoing the worst period of the First Punic War. In 237 BC, when Hamilcar was about to take his army to Spain to carry out his great plan, Hannibal, then nine years old, wanted to accompany him. Hamilcar was preparing to offer sacrifice, to ensure the success of his venture, and made his son swear an oath, with his hand on the sacrificed animal, that when he grew up he would never forget that Rome was the deadly enemy. This story, in spite of its Roman source in Livy, was probably not invented, for the humiliation which the whole Barca family felt at the shameless way in which Rome used power politics to violate the peace treaty was reflected in the spirit with which not only Hannibal, but all his brothers, honoured the oath which he had sworn.

Once he was in Spain, Hannibal took to military life like a duck to water. He soon showed a genius for tactics, man-management, command, and leadership. His horses and his horsemanship were superb, and his weapons and equipment were the object of his constant care. In his clothing he showed no rank-consciousness, but wore the ordinary dress of an officer. Abstemious of wine and women, indefatigable in mind as well as in body, he could endure extremes of heat and cold, fatigue or hunger, and instead of sleeping in a bed he was often seen by the pickets and sentries sleeping among them, on the ground, covered only by his cloak. Supreme at fighting, with a total disregard of danger, it is not surprising that all these qualities endeared him to his men to a fanatical extent. This information comes from a Roman, Livy.

On one occasion in Spain, when a column of Hannibal's horsemen became detached and cut off from him by a river, he swam the river himself and encouraged his men after him. He inspired them all with confidence and audacity; they would do anything for him, and, as will be seen, they did. This personal background has to be borne in mind when considering the tasks which Hannibal set his men, and how they accomplished them, in spite of the fact that they were not a patriotic national army, but a motley crowd of mercenaries, from Carthage, Numidia, Spain, the Balearic Islands, Gaul, and elsewhere, fighting not for their native land, but for their personal devotion to their leader.

95

Presumed portrait busts of Hannibal, according to Gilbert Charles Picard, based on head-shape, features, hair, and comparison with Carthaginian coins: (left) marble head at the Ny Carlsberg Glyptotek, Copenhagen; (right) bronze head from Volubilis, Morocco

Little more is known of Hannibal's personal character. Cornelius Nepos related that he was a scholar as well as a soldier, and this quality agrees with the acts of statesmanship which he afterwards accomplished. He was taught Greek by Sosilos and is reported to have written books in Greek, including one addressed to the Rhodians on the deeds of Cnaeus Manlius Vulso in Asia.

Much as the Carthaginians disliked the Greeks, some, and in particular Hannibal and his family, appreciated fully the Greek contribution to thought. This may be detected in the fact that the Barca family established a pantheon of their own particular gods, not identical with those of Carthage itself. This, as Gilbert Charles Picard has shown, would explain why the treaty which Hannibal later concluded with Philip V of Macedon, invoked as witnesses not only the gods of Carthage and Macedon as a matter of form, but also Baal Shamim who was the equivalent of Zeus, Melqart or Heracles, and Reshef or Apollo. The tapping of the sources of Greek inspiration may also be seen in the coins which Hamilcar and Hannibal struck in Spain, and this leads on to a consideration of Hannibal's personal appearance.

Reverse of a silver double shekel struck at Carthagena c. 220 BC, showing beardless head of Melqart generally regarded as a portrait of Hannibal

Little reliance can be placed on antique busts said to represent Hannibal, with the possible exception of a bronze head found at Volubilis in Morocco, as Picard has made clear. The best evidence of what he looked like is provided by the beautiful silver coins minted at Carthagena. Some of these, bearing on the obverse the head of bearded Melqart, represent Hamilcar, in the opinion of E. S. G. Robinson and others. Later coins, from the time when Hannibal succeeded to the command, show a beardless head with a strong facial resemblance to the bearded type, and this has been attributed to family resemblance of Hannibal to his father. If this was correct, Hannibal had a straight nose, a very strong forehead, a bright and open expression, and a twinkle in his eye. The head found at Volubilis resembles it closely.

After Hasdrubal the Handsome was murdered in 221 BC, the army, unanimously, acclaimed Hannibal as their general. Here may be seen a reflection of the fact that the Carthaginian leadership in Spain was a sort of personal dictatorship vested in the Barca family, with a large degree of independence from the Senate at Carthage, which accepted the *fait accompli* of the army's choice. The episode also provides a preview of what was to happen centuries later in Roman history, when a commander acclaimed by the army in a distant province imposed his will on Rome.

Hannibal's army was composed of professional soldiers who served for the attractions of pay and plunder, and a fixed occupation. So far as is known, the infantry was at first organized on the tactical principles of the Greek phalanx; Xanthippus had commanded the Carthaginian army during the First Punic War, and his reorganization must have been based on Greek military methods. The phalanx was a solid body of heavy infantry, the men standing nearly shoulder to shoulder, in two hundred and fifty-six files, each sixteen men deep, or just over four thousand men. They were armed like hoplites with swords and spears, heavy shields and armour, and the object of the formation was to give a heavy shock, but it lacked flexibility, particularly over uneven or broken ground. The men were drawn to a small extent from Carthage, and more from the neighbouring regions of Africa and from Spain, all these providing the best troops. There were also Gauls, who fought with great dash, but were unreliable. In addition to the heavy infantry, there were light infantry, peltasts or targeteers with light shields, and psiloi, lightly armed, with no armour.

The most distinctive feature of Carthaginian infantry were the slingers, or Balearic Islanders, who were organized in corps of two thousand men, armed with two types of sling, one for long-distance fire and the other for close-quarters shooting. The missiles which they threw were stone pebbles or leaden bullets, and their accuracy was such that they could hit a hair set up as a target. Their fire-power was superior to that of the best contemporary archers.

The cavalry consisted of heavy units, composed of Spaniards who commonly rode two men on a horse, one to fight on horseback and the other on foot, and auxiliary squadrons of Gauls. The best troops of the Carthaginian army, however, were the Numidians, from the north coast of Africa west of the Carthaginian domains, Algeria and Morocco. The name Numidian means nomad, and they were born horsemen. Armed with a spear and javelins, they were lightly clad, mounted on sturdy little horses, without saddles or bridles, and guided by the

Punic armour, decorated breast- and back-plates with shoulder braces and belt, from a tomb at Ksour-es-Sad, Tunisia, third century BC. The work and motif of the goddess's head appears to be Campanian, and the armour may have belonged to an Italian mercenary in Hannibal's army

Hoplites (heavy infantry) depicted on the Chigi vase found at Veii. The men are armed with spears, helmets, breast-plates, grieves, and round shields decorated with pictorial devices. On the left a flautist plays the double pipe. Protocorinthian, mid-seventh century BC; height of frieze, approx. 2 in.

Reverse of a coin minted at Carthagena c. 220 BC, showing a palm-tree and a horse, a favourite emblem of Hannibal's

voice and stick of the rider. Their tactics were to charge enemy troops with great dash, but not to engage if the enemy was heavily armed; instead, the Numidians withdrew to charge again and again, and to harass the enemy like a swarm of hornets. Endowed with phenomenal powers of endurance in man and horse, accustomed to mountainous country, they were as effective in that as on the flat, and adept at taking cover behind obstacles and at laying and emerging from ambushes: the best light cavalry.

The Carthaginian army also, of course, had elephants, as in the First Punic War; but elephants are so closely associated with Hannibal in the public imagination that a consideration of them as fighting animals is best placed here, in the following chapter.

ELEPHANTS

MAN'S KNOWLEDGE OF ELEPHANTS goes back a long way, for at Salayah in the Libyan desert there have been found scratched representations of elephants attributed to Neolithic times, before 4000 BC. There is also a representation of an elephant on the early dynastic statue of Min in Egypt. An inscription of Amenemheb, who was in Syria with Thothmes III in 1470 BC, records that he was chased by an elephant. Ashur Nasirpal and Shalmaneser in the ninth century BC received tribute of elephants from Syria (Black Nimrud obelisk).

The first introduction of Europeans to the use of elephants in war was probably at the battle of Gaugamela, 331 BC, when Alexander the

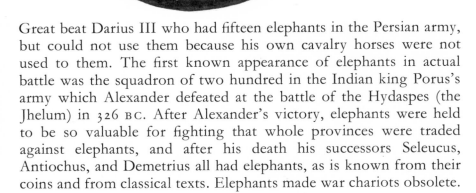

Reverse of a tetradrachm of Seleucus I of Syria, minted at Pergamum c.280 BC (at the time of Pyrrhus's invasion of Italy), showing an Indian elephant

Decadrachm showing Alexander the Great on horseback attacking Porus riding an Indian elephant; minted at Babylon to commemorate Alexander's victory and conquest of the Punjab

Great beat Darius III who had fifteen elephants in the Persian army, but could not use them because his own cavalry horses were not used to them. The first known appearance of elephants in actual battle was the squadron of two hundred in the Indian king Porus's army which Alexander defeated at the battle of the Hydaspes (the Jhelum) in 326 BC. After Alexander's victory, elephants were held to be so valuable for fighting that whole provinces were traded against elephants, and after his death his successors Seleucus, Antiochus, and Demetrius all had elephants, as is known from their coins and from classical texts. Elephants made war chariots obsolete.

101

All the elephants so far referred to were of the Indian species, *Elephas indicus*, then common in Syria as well as in India. Pyrrhus had some in his army at the battle of Heraclea in Italy, the Romans' first introduction to them, in 280 BC, and the Roman *aes signatum*, minted shortly after that date, depicts them, as does a plate from Capena.

There is another elephant still extant, the African, and this was pressed into service by the Egyptians and the Carthaginians. It was of the small species *Loxodonta africana* variety *cyclotis*, known as the forest elephant to distinguish it from the great bush elephant found in central and southern Africa. The Carthaginians found their forest elephants fairly close at hand, at the foot of the Atlas mountains and on the coast of Morocco, and they were also plentiful round the oasis of Ghadames, south of Tunisia. At the present time, the forest elephant is not found in western Africa north of the Senegal river. They were first used in the Carthaginian army during the First Punic War at Acragas (Agrigentum) in 262 BC.

The Egyptians obtained their elephants, also of the small forest variety, from the coastal belt of the Red Sea and Eritrea. Ptolemy II established a base at Ptolemais (near Aqiq, Sudan) for hunting and shipping elephants to Egypt. They were still to be found in that region at the time of Napier's expedition to Magdala in AD 1868, but are now extinct north of the Sudan.

Terracotta figurine of an elephant of Antiochus I of Syria (280–261 BC) crushing a Galatian warrior. The elephant is Indian and carries a castle on its back

Painted dish from Capena, in Campania, of Etruscan style, third century BC. It shows an Indian elephant with driver (mahout) and a castle (howdah) and two Macedonian warriors, followed by a baby elephant

Silver phalera (military decoration) showing an Indian elephant bearing a driver with goad in hand, and a castle with two soldiers

Reverse of a tetradrachm of Antiochus III of Syria showing an Indian elephant

Roman mosaic of the Imperial ▶
period at Ostia, showing an African
elephant; by this time the Romans
had their own African elephants

In 217 BC the army of Ptolemy IV, with seventy-three elephants, fought the battle of Raphia near Gaza against Antiochus III whose army contained one hundred and two Indian elephants. Polybius has described the battle: 'The armed crews of the elephants put up a splendid fight, and the elephants themselves an even better one, pushing with all their strength and clashing head to head. Elephants fight in the following manner; they interlock their tusks and press against each other's heads, wrestling, until one, overpowering the other, presses its trunk aside and jabs it in its flank with its tusks.' Polybius continued, 'Most of Ptolemy's elephants shirked the fight, as African elephants are wont to do, because they cannot bear the smell and the trumpeting of the Indian elephants. Furthermore, I believe that they are dismayed by the greater size and strength of the Indian elephants, with the result that they run away.'

These lines of Polybius have been the subject of much uninformed adverse criticism by modern commentators who were ignorant of the difference between the bush and the forest varieties of African elephants. Polybius's account has been completely vindicated; the heights at the shoulder of the three elephants are approximately 7 feet 9 inches for the African forest elephant, 9 feet 6 inches for the Indian elephant, and 11 feet for the African bush elephant. The size of the Indian elephant made it possible to mount howdahs or 'castles' on its back, containing archers. The African forest elephant was too small and seems never to have carried a castle, but to have been ridden bareback. Indian and African elephants have been depicted on coins and mosaics,

and the differences between them are so clear-cut that they can easily be distinguished. The African forest elephant differs from the Indian in the following features: 1, the ear is enormous, whereas the Indian elephant's ear is small; 2, the back has a concave dip between a high point over the shoulder and another high point over the hind quarters, whereas the back of the Indian elephant is an unbroken convex dome from front to rear; 3, the hind quarters are almost flat, whereas the Indian elephant's hind quarters project backwards at a fairly sharp angle; 4, the head is carried high, while the Indian elephant carries its head low; 5, the forehead is flat, instead of showing the Indian elephant's concave profile; 6, the trunk is marked by transverse ridges, instead of being smooth; 7, the tip of the trunk has two 'fingers' instead of only one as in the Indian elephant; 8, the upper part of the front edge of the hind leg is masked by a fold of skin forming a skirt, whereas the front edge of the hind leg of the Indian elephant is uncovered right up to the groin.

105

Reverses of Punic silver coins from Hannibal's time showing African elephants. A comparison of the cloaked driver (left) and his mount demonstrates how small the elephant was; the elephant on the right shows the markedly concave back of this variety; both show the typical ribbed trunk, 'skirt', flat hind-quarters and big ears

Hannibal's elephants, as the coins show, were mostly African. The fact that their drivers were referred to in classical texts as 'indoi', Indians, is due to the practice of the Egyptians, when they started training elephants, of importing Indian tamers, trainers, and drivers, and in no way invalidates the African nature of the elephants, as is proved by the beautiful coins minted at Carthagena in about 220 BC. The relatively small size of the African forest elephant means that they were not much bigger than horses, and their passage over mountains cannot have been attended with as much difficulty as the Indian variety would have encountered. Nevertheless, there is evidence, which will be presented in due course, to show that Hannibal must have had one or more Indian elephants with him. These Carthage must have obtained from Egypt, with which it enjoyed friendly and close relations. Ptolemy I captured some in 321 BC when Perdiccas invaded Egypt with Indian elephants and was defeated. At the battle of Gaza in 312 BC, Ptolemy captured all forty-three of Demetrius's Indian elephants; and in the Third Syrian War, 246 to 241 BC, Ptolemy III defeated Seleucus and captured more of this type. It is known that during the First Punic War, Ptolemy II lent Carthage large sums of money, and it must be concluded that he sent Indian elephants as well, which he could well have done before Rome acquired sea-power.

As will be seen, Hannibal used his elephants primarily to strike terror into native tribes which had never seen them before, and against

Roman cast bronze bar (aes signatum), *weight about 5 lb. The reverse shows an Indian elephant, the obverse a sow. Probably commemorating the Roman victory of 274 BC at Beneventum when some of Pyrrhus's elephants were panicked by pigs in the Roman camp*

cavalry whose horses had not been trained to meet them. In set battles, however, as Pyrrhus had experienced, and especially against Roman troops, the elephants were apt to do as much harm to their own side as to the other, and as part of their equipment their drivers were eventually provided with a chisel and mallet to pole-axe them and kill them before the damage which they did was irreparable. This also was usually unsuccessful.

SAGUNTUM

AFTER TAKING OVER COMMAND, and before embarking on wider schemes, there was still some consolidation work for Hannibal to do in Spain, to complete the task undertaken by his father and brother-in-law. In 221 BC, he laid siege to the town of Carteia (site unknown), capital of the tribe of the Olcades, south of the Ebro, and stormed it. It was in the Carthaginian sphere of influence, but not yet under Carthaginian control, and by attacking it, Hannibal moved a step nearer to his objective without disclosing it. He returned to winter quarters in the south.

In the following year he extended his operations further to the north. His line of march has been traced by F. W. Walbank as crossing the Sierra Morena by the Peñarroya Pass, past the site of Merida to Salmantica (Salamanca), which he captured. He subdued the Vaccaei, a tribe living in the middle reaches of the river Douro, and turned south again, probably across the Puerto de Guadarrama, to the Tagus near Toledo. Those Iberians who got away from Salmantica joined forces with the Olcades whom Hannibal had defeated the previous year, and, together with another tribe, the Carpetani, combined in his rear to attack him when he crossed the Tagus. By means of a night march, Hannibal slipped past the enemy, crossed the Tagus by a ford higher up the river, and came down it again to face the enemy from the other bank. They began fording the river in small parties, and when they were in the water Hannibal set his cavalry at them and cut them to pieces as they floundered about without firm foothold, and were carried away by the current. The well-trained Carthaginian cavalry were firm on their mounts. Hannibal then led his infantry across the river and completed the rout of the enemy. The Carpetani surrendered, and the whole of the Iberian peninsula south of the Ebro was then under his dominion, with the exception of the Greek city of Saguntum. Hannibal returned to the south, probably by the Valdepeñas Pass through the Sierra Morena. He was now able to turn his thoughts wider afield, as events were soon to show.

By 220 BC, Hannibal's army was recruited, trained, and equipped to carry out the plan which Hamilcar had laid but Hannibal was now to implement. It combined the elements of initiative and surprise with that of psychological shock, for its main feature was that the Roman army must be fought on Italian soil. This was all the more desirable because the Gauls in the north of Italy were seething with revolt, in anger against the treatment which they had received at the hands of the Romans during the previous few years. An opportunity had arisen which must not be missed. Only five years previously, in 225 BC, the Boii had joined with the Insubres, Cenomani and other Gallic tribes, including some from the western side of the Alps, and to the number of some seventy thousand they invaded Etruria, ravaging and burning everything in their path, and defeated a Roman army near Faesolae (Fiesole).

Rome had had her fill of Gallic tumults and took extreme measures. The Sibylline Books were consulted, and it was found that the soil of Italy was destined to be occupied twice by foreigners. By means of a sort of do-it-yourself anticipation of the prophecy of invasion, the Senate ordered that a Gaulish man and a Gaulish woman and a Greek man and a Greek woman should be buried alive in the Forum. In Etruria, the Gallic army avoided a Roman army under Lucius Emilius Papus by turning westwards towards the Tyrrhenian Sea; but there they were confronted by another Roman army under Caius Attilius Regulus which had just returned from Sardinia. Caught between the two, the Gaulish hordes were annihilated in a terrible battle at Telamon (Talamone).

To put an end to these Gallic incursions, Rome then determined to invade and conquer Cisalpine Gaul. Caius Flaminius crossed the Po with his army, but got into such difficulties that he was obliged to make terms with the Insubres. Then he attacked again and the situation caused by his faulty dispositions was saved by the courage of his troops. Rome insisted on unconditional surrender, which the Gauls refused. The Insubres called to their aid some Gauls from the western side of the Alps, who came, to the number of thirty thousand, but they were badly defeated by the Consul Marcus Claudius Marcellus at Clastidium (Casteggio) in Piedmont. The other Consul, Caius Cornelius Scipio, routed them in another battle, and joining his army to that of Marcellus, he occupied the Insubrian capital Mediolanum (Milan) and Comum (Como). In this sanguinary manner, Rome established a foothold in what was to become yet another Province, Cisalpine Gaul. In order to consolidate her hold on it, she established Latin colonies at Placentia (Piacenza) south of, and Cremona north of the Po to keep the Insubres in check, and at Mutina (Modena) to subdue the Boii, in about 220 BC.

The Gauls were smarting under all these blows, and Hannibal knew it, and determined to profit from this unrest. He also expected that Rome would have trouble on her other flank, in Illyria and in Greece. It never occurred to the Romans, or to anybody else, except Hamilcar,

Saguntum, general view of the site of the ancient city captured by Hannibal in 219 BC; in the foreground is the Roman theatre built later, and beyond the citadel

that the Carthaginian army would or could make the overland journey from Spain, across the Ebro, the Pyrenees, Gaul, the Rhône, and the Alps to reach Italy. This was precisely what Hannibal had decided to do, taking advantage of all the preparations which Hamilcar had made when he developed Spain as a base, and a source of supplies and man-power.

The operations were planned in great secrecy and required the collection of much information. There was first of all military intelligence, of the nature of the country and the obstacles which the army would have to circumvent on its way to Italy, and the fighting capacities and tactics of the inhabitants through whose territories it would have to march. This was obtained from military missions which he requested the various Gallic tribes to send to him. Of equal if not greater importance was political intelligence, regarding the opinions, aspirations, and aversions of the various tribes, the maintenance of their opposition to Rome, their powers of resistance to Roman pressure, the numbers of their populations, and the likelihood or otherwise of their granting him support, supplies, and men to join his own army, which, when he reached Italy, would be cut off from its base by one thousand five hundred kilometres.

Finally there were questions of logistics and commissariat to be studied and answered. How was the army to be fed during its march across the Pyrenees, the south of Gaul, and the Alps, until it reached the prospective allies, the Gauls in the north of Italy? Some districts were fertile, but others, like the high alpine valleys, were barren, and one of Hannibal's staff-officers, Hannibal Monomachus, suggested that the men of the army should be trained to live on human flesh. Hannibal refused to consider this proposal of cannibalism, but it is historically of interest because of the similarity of his name to that of Monomachus, and Polybius recognized that the reputation for ferocious cruelty which the Romans attached to Hannibal may in reality have been due to his having been mistaken for Hannibal Monomachus.

All these items were taken into consideration, and plans were laid for the great march. But Hannibal had one more difficulty to overcome nearer home. He had wide popular support, but the Carthaginian Senate contained a number of appeasers, peace-at-any-price men, very fond of money, animated by jealousy and hatred of Hamilcar's family, who dreaded the idea of antagonizing Rome and thereby endangering their lucrative business and trade. The Senate could hardly be relied on to declare war against Rome. Yet war it must be, and quickly, to take

Fifteenth-century illuminated miniature depicting the siege of Saguntum. The Saguntines, of Greek origin, determined that no man, woman or child, nor their possessions, should fall into the hands of the barbarous Africans. The picture shows the fire lit, the destruction of precious goods, and the immolation of inhabitants

advantage of the circumstances. Hannibal therefore undertook a psychological warfare exercise against the government of Carthage. The opportunity was provided by the town of Saguntum (its modern name of Murviedro is derived from the *muri veteres, muros viejos,* of Saguntum).

Neighbours of the Greek inhabitants of Saguntum were the tribe of the Turdetani, Iberians, whose opposition to the Saguntines Hannibal skilfully fanned into a flame. Fearing that Hannibal would soon pass to hostile action, the Saguntines appealed to their protectors the Romans. Rome sent envoys to study the situation and interview

Hannibal, to warn him that Saguntum was under Roman protection, which he knew very well. Meanwhile Hannibal had started on the siege of Saguntum, 219 BC. The Roman envoys arrived, and Hannibal treated them with studied coldness, saying that he had no time to give them an audience, in the hope that they would then and there declare war. The Roman envoys withdrew and went to Carthage to complain that Hannibal was violating the agreement on spheres of influence in Spain. Hannibal wrote to forewarn his friends in the Carthaginian Senate, which stood by him when the Roman envoys demanded the surrender of his person. Instead, the Carthaginians laid the blame on the Saguntines, adding that it would be Rome who acted unwisely if she allowed her protection of the Saguntines to take precedence over the good relations that had existed between her and Carthage for over twenty years.

The siege of Saguntum went on, bitterly contested, and it lasted for eight months before the city fell, with all the horrors of massacre and destruction. Its great riches passed into Hannibal's hands, and he astutely sent the booty to Carthage to strengthen his supporters. The news of the fall of Saguntum reached Rome at the same time as the envoys returned from Carthage with their negative message. Rome decided on a declaration of war, but before embarking on hostilities she sent yet another delegation to Carthage, composed of men of the highest standing, with instructions to ask whether it was in accordance with the policy of the Carthaginian Senate that Hannibal had attacked and destroyed Saguntum. The Carthaginians replied with a legal argument, saying that the treaty between Carthage and Rome which provided that neither side was to interfere with the allies of the other made no mention of Saguntum, which was not at that time an ally of Rome. Furthermore, the treaty had not been ratified by the Roman Senate, nor approved by the Roman people. It was therefore in the same case as Hasdrubal's understanding about spheres of influence in Spain, which had not been endorsed by Carthage, and had neither more nor less validity.

The Carthaginians then invited the Romans to state what was really in their minds, and Quintus Fabius Maximus gathered his toga into a fold over his chest, saying, 'Here we bring you peace or war. Choose which you prefer.' The Carthaginians replied that the Romans could choose. Fabius said 'War', and the Carthaginians added 'So be it.' The Second Punic War had been declared.

After the operations at Saguntum, Hannibal returned to winter quarters at Carthagena. In the spring of the fateful year 218 BC he went to Gades to offer sacrifice to Melqart and returned to concentrate his army. He addressed his men, appealing to their highest and lowest instincts, the former by telling them that Rome had demanded the surrender of his own person, their general, which raised their indignation; the latter by painting in glowing colours the richness and fertility of the countries through which he was going to lead them, which whetted their appetite for plunder. A day was appointed for the start of operations in May.

Shortly before this time, Hannibal had married a lady called Imilce, a native of Castulo on the Baetis (Guadalquivir). If Silius Italicus was correct, this town was founded by Imilce's ancestor Castalius, a native of Delphi, and Imilce would have been of Greek descent. Their married life spent together was not long. Their son was born during the siege of Saguntum. As there was to be war, a campaign was no place for a wife, at any rate in Hannibal's army. Silius's poem relates how Imilce appealed to her husband to let her accompany him in the field, saying, 'Do our union and our nuptial joys make you think that I, your Wife, would fail to climb the frozen mountains with you? Have faith in a woman's hardihood.' Hannibal remained inexorable, and sent his wife and child to Carthage.

THE SECOND PUNIC WAR BEGINS

THROUGH HANNIBAL'S POLITICAL ASTUTENESS, it was the Romans who declared the Second Punic War and could, therefore, on a possible interpretation of the facts be regarded as having violated the peace treaty with Carthage. For the year 218 BC, Rome had appointed as Consuls Tiberius Sempronius Longus and Publius Cornelius Scipio. The former received Sicily as his province, which in view of the war with Carthage was the place nearest to the enemy where Rome could concentrate an army. Scipio received as his province Spain. The reason for this was not only the importance of safeguarding the line of the Ebro and the Pyrenees, but also the anti-Roman feeling that had developed north of the Ebro. Hannibal had known very well what he was doing when he besieged, stormed, and destroyed Saguntum. A Roman mission sent to northern Spain found that the prestige of Rome had sunk very low, for there was Saguntum to prove that in spite of Roman protection, Rome had done nothing to save the Saguntines from Hannibal's attack, and, following the time-honoured practice of rushing to the aid of the victors, the Spanish tribes preferred to side with the Carthaginians and told the Romans so, and asked the mission to get out; this it did, and went to Gaul.

In Gaul, the Roman delegates had a reception only a little better than that which they had received in Spain, for the Gauls maintained proudly that as they had never had any help from Rome, nor suffered any harm from Carthage, they would not take sides in the forthcoming struggle. Furthermore, the Gauls in Gaul had learnt that their brethren the Gauls in Italy had recently been the victims of very severe repressive measures by Rome, expelled from their territories, obliged to submit to the establishment of Latin colonies, beaten in battle and forced to pay tribute. The wretched Roman delegates, on their way home with nothing but failure to report, received no word of comfort until they reached Massalia which remained firm in friendship. These were the reasons why it was decided to send Scipio with his army to Spain.

This is the appropriate place to consider briefly the organization of the Roman army at the time of the outbreak of the Second Punic War. The Roman army was based on the principle of personal service by the citizens defending their state and their homes. It was not yet a professional army. The word Legion means selection, and it was an honour to serve. The legion, as a tactical unit, was the equivalent of the modern division. It was divided into ten cohorts, equivalents of battalions. In each cohort there was one maniple of *hastati,* younger men, 120 in number, armed with sword, javelin, and lance; one maniple of *principes,* slightly older men, also 120 in number, similarly armed; and one maniple of *triarii*, mature middle-aged men, 60 in number, who were armed with sword and pike and constituted an old guard of veterans.

The maniples were drawn up in order of battle, the *hastati* in front, each maniple of twelve files, ten men deep, with intervals between the maniples equivalent to the frontage of a maniple. In second line came the maniples of *principes,* also twelve files, ten men deep; but the maniples of *principes* were stationed behind and facing the intervals between the maniples of *hastati,* in chequerboard fashion, so that the second line could advance and reinforce or replace the first line without any confusion or obstruction.

This tactical formation, said to have been originated by Marcus Furius Camillus out of the previous solid formation of the phalanx, conferred valuable flexibility on the legion's power of movement, reinforcement in attack, fighting in retreat, and negotiating broken ground. The third line, the maniples of *triarii,* each of six files ten men deep, likewise covered off the intervals between the maniples of *principes.* The cohort also contained a corps of *velites,* 120 men strong, light infantry armed with a round shield and several darts. They could be stationed between the maniples in the intervals, or in the rear or on the flanks. Lastly each cohort had attached to it a *turma* of cavalry, consisting of 30 mounted men armed with lance and darts, and bridled horses.

A legion was therefore about 4,500 men strong, and the regular composition of a Consular army was two Roman legions. But attached to each Roman legion was an allied legion, recruited from the cities of the Roman confederacy. The total strength of a Consular army was thus four legions, to which were attached auxiliary troops, raised from Gauls or other tribes. In each army, the allied legions detached 200 horsemen and 800 infantry to form a reserve, the *extraordinarii,* who supplied the body-guard of the Consul.

The legionary was heavily laden, for in addition to his weapons, shield, armour, and helmet, he carried digging tools and two palisades for the fortification of the camp which was built each night after the day's march. He also carried a cooking pot, and his rations which consisted of two pounds weight per day of unground wheat, which he cooked himself to make cakes or porridge, and some meat.

The traditional tactic of the Roman army was to attack, and after throwing javelins and darts, to close with the short sword which was designed for thrusting as well as slashing. The men stood sufficiently far apart to swing their swords without getting in one another's way, twice as far apart as the men in the Greek phalanx. It will be seen how these tactics had to be modified in the ensuing war. The Roman cavalry was not outstanding, for the men were not born horsemen like Numidians and Gauls.

The mainstay of the Roman army was its wonderful centurions, the backbone of the legions, tough, professional long-service senior non-commissioned officers, two to a maniple, devoted to the army and to the State, who by their drill and discipline licked the legionaries into shape. Their records of service, quoted by classical authors, or found inscribed on stone tablets and monuments, make inspiring reading.

The Roman army had, however, a handicap, the system by which the command changed every year, a measure designed to prevent the danger of military usurpation of power, but which made continuous and coherent strategy impossible if a war lasted more than one year.

Bronze statuette of a Roman legionary wearing a cuirass of overlapping metal bands, helmet with cheek-pieces, and a kilt of leather and metal strips

Inscribed funerary stele of Favonius Facilis, centurion of the XXth legion in Britain, with his vine-wand; probably killed in Boadicea's rebellion

In a war which lasted as long as that fought against Hannibal, circumstances eventually compelled a relaxation of this system, but the relaxation contained within itself the seeds of trouble to come, when, a century and a half later, it led to the abuse of military dictatorship. These were the characteristics of the armies which Sempronius concentrated in Sicily and Scipio prepared to lead to Spain. Meanwhile, Hannibal had not been idle.

View from Montdauphin looking north across the upper basin of the river Durance towards the Col du Mont-Genèvre, which may have been Hannibal's intended pass. The configuration of the mountains suggests that there is no way through in this direction

III Over the Alps and Far Away

HANNIBAL'S MARCH BEGINS

HANNIBAL REALIZED VERY WELL that while he was on his march to
Italy the Romans might not only take advantage of their possession of
Sicily to mount an attack against Carthage, but also undertake operations in Spain to undermine the recently obtained loyalty to him of the
Iberian tribes. Accordingly, he sent a force of some fifteen thousand
men, slingers, targeteers, and cavalry to Africa, and raised four
thousand picked men to reinforce the garrison of Carthage. In Spain,
he placed his brother Hasdrubal Barca in command, with another
army of fifteen thousand men, twenty-one elephants, and a small
fleet. His policy was to employ Spanish, Balearic, and Ligurian troops
in Africa, and African troops in Spain, as mutual guarantees of loyalty
and good conduct.

Under his own command, Hannibal had ninety thousand foot soldiers,
twelve thousand horsemen, and many elephants, with which, towards
the end of May 218 BC, he advanced from Carthagena to the Ebro,
which river he crossed in July. He was then in Catalonia, a hilly country
inhabited by stubborn tribes whose resistance he must overcome if
he was to carry out his plan of crossing the Pyrenees. His army
advanced in three divisions. Several tribes were subdued and some
towns stormed at the cost of considerable loss to his own troops.
Hannibal then entrusted ten thousand men and one thousand horses
to his brother Hanno to control the passes over the western Pyrenees
between Spain and Gaul.

After he had passed Emporiae (Ampurias), Hannibal started to cross
the Pyrenees. By this time, in spite of secrecy and security measures,
many of the foreign contingents in his army had guessed that the
destination of the army was Italy, and they were appalled at the prospect of having to cross the Alps at the end of such a long march. One
contingent of three thousand men refused to proceed any further.
Hannibal refrained from recalling them or compelling them, because

of the injurious effect that such a measure would have had on his other foreign troops. Instead, he dismissed more than seven thousand of those whose reliability he mistrusted, and proceeded with his army now reduced to some fifty thousand men in the infantry, nine thousand cavalry, and thirty-seven elephants.

The exact pass or passes by which the army went over the eastern spurs of the Pyrenees is not known, but J. Colin was of opinion that it was by the Col de Banyuls, about 360 metres high, 37 kilometres from Emporiae and 33 to Illiberis (Elne), where Hannibal encamped. The Gauls also knew that Italy was Hannibal's destination, and as they did not wish to undergo the fate of the Catalonian tribes through whose country Hannibal had just passed, they concentrated their forces near Ruscino (Castel-Roussillon). Hannibal's chief concern was to avoid delay, so he invited the Gallic chiefs to a conference, and succeeded in convincing them that he came as a friend and not as a foe, after which they let him proceed through their country.

Hannibal's line of march through Languedoc, in the south of Gaul, is not exactly known. There were marshes and lagoons along the coast, but he must have kept as close to it as possible, and neutralized the town of Agde, colony of Massalia, allied to Rome. No Roman

The mountains of the Pyrenees at their eastern extremity near Banyuls. The route followed by Hannibal's army from Ampurias in Spain to Illiberis in Gaul is not known in detail, but must have been through mountainous country of this nature

roads had at that time been built through the country, which did not become the Roman Province until 121 BC, after which Cnaeus Domitius Ahenobarbus built the Via Domitia. But there is one source of information which helps indirectly to identify, albeit roughly, Hannibal's line of march. Polybius, writing about 150 BC, gave distances between selected points on this march, expressed in round figures, in Greek stadia. The text of Polybius's book, as it has come down to posterity, contains the sentence, 'these distances have been carefully measured by the Romans in units of 8 stadia to the Roman mile.' This would make the stadium equal to 185 metres. But the Romans did not build their road until after Polybius's death, and Strabo, writing in the first century BC, stated specifically that Polybius had calculated $8\frac{1}{3}$ stadia to the Roman mile, which makes the stadium 177·5 metres. It appears that it was Artemidorus, fifty years after the Roman conquest of Greece, who rationalized the length of the stadium as one eighth of a Roman mile. For present purposes, therefore, the length of Polybius's stadium must be taken as 177·5 metres.

Polybius's distances are as follows: from Carthagena to the Ebro 2,600 stadia (461 km.); from the Ebro to Emporiae 1,600 stadia (285 km.); from Emporiae to where Hannibal crossed the Rhône 1,600 stadia (285 km.); from the crossing of the Rhône to 'the ascent towards the Alps' 1,400 stadia (248 km.), and from that point to the plain of Piedmont, across the Alps, 1,200 stadia (213 km.). The total comes to 8,400 stadia, from Carthagena to Piedmont, or nearly 1,500 kilometres. But a slight complication then arises, because in another place in his text Polybius referred to the total as about 9,000 stadia, which is 600 stadia, or 106 km., more than the separate items added together. The difference is probably not significant, in view of the imperfection of geographical knowledge and of methods of surveying then available. The conclusion to be drawn is that Polybius's distances are an approximate guide. Those commentators who have ignored Polybius's distances altogether have merely substituted their own fanciful imagination for what historical evidence exists.

From Emporiae to the point of crossing of the Rhône, the distance of 285 km. given by Polybius agrees roughly with the distance of 290 km., by the shortest route, from Emporiae to Fourques, opposite Arles, immediately above the point where the Rhône divides into its distributaries, the Petit Rhône on the west, and the Grand Rhône on the east, which enclose the marshes of the Camargue.

There are numerous reasons, in addition to this rough correspondence of distance, for believing that Hannibal's crossing-place was indeed

Ruins of the ancient Greek settlement of Emporiae (Ampurias)

Fourques. One is Polybius's statement that Hannibal crossed the Rhône where it is a single stream, four days' march from the sea. Coming along the coast from the west, and leaving the sea near where the Petit Rhône runs into it, Fourques is the first place where the Rhône is a single stream. In his operations in the Rhône valley, the speed of march of Hannibal's army is given by Polybius as 80 stadia, or 14 km. a day; and 56 km. is about the distance from the sea near Aigues-Mortes to Fourques. A further reason is that the crossing point was the same distance, four days' march, from another point which will be described below. For reasons which will become obvious when the actual method of getting Hannibal's army across the Rhône is considered, it is clear that he crossed the river where it is least swift and therefore most shallow; that is necessarily where it is widest and where the slope of the river-bed is least steep, which is nearest to the sea. All these conditions are met opposite Fourques, but not further upstream where the Rhône is faster, narrower, and deeper. Finally, when itineraries came to be written, the road from Gades to Rome given in the Gaditanian Vases, the itinerary from Bordeaux to Jerusalem, and the Antonine Itinerary, place the crossing of the Rhône at Fourques, doubtless for the same reasons as those which applied to Hannibal. It is the later descriptions, given by Strabo, the Peutinger Table or Map, and the work of the Anonymous Geographer of Ravenna, which place the crossing of the Rhône between Beaucaire and Tarascon, 17 km. further north than Fourques, and where the river would have occasioned much greater difficulties for Hannibal, even if his crossing had been possible at all there. Some commentators have wanted to make Hannibal cross the Rhône still higher up, at Roquemaure, or Pont-Saint-Esprit, which was even more impossible.

The Romans have the credit for establishing a network of roads in western Europe, and these, many of which still exist or are traceable, are enumerated in the various Latin Itineraries; but they are all military roads, built for strategic purposes. Before their time, there had been numerous roads or tracks ever since the Bronze Age serving purposes of trade and transport, as is proved by the finds of Greek, Etruscan, and other imported objects in Gaul (and in Britain), especially in the Rhône valley and along the Mediterranean coast. These tracks also served for migrations and wars, and were opened rather than built by the Ligurians and Iberians, and by the Gauls when they had driven the Ligurians back to their foothills and mountain fastnesses in the Pyrenees and Alps. There was a wealth of possible tracks for Hannibal to choose from.

HANNIBAL CROSSES THE RHÔNE

IN VIEW OF THE IMPORTANCE of speed in Hannibal's plans, not only to get across the Alps before the winter but also to disconcert the Romans, he lost no time in preparing to cross the Rhône at the first place where he came to it, which was also the most advantageous for him. It was an operation of no mean calibre to cross a river nearly one km. wide, with fifty thousand foot, nine thousand horse, and thirty-seven elephants. Moreover, the crossing was opposed. The Gaulish tribe

The river Rhône looking from Fourques towards Arles just upstream from the point where it splits into its distributaries the Grand and Petit Rhône; here the river is most shallow and its current slowest

The Rhône opposite Avignon, where the Île de Bartelasse divides it into two swiftly flowing streams. It is possible that Hanno crossed the river here with his light troops, without horses or elephants

of the Volcae owned territory on both sides of the river, and although Hannibal not only professed friendship towards the Gauls but had undertaken his whole expedition in part to free the Gauls in northern Italy from the Roman yoke, the Volcae did not take kindly to his approach, and concentrated their forces on the left or eastern bank of the river to oppose him.

From such local tribesmen as had not left their homes on the western bank, Hannibal succeeded by means of presents and bribes in collecting all available river craft (which were numerous because of the trade that was carried on in the lower reaches of the Rhône), and in having rafts constructed and tree-trunks hollowed out. In two days, a fleet sufficient for the army to cross had been collected.

Meanwhile, the hostile Gauls were massing on the opposite bank, both foot and horse. Hannibal's operation was in any case going to be delicate, and the army vulnerable while it was being carried out. He therefore undertook one of his tactical devices to deal with the opposition. He sent Hanno, son of Bomilcar, with a party of Spanish troops up the right bank of the river, to his left, a distance of 200 stadia, 35 km., to a place where an island in the middle of the Rhône divided the water into two streams. There Hanno was to cross by means of improvised rafts made from the trees which abounded on the spot. There is no guarantee that in the course of the two thousand years that have elapsed since this operation the islands in the Rhône have persisted exactly in the same places, but islands there certainly were, and it may be noted that today, between Vallabrègues and Aramon, there is a group of islands about 24 km. from Fourques, and at the distance of 35 km. there is the Île de Bartelasse between Villeneuve-lèz-Avignon and Avignon. Whichever island it was, the river was there divided into two streams, each narrower, and at least one of them faster and deeper than at Fourques; but this presented little difficulty to Hanno because his force was small, had no horses or elephants, and was unopposed. The Spaniards swam across supported by their shields.

After making his crossing, Hanno turned southwards on the left bank of the Rhône and took up a position in the Volcae's rear. On the following morning he made a smoke signal to Hannibal, who ordered his men to begin to cross. It was at dawn on the fifth day since his arrival on the right bank. For the infantry, rafts and tree-trunks were ready; the cavalry got across either by embarking the horses in larger boats, or by horses and men swimming across together, or by the horses swimming with their bridles held by men in the stern of boats, three or four horses at a time, while larger boats stationed on the side upstream acted as a sort of break-water and reduced the strength of the current.

Suddenly, as the Volcae were shouting and brandishing their spears, and shaking their shields above their heads, Hanno and his men, who had captured the Volcae's camp, fell on their rear and drove them away in confusion after a brief show of resistance. This action not only enabled Hannibal's army to complete its crossing of the Rhône without further opposition, but it also gave him a modest opinion of the fighting qualities of the Gauls, his future allies during the campaign in Italy.

Hannibal was now able to get his elephants across. The method adopted was to build piers, about sixty metres long, jutting out into the river, and secured against the current by means of ropes attached to trees upstream on the river bank. To the end of each pier there were fastened rafts, about twelve metres wide, with floats made fast on either side. The piers and the rafts were covered with earth, to make the elephants believe that they were still on dry land when they were led on to them, cow elephants first, followed by the bulls. When they were on the rafts, these were cast off from the piers and towed across the river. Some of the elephants panicked, stampeded, upset their rafts, and fell into the water. But the river there was so shallow that they were within their depth. With their trunks held up over the surface of the water, they waded across safely, and not a single elephant was lost. As the majority of the elephants were of the small African forest variety, about 7 feet 9 inches high at the shoulder, the depth of the river cannot have been much more than 9 feet, and this is one of the reasons for concluding that the crossing of the Rhône took place where it was widest, opposite Fourques.

His army assembled on the left bank of the Rhône, Hannibal encamped. He had just learnt a surprising piece of news: Scipio, with his Consular army, had arrived near the eastern mouth of the Rhône (the Grand Rhône), and disembarked it. The surprise was mutual, for Scipio knew that Hannibal had crossed the Ebro, but was not certain that he had crossed the Pyrenees, and did not know what his objective was. Now he learnt that Hannibal was crossing the Rhône, and it was clear that his objective was none other than Italy. This information was

An eighteenth-century engraving depicting Hannibal's crossing of the Rhône: in the fore- ▶
ground, the pier onto which elephants are unsuspectingly led; in midstream a raft bearing an
elephant, with another wading across; on the opposite bank, elephants and troops and
Hannibal's camp

confirmed to Scipio by a force of 300 cavalry which he sent out to reconnoitre. Hannibal met it with 500 Numidian horsemen, and there was a savage little skirmish with heavy losses on both sides. The Romans had almost reached the end of their resistance, when the Numidians broke off the fight, turned and retreated. The Romans were then able to see Hannibal's camp, and returned in haste to report to Scipio. As soon as Scipio had received the information from his scouting party, he immediately set out to advance with his army, up the left bank of the Grand Rhône to attack Hannibal; but when he reached the place where Hannibal had crossed the river, he found the camp deserted, and learnt that Hannibal had marched away northwards three days before, the day after the cavalry skirmish. This fact is very important geographically, for it means that Scipio's army had reached Hannibal's crossing-point in three days' march, the distance being approximately the same, some 60 km., as Hannibal had covered in four days from the point where he had left the sea. Scipio's army was not composed of professional soldiers, but of citizens. In accordance with the invariable Roman custom, they constructed an entrenchment to fortify their camp every night after the day's march, and 20 km. is certainly as much as they could have covered in a day. This is further evidence that Hannibal's crossing-point was not more than 60 km. from the sea, and, as will shortly be seen, it makes nonsense of claims to the contrary.

Hannibal, for his part, after he had completed his crossing, received a delegation from the Boii, under a chief called Magalus who offered to provide guides and expressed the hope that Hannibal would concentrate all his energies on reaching Italy as soon as possible, and that he would not be deflected from this purpose, and incur losses, by fighting Scipio's army on the bank of the Rhône. This view coincided entirely with Hannibal's own policy, of striking the first real blow against the Romans on Italian soil, where it would have the greatest effect. It was for this reason that on the day after crossing the Rhône he had already started to march northwards up the left bank of the river, and avoided a battle with Scipio.

Magalus with his military mission from the Boii had arrived just in time to help Hannibal to keep up the morale of his army, for the troops were beginning to show nervousness at the length and difficulties of the march before them, and especially at the crossing of the Alps. Nor had they forgotten that it was the Romans who had won the First Punic War. Hannibal harangued his men and pointed to Magalus and his party as descendants of the Gauls who had crossed these selfsame

Alps with their wives and families two centuries before. Bellovesus had led his tribe of Insubres over the 'Taurine Pass' and founded Mediolanum (Milan) at that time. He was followed by Elitovius who led the Cenomani over the Alps to establish themselves near Brescia and Verona. Then came the Boii, the Lingones, and the Senones. Twenty years before, the Boians Atis and Galatas had called more Gauls over the Alps, and only seven years before, Concolitanus and Aneroestus and their men had crossed into Italy to help their Gallic brethren against the Romans.

Why, Hannibal asked, were his men now nervous? In Spain under his leadership, they had been victorious everywhere. They had taken Saguntum (memories of plunder). They had crossed the Pyrenees. They had forded the Rhône against opposition by the Volcae, Gauls; and it was Gauls who had captured Rome itself less than two hundred years before. Magalus and his companions had just crossed the Alps and come to meet them, and they did not need to fly through the air to get across. What were they afraid of? Such was the oratory with which Hannibal steeled his men to continue the march.

To return now to Scipio; on finding the Carthaginian camp deserted and the army gone, he was greatly surprised, for he could scarcely bring himself to believe that Hannibal would try to cross the Alps and reach Italy through barren regions occupied by powerful and treacherous tribes. But that was clearly what Hannibal had set out to do, and as Scipio realized that he could not overtake him, he marched back to the eastern mouth of the Rhône, re-embarked his army which he sent on to Spain under the command of his brother Cnaeus, and himself sailed back to Italy where he intended to take command of the troops in Cisalpine Gaul, then under the Praetors Lucius Manlius and Caius Attilius, and be in a good position to oppose what was left of Hannibal's army in the valley of the Po, if Hannibal did succeed in crossing the Alps.

'THE ISLAND'

ALL THE FOG that has hung for four hundred years like a cloud over the problem of the route which Hannibal took, and the pass over the Alps which he crossed, can be traced to some stupid blunders and faults of scholarship on the part of the editors who first printed the manuscripts of Polybius and Livy in the sixteenth century.

In order to bring the problem into true perspective it will now be necessary to examine in some detail the essential background and show that a close analysis of the ancient texts in the light of recent findings provides a clear indication of the route taken by Hannibal's army after crossing the Rhône.

The problem is quite simple. Both Polybius and Livy, who copied him closely, state that after making good his crossing of the Rhône, Hannibal marched north up the left or eastern bank of the river for four days until he came to a place which, in Greek and in Latin respectively, they called 'the Island'. This was described as a region shaped like the Delta of the Nile; in other words, an equilateral triangle, densely populated, very fertile, and wheat-growing, which means that it was low-lying and liable to flooding. It was enclosed between the Rhône on one side (the west), another river on the second side (south-east), and a range of mountains on the third side (north-east). It was therefore not an island totally surrounded by water, but there are many examples of pieces of land bearing the name of 'island' with water on many sides without being completely surrounded by it. In Provençal speech today, *iscle*, 'island', means land liable to flooding. The trouble began with the name of the second river, which, in the manuscripts (and the fact that they are manuscripts must be stressed) of Polybius is called the *Skaras,* while in the manuscripts of Livy it is called the *Arar.* The oldest extant copies of these manuscripts date from the tenth and eleventh centuries, long before scribes and scholars began tinkering with the texts. The name *Skaras* defeated the sixteenth-century editors, and when Perotti published a Latin translation of Polybius's *History,* he calmly altered *Skaras* into *Arar* to make it agree with Livy. Carlo Sigonio followed suit in a footnote to his edition of Livy in which he also altered Polybius's *Skaras* into *Arar.* Isaac Casaubon, in his printed edition of Polybius in Greek, similarly altered *Skaras* into *Araros,* thereby giving the name of the river a spurious Greek form for which there is no manuscript authority whatever.

Presently, these early editors became worried, because they remembered from Caesar's *Gallic War* and other sources that *Arar* was a name for the Saône, which flows down from the north into the Rhône at Lyons; and Jacob Gronovius realized that the Saône did not fit the geographical requirements of the text at all, for the troublesome river was said by Livy to rise in the Alps, which the Saône certainly does not, and in no circumstances could the land enclosed between the Rhône and the Saône be said to form an equilateral

Stele found at Kleitor in Arcadia, said to represent Polybius (202–120 BC), born at Megalopolis in Arcadia. He was the Greek general and historian who followed Hannibal's route across the Alps, lived in the house of the Scipios, and was present at the final destruction of Carthage

triangle, shaped like the Delta of the Nile, with a range of mountains along its third side.

With their patchy knowledge of geography, the editors then noticed that there was a river, the Isère, which flowed into the Rhône, from the Alps, at a place where they imagined that Polybius's *Skaras* and Livy's *Arar* ought to be. As the Latin name for the Isère, *Isara*, has many letters in common with *Arar*, Philip Cluver substituted *Isara* for *Arar* in his work on the antiquities of Italy. His excuse for this was that in the manuscripts, the word *Arar* is preceded by the adverb *ibi* (there), and in some manuscripts there is something that looks like an *s* between *ibi* and *Arar*, giving *ibi sarar*. By knocking off the first two letters and the last *r*, the word *Isara* is conjured up.

The country near Buis-les-Baronnies, showing the mountains forming the boundary on the north-east-side of 'The Island'

The river Rhône looking towards ▶ 'The Island', the low-lying, fertile, densely populated triangular area of land liable to flooding. In the distance, the Baronnies mountains

But there was still Polybius with his *Skaras,* which had already been altered by Casaubon into *Araros* to make it agree with what was (rightly) originally thought to be Livy's text. Nothing daunted, Cluver altered it again, into *Isaras* to make it agree with the alteration in Livy's text. The scholars congratulated themselves on these exploits, and Holsten provided an explanation of how the manuscripts had allegedly been falsified by supposedly ignorant copyists, who transcribed the Greek capital letters OICARAS (= Isère) into CKORAS (= Skaras). It never occurred to these editors that *they* were the falsifiers, and they might easily have discovered the fact for themselves. Silius Italicus in his poem on the Punic War followed the text of Livy closely in the names of places, rivers, and tribes which he mentioned, and Silius wrote *Arar*. There is no getting away from that, because Silius wrote Latin poetry, and the accuracy of the reading *Arar* is guaranteed by the metre of the poem.

It also never occurred to the editors as strange that the copyists of the Greek text of Polybius and the copyists of the Latin text of Livy, should, independently, have made different mistakes at exactly corresponding places in the two texts. The odds are heavily against such an occurrence, and the editors would have done better to print the texts of the manuscripts as they were, without attempting to improve on

them, even if they did not understand the meaning of the names of these rivers.

The result of all these tamperings with the texts has been that almost all printed editions of Polybius and Livy available for the last three hundred years give the name of the second river of 'the Island' as the Isère, most of the editions without any indication at all to show and warn the reader that Isère is not the transcription of what Polybius and Livy wrote, but merely the guesses of the sixteenth-century editors. Anyone working on these editions is misled from the start, for the guesses were bad, and quite unnecessary.

It will be remembered that Hannibal's point of crossing the Rhône was four days' march from the sea, and it was also four days' march from 'the Island' according to both Polybius and Livy. Making use of Polybius's statement that the speed of Hannibal's army during this part of the march was about 14 km. a day, the *Skaras* or *Arar* should be about 112 km. from the sea. That is just the distance from the sea at which a large river, the Aygues, which rises in the foothills of the Alps, flows into the Rhône, from the north-east at an angle of 60°, enclosing a densely populated, very fertile triangular-shaped piece of land, between itself, the Rhône, and on the third, north-east side, a low range of mountains, the Baronnies.

The geographical requirements of the *Skaras* or *Arar,* the second river bordering 'the Island', are therefore perfectly met, in accordance with Polybius's and Livy's statement, by the Aygues. There is only one point of disagreement, i.e. the statement that 'the Island' was of the same size as the Delta of the Nile. As there is no piece of land whatever on the eastern side of the Rhône, enclosed between it and any river, approaching anything like the size of the Delta of the Nile, this must be an error somehow introduced in the texts.

The proof that the *Skaras* is the Aygues is provided by the old names for that river, which the sixteenth-century editors would have been well advised to consider. It is found in manuscripts of the tenth century as *Icarus, Equer, Equeris* in A D 1218, *Ecaris* in 1272, *Ycaris* in 1321, *Aqua Iquarum* in 1393, and *Egue* in the same year. There can be no doubt about it. Polybius's *Skaras* became transformed into *Icarus,* etc. in accordance with well-known rules of Romance philology, by loss of the initial *s* and prefixing of *i* or *e*, as in countless other words, such as *stella*—étoile, *scala*—escalier, *schola*—école. There is one more point to notice, in the form *Aqua Iquarum,* for it is *Aqua,* 'water', that has become Aygues, as in numerous other place-names, Aigue-belle, Aiguefonde, Aigueperse, Aigues Mortes. Moreover, in Provençal speech today, 'water' is *aigue*.

The Aygues is therefore quite certainly identified as the *Skaras* of Polybius, and 'the Island' as the very fertile land enclosed between the Rhône, the Aygues, and the Baronnies mountains, close to the town of Orange. It is no unusual thing for a river to bear more than one name. Indeed, as Charles Thomas has pointed out, for many rivers it was the rule, for rivers were gods and the mention of their names was taboo, and substitute names were applied. In addition to *Icarus, Ecaris* and the other similar names just mentioned, it is found that the Aygues also bore the name *Araus,* very similar to the old original name of the town of Orange, *Arausio,* close to the Aygues. J. Colin gives a variant of this name as *Arauris,* and this must have been the origin of Livy's *Arar*.

The guess that the *Skaras* or *Arar* was the Isère can be shown to be absurd in many ways. The land enclosed between it and the Rhône is not triangular in shape, has no range of mountains shutting off the third side of the equilateral triangle, is not low-lying or liable to flooding, is rocky and stony and not fertile, growing vines and chestnuts, and is sparsely populated even today. The error of regarding the Isère as the *Skaras* is even more glaring when distances are considered. The Isère is 200 km. from the sea. It will be remembered that the point

136

The river Rhône at Tournon, showing the rocky, infertile and sparsely populated area between the Rhône and the Isère, not liable to flooding and bearing no resemblance to 'The Island' as described by Polybius and Livy

where Hannibal crossed the Rhône was four days of his march from the sea and from 'the Island', half-way between them, or on this showing 100 km. distant from either. These 100 km. would then have to have been marched by Hannibal's army at 25 km. a day, instead of 14, and by Scipio's army at 33 km. a day, crossing on the way the secondary channels of the Durance which then flowed into the Rhône below Arles, the main channel of the Durance, the Sorgues, the Ouvèse and the Aygues, all of which flow into the Rhône from the east. This rate of march was quite impossible for a Roman non-professional army with heavy infantry, entrenching itself each night.

There are even worse consequences of identifying the *Skaras* with the Isère, for this would have placed the point where Hannibal forded the Rhône at or near Pont-Saint-Esprit, where he would not have succeeded in getting his horses and elephants across the river as he did, and where the distance from Emporiae, 1,600 stadia or 285 km. according to Polybius, would have been greatly exceeded.

In addition to these conclusions based on geography, there are confirmatory facts contained in the texts of the classical authors which put the Isère completely out of court; they will be presented when the next stage of Hannibal's march is described.

IN THE FOUR DAYS' MARCH from the crossing of the Rhône to 'the Island' there are two special points of interest. Hannibal's route must have taken his army near the site of the village of Maillane, 7 km. south of the point where the river Durance of today flows into the Rhône. At Maillane, in 1777, Barthélémy Daillan discovered a copper medallion and the skeleton of an elephant embedded in the ground. At first thought to be the remains of a human giant, 12 feet tall, it was recognized as an elephant when two of its molar teeth were shown to Claude-François Achard, who recorded the discovery in his *Description historique de la Provence* (tome 2) in 1788. M. Daillan fixed the copper medallion to the handle of his pick, but the bones of the elephant were broken in getting them out. In 1824, however, the Comte de Villeneuve wrote in his *Statistique du Département des Bouches-du-Rhône* that Daillan's widow still possessed one of the molar teeth of the elephant, and that M. Toulousan had seen a part of its thigh-bone in a farm-house near Saint-Etienne-du-Grès, a few kilometres away. The Comte de Villeneuve added that the most probable explanation of the find was that the skeleton was that of one of Hannibal's elephants.

More recently, Theodore Andreas Cook in his *Old Provence* referred to the elephant and called it African. If only Claude-François Achard had described the molar teeth, it would be possible to determine immediately whether this was so or not; as it is, the association of the elephant with Hannibal, and the fact that Hannibal was African, must be suspected as the reason for labelling the elephant also as African. Even if it were, however, it would not be proof that it had belonged to Hannibal's army, because the Romans used African elephants in Provence a century later, when they annexed the *Provincia Narbonensis,* Provence, in 121 BC, and its governor Cnaeus Domitius Ahenobarbus rode about on an elephant to show the flag. The province of Africa then belonged to Rome.

Even if the elephant of Maillane had turned out to be Indian, it would still not have ruled out the possibility of its having belonged to Hannibal's army, for he had some Indian elephants, as will be seen below. The lost key to the problem of the elephant of Maillane is the copper medallion found with it, which would certainly have made it possible to determine whether its owner was Carthaginian or Roman; but it has been lost. At least, this medallion has served to prove one fact, that the elephant was buried, and was not the fossil remains of an extinct mammoth or other species of elephant, such as are occasionally found in river terraces.

The other point concerns the river Durance. At the present day, all the waters of this river flow into the Rhône just south of Avignon. Two thousand years ago, however, as Ernest Desjardins showed, this was not the case. Then the Durance had three other outlets. The first of these was a break-away from the main stream near Malle-mort, which flowed southwards to Salon-de-Provence and there divided into two; one of the branches flowed into the Etang de Berre and so directly into the sea; the other ran westwards over the boulder-strewn flood-plain of La Crau, and flowed into the marshes and pools near Arles, and so into the Grand Rhône south of that town. It was therefore not on Hannibal's route, but it was on that of Scipio. The course of this branch is seen today in the Canal de Barbegal which the Romans built, but is now dry.

A second break-away from the Durance left its channel at Orgon and flowed into the marshes near Arles. It was also canalized by the Romans and is known as the Vieille Durance. The third outlet was the biggest

Air view of Saint-Martin-de-Crau and the plain of La Crau. The sheet of water in the foreground is the Etang des Aulnes into which one of the old channels of the river Durance flowed, from Mallemort, across the flood-plain of La Crau

The flood-plain of La Crau near Salon-de-Provence; the plain is covered with water-worn pebbles

of all. It left the Durance between Chateaurenard and Rognonas, spilled into the plain of Maillane, and also finished in the marshes near Arles. Its course was indicated by the river Duransole which dried up in AD 1636.

Since Hannibal's time, therefore, all these three outlets of the Durance have become silted up and dried, and the existing channel, now the only mouth, carries all the water and has become widened. When Hannibal's army crossed it there can have been little difficulty, not only because it carried less water than at present, but also because at the time of year in question, September, there can have been only little water.

When he reached 'the Island', Hannibal found a civil war in progress, with two brothers fighting for the kingship. The elder, Brancus, had been king, but his brother and a clique of young nobles were attempting to depose him. When Hannibal arrived, both sides appealed to him to arbitrate and resolve the quarrel. He discovered what were the views of the rival chiefs and the council, and decided that the throne must be restored to Brancus. The younger brother was driven out, and Brancus, full of gratitude, not only supplied the Carthaginian army with clothing and footwear for crossing the Alps, wheat and other provisions, but provided an escort of his men to protect Hannibal's rearguard against attacks by the Allobroges on his next march. Re-equipped, the army set off again, to 'the ascent towards the Alps'. The route can be made out with the help of the classical authors.

HANNIBAL'S ROUTE

IF IT WERE not for two archaeological finds, there would be no evidence that Hannibal had ever existed at all except for the texts of the classical authors, which brings home the importance of analysing them and respecting them. The two archaeological finds are the graves, weapons, and incineration-pits found on the battlefield of Lake Trasimene, and a Latin inscription from Brundisium (Brindisi). Even the inscription in Greek and Punic which Hannibal had placed in the temple of Hera Lacinia is known only through the text of Polybius, who saw it with his own eyes.

The classical texts are much more numerous, and although the earliest that has come down to posterity was not written until sixty years after the events, and they all contain and reflect different traditions, it is astonishing, not that they differ, but that they agree in general so well. Polybius's account is the most valuable because he himself followed Hannibal's route, c. 160 BC. Polybius was born in Arcadia in 202 BC, and his life overlapped that of Hannibal by nearly twenty years; he was himself a soldier, a cavalry general in Greece, and it was he who carried the urn containing the ashes of Philopoemen, the last great soldier of classical Greece. Polybius came to Rome as a hostage in 168 BC, and lived in the house of Aemilius Paullus, son of the Consul who fought and died at the battle of Cannae. Polybius was also the tutor of Scipio Aemilianus, the conqueror of Carthage at the end of the Third Punic War in 146 BC, at which Polybius was himself present. He must therefore have had good opportunities of meeting survivors of the war against Hannibal. Concise and well imbued with the importance of causality in historiography, his *History* is the foundation of what is known of Hannibal's campaign, and particularly of his passage over the Alps.

The only reproach that can be levelled at Polybius is of having been too laconic, and giving too few details of names of places and peoples. This lack of information is largely made good by Titus Livius, who was born at Patavium (Padua) in 59 BC. When writing his *History of Rome,* he relied on Polybius greatly for the Hannibalic War. His text is interlarded with additional pieces of information, not always in scale or in perspective with neighbouring passages of the text, but of value because of the details which they provide. Livy's countryman, Silius Italicus, was born in AD 25, and his epic poem on the Punic Wars derived much of its information from Livy, so that he provides a check on the readings of names in the text of that author.

Scraps of information on the passage of the Alps are given by other authors, whose works are known from fragments quoted by later writers. Marcus Terentius Varro, born in Sabine country in 116 BC, held by Quintillian to be 'the most learned of Romans', left a list of Alpine passes with an indication of which was that used by Hannibal, preserved in a commentary on Virgil's *Aeneid* by Servius Marius Honoratus, written about AD 400. Since Varro was born only a few years after Polybius died, and was selected by Caesar for the post of librarian in the public library of Rome, his statements deserve respect. Another list of Alpine passes with an indication of which was Hannibal's, based on an otherwise unknown passage of Polybius, was given by Strabo in the first century BC.

Timagenes of Alexandria came to Rome, where he earned the protection of Augustus, in 54 BC. His work is lost except for fragments which include a thumb-nail sketch of Hannibal's passage of the Alps, preserved by Ammianus Marcellinus of Antioch who wrote a continuation of Tacitus's histories in AD 390. Hannibal's passage of the Alps appears, of course, in the works of many Roman authors, Cornelius Nepos (first century BC), Trogus Pompeius (first century AD), Justin and Appian (second century AD), and Eutropius (fourth century AD), to mention only the more important; to which must be added the magnificent descriptions of episodes and anecdotes in Hannibal's life given by Plutarch.

It will be observed that every one of these sources was either a Roman or a Greek romanized author. Not one single Carthaginian source has been preserved, although it is known that originally there were some, including Sosilos who taught Hannibal Greek and, according to Cornelius Nepos, afterwards wrote his life. There was also Silenos who accompanied Hannibal's army on its march, and whose writings, according to Cicero, were translated by Lucius Coelius Antipater. Echoes of these Carthaginian traditions are to be found in the work of Polybius, as F. W. Walbank and others have shown.

In their accounts, Polybius and Livy fortunately agree on most important points, but differ on one: Polybius places Hannibal's first battle at 'the ascent towards the Alps' out of the Rhône valley, whereas Livy places it many days later in the march, after Hannibal had crossed the Durance. For many reasons, of topographical detail concerning the terrain over which the battle was described as having been fought, and of time-table for which Polybius gives information for all the fifteen days that the passage across the Alps occupied, Livy's account must here be mistaken. The description that follows is based on

Polybius's text, with additional details supplied by other authors inserted where necessary.

Regarding Hannibal's route after leaving 'the Island', there are three pieces of information which enable it to be determined. First, Polybius's statement of distances gives that between the crossing-point over the Rhône and 'the ascent towards the Alps' as 1,400 stadia or 248 km. Additional details are that, of these 1,400 stadia, 800 or 142 km. were marched in ten days 'along the river', but without specifying which river it was, or which part of the 1,400 stadia the 800 represent. One part of this march was 'close beside the river', implying that there was a defile between cliffs and the river, through which the army marched.

Map of the Alps to illustrate the route taken by Hannibal's army on the crossing into Italy ▶

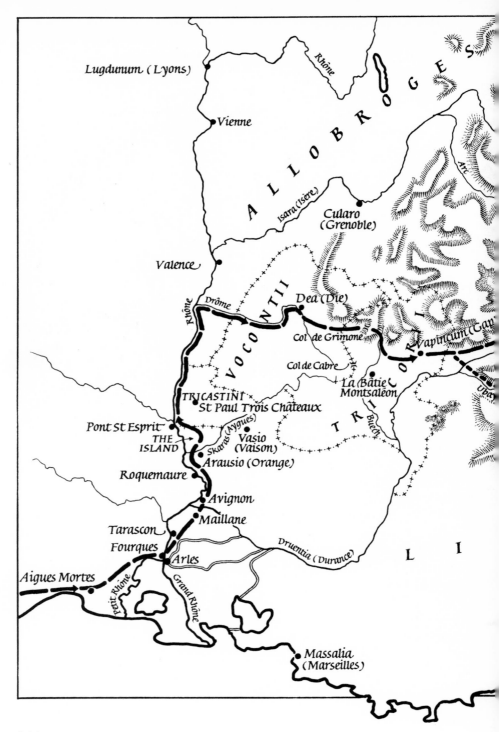

Lugdunum (Lyons)

Rhône

ALLOBROGES

Arc

Vienne

Isara (Isère)

Cul, aro
(Grenoble)

Valence

Drôme

Dea (Die)

Rhône

VOCONTII

Col de Grimone

Vapincum (Gap

Col de Cabre

TRI OR

Ubay

La Bâtie
Montsaléon

TRICASTINI

St Paul Trois Châteaux

Buech

Pont St Esprit

Skaras (Aygues)

Vasio
(Vaison)

THE
ISLAND

Skaras

Arausio (Orange)

Roquemaure

Avignon

Maillane

Druentia (Durance)

Tarascon

LI

Fourques

Arles

Aigues Mortes

Petit Rhône

Grand Rhône

Massalia
(Marseilles)

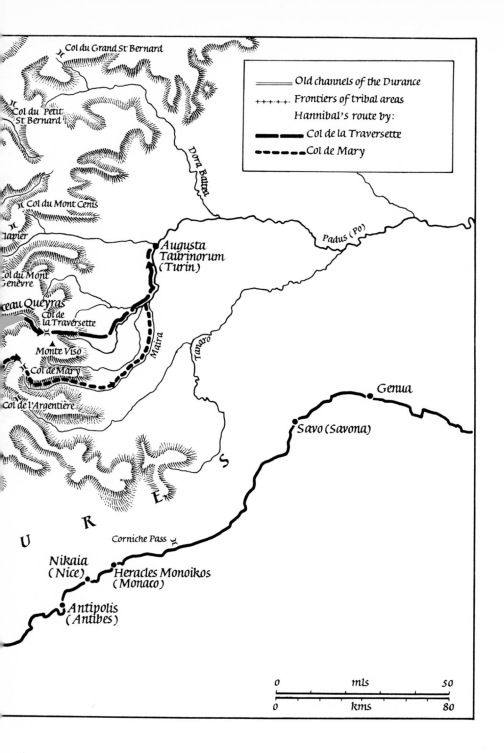

Col du Grand St Bernard

Col du Petit
St Bernard

Col du Mont Cenis

Dora Baltea

Japier

Col du Mont
Genèvre

Padus (Po)

Augusta
Taurinorum
(Turin)

eau Queyras
Col de
la Traversette

Col du Mont

Monte Viso

Maira

Tanaro

Col de Mary

Col de l'Argentière

Genua

Savo (Savona)

S

E

R

U

Corniche Pass

Nikaia
(Nice)

Heracles Monoikos
(Monaco)

Antipolis
(Antibes)

Old channels of the Durance
+ + + + + + Frontiers of tribal areas
Hannibal's route by:
━ ━ ━ Col de la Traversette
- - - - Col de Mary

0   mls   50
0   kms   80

145

The place described as 'the ascent towards the Alps' was clearly a pass over which, as will be seen, the first battle in the Alps was fought, Hannibal's army going up one side and down the other. This introduces an important point in the geography of the south-east Gaul, between the Rhône valley and the watershed of the Alps which separates Gaul from Italy. The Alps here form a belt, 200 km. broad, of mountains increasing in height from the border of the Rhône valley to the main watershed. Through this belt there are only two approaches from west to east, along river valleys which would lead to the main watershed without crossing any other pass beforehand. These are the valleys of the Durance in the south and of the Isère in the north. Everywhere in between these, it is impossible to get out of the Rhône valley and to travel eastwards towards Italy without crossing a low pass, out of the Rhône valley and into that of a tributary of either the Durance or the Isère.

That Hannibal did not march up the lower reaches of the Durance is clear from the fact that after crossing the Rhône he marched up its left bank to 'the Island', past the Durance. That he did not march up the valley of the Isère is equally clear from the welter of evidence about to be presented, and the fact, already mentioned, that the texts which suggest that he did were made to conform with preconceived notions. Hannibal must therefore have crossed a low pass out of the Rhône valley, and this was appropriately described by Polybius as 'the ascent towards the Alps'.

The problem therefore is to find a low pass leading eastwards out of the Rhône valley, north of the Durance, and south of the Isère. There are several such passes, at the heads of the little valleys of the Ouvèse, the Aygues, or the Drôme, but the one required must be 1,400 stadia or 248 km. distant from the crossing-point of the Rhône opposite Fourques. Fortunately, there are other helpful indications.

Livy stated that when Hannibal was in 'the Island' and ready to march to Italy, he did not take the direct route towards the Alps (which, from near Orange, would have been up the valley of the Aygues and across the Col de Palluel to Serres, the river Buëch and the middle reaches of the Durance), but, instead, turned to his left, and passed through the territory of the Tricastini, the far edge of the territory of the Vocontii, and entering the territory of the Tricorii came to the Durance. There is little room for mistake in this, because Silius Italicus mentions the Tricastini, the Vocontii, and the Durance as the line of Hannibal's march; and Timagenes gives his route as passing through the country of the Tricastini, skirting the country of the Vocontii, and making his

146

The Roman walls of Dea Vocontiorum, modern Die, seat of one of the two dioceses which occupy the territory of the Vocontii. Situated in the valley of the Drôme, Die is situated on Hannibal's route from the Rhône to the Col de Grimone

way to the gorges of the Tricorii. Here, then, are the names of three tribes, and where they lived is well known.

Auguste Longnon pointed out that when in 121 BC the Romans conquered the province in Gaul that goes by the name of Provence, they kept in being the organizations of the Gallic or Ligurian tribes which they had conquered as the basis of the Roman organization of *civitates,* or states. This means that the *civitates* preserved the intertribal frontiers. Then, when the early Church was established in Gaul, the frontiers between the *civitates* were used as the boundaries between the dioceses. In this manner, the delimitations of the dioceses serve to show where the frontiers originally ran between the tribes, and the locations of those just mentioned can be given with accuracy.

The territory of the Tricastini became the diocese of St-Paul-Trois-Châteaux, the very name of which proclaims its origin. It is situated to the north-west of the Aygues, its western border running along the left bank of the Rhône almost as far north as Montélimar, and its eastern border including the town of Grignan, so familiar to readers of the Letters of Madame de Sévigné.

Air view of the ruins of the medieval castle of Vaison-la-Romaine, ancient Vasio Vocontiorum, the birthplace of the Roman historian Trogus Pompeius. Vaison is the seat of the other diocese which occupies the territory of the Vocontii. The surrounding hills are part of the Baronnies mountains

The territory of the Vocontii became split into two dioceses, that of Dea Vocontiorum or Die, and that of Vasio or Vaison-la-Romaine. This region lies to the east of the territory of the Tricastini and covers the upper part of the valley of the river Drôme, and extends eastwards to the upper waters of the Buëch, tributary of the Durance, at Lus-la-Croix-Haute. From the valley of the Drôme leading to the valley of the Buëch, there are two passes, the Col de Grimone and the Col de Cabre, the former near the northern or further border of the territory of the Vocontii.

The territory of the Tricorii is represented by the diocese of Gap, in the fertile basin of the middle reaches of the Durance, a fact of great importance. As late as the sixth century A D, the bishop of Gap sued the bishop of Vaison for the return to his diocese of the little valley of Sainte-Jalle because it had belonged to the Tricorii, of which tribe the bishop of Gap was the legatee.

148

Of other tribes whose location is of importance, the Allobroges occupied all the territory north of the Isère and east and south of the Rhône, as far as the Lake of Geneva. Their territory became the diocese of Vienne. The Cavari, who have given their name to Cavaillon, lived between the Durance and the Aygues in what is now the diocese of Avignon. The Segallauni lived south of the Isère and north of the Drôme and occupied the present diocese of Valence.

The application of Longnon's principle of correspondence between the territories of the tribes and the dioceses depends on there having been no great changes or migrations between Hannibal's time and the incorporation of the Roman Province a century later. After that date, there were attempts at migrations by tribes such as the Arverni, the Helvetii, the Teutones, and the Allobroges, but they were sent home again by the Romans, and the inhabitants of south-east Gaul during the second century BC may be taken as having remained in their respective territories.

The location of tribes by means of the dioceses also agrees with the descriptions of the early geographers, although their statements are somewhat vague. Strabo described the territory of the Vocontii as 'above' that of the Cavari, and that of the Tricorii as 'above' that of the Vocontii, which is the order in which they stand when considered from the Mediterranean, the Cavari nearest on low ground, the Vocontii coming next behind them on higher ground, and the Tricorii still further away. Claudius Ptolemy described the Tricastini as living south of the Allobroges, east of the Segallauni, and north of the Vocontii; this description, though slightly confused, provides a recognizable location.

To return now to Livy, Silius Italicus, and Timagenes. When Hannibal was in 'the Island', instead of making his way straight for Italy, eastwards across the Col de Palluel, he turned to his left; that is, to the north, through the territories of the Tricastini, the edge of that of the Vocontii, to that of the Tricorii, where he was in the valley of the Durance. As the territories of the Tricastini and Vocontii lie north of 'the Island', and south of the Isère, and Hannibal reached them by marching north from 'the Island', the latter must have been south of the Isère, and the *Skaras* cannot have been the Isère. On this point the evidence is conclusive.

It will be remembered that 'the Island' was bordered on its north-east side by hilly country, the Baronnies and the prolongation of their spurs which end in cliffs bordering on the Rhône, with only a narrow defile separating them, the Défilé de Donzère. Marching northwards along this stretch, Hannibal's men must almost have had their left feet in the water. This gives point to Polybius's statement that part of the march was 'close beside the river itself'.

If the 248 km. given by Polybius are measured straight up the Rhône from the point where Hannibal crossed it, they reach to Vienne, nowhere near the territory of the Vocontii or any 'ascent towards the Alps' by which he could have reached the territory of the Tricorii, and from which he could have reached the plain of Piedmont, on the eastern side of the Alps, in 1,200 stadia or 213 km. To reach the territory of the Vocontii from the Rhône valley it is necessary to turn up the valley of the Drôme, at the head of which, as already mentioned, there are two passes, the Col de Cabre and the Col de Grimone. They are both roughly 213 km. from the crossing-point over the Rhône, and although the latter is near the further edge of the territory of the Vocontii, it would be difficult to choose between them were it not for a statement mentioned by Livy, although rejected by him. This was that Lucius Coelius Antipater, who obtained his information from Silenos, a companion of Hannibal's, on the march, said that Hannibal crossed the *Cremonis jugum*. The difficulty was that no other classical author mentioned this name, not that in principle this gives any *a priori* ground for rejecting it, as Cecil Torr pointed out in respect of many other names which are only mentioned once in classical texts. Livy thought, for reasons unknown, that *Cremonis jugum* meant the pass known as the Petit Saint-Bernard, on the watershed between Gaul and Italy, and he rightly rejected this because it would have led Hannibal down into Italy in the wrong place, into the territory of the Salassi, and not 'into the territory of the Taurini, into which everybody agrees that he came'. But *Cremonis jugum* is the old name for the Col de Grimone, found in early manuscripts, such as the cartulary of the abbey of Durbon. Livy might have been right in rejecting the Petit Saint-Bernard as part of Hannibal's itinerary, but mistaken in thinking that by *Cremonis jugum* Coelius meant the Petit Saint-Bernard; Coelius, whose testimony because of its authoritative source is not to be ignored, may have been right in stating that Hannibal crossed the *Cremonis jugum,* without implying that it was on the main watershed of the Alps; and the *Cremonis jugum* has an undeniable identification in the Col de Grimone. An attempt made to identify the *Cremonis jugum* with the Mont Cramont, an outlying spur of the Mont-Blanc range, is not worth any time spent on it.

As will shortly be seen the Col de Grimone answers further requirements in Polybius's narrative, and it may be taken as his 'ascent

The Défilé de Donzère, where the cliffs on the left bank of the Rhône come so close to the river that there is barely room for the road. At this point Hannibal's army after leaving 'The Island', marched 'close beside the river itself'

towards the Alps', the place where the route no longer lies along a river, but ascends out of the Rhône basin to a pass, the pass where the First Battle in the Alps was fought.

THE FIRST BATTLE IN THE ALPS

POLYBIUS'S NARRATIVE of what happened on each day of the fifteen days which Hannibal took to march from 'the ascent towards the Alps' to the Plain of Piedmont, covering 1,200 stadia, 213 km., is simple and straightforward. The first three days, considered in this chapter, concern the First Battle in the Alps and the conquest and occupation of the enemy's town.

After marching 800 stadia, 142 km., along the river in ten days, Hannibal began the ascent towards the Alps and ran into danger. During the time that the army was in the Rhône valley, the Allobroges kept at a distance, because of the horses and the escort which Brancus had provided to accompany the Carthaginian army. The fact that the source of danger was the Allobroges shows, in itself, that from 'the Island' Hannibal marched northwards, and Livy's statement that the inhabitants of 'the Island' were, themselves, Allobroges must be a confusion. When Brancus's escort left the army and went home, and Hannibal's men began to negotiate difficult country, the Allobroges collected sufficient men and occupied the heights commanding the

The approach from the west to the Col de Grimone; this was the route taken by Hannibal on the 'ascent towards the Alps' from the basin of the Rhône

route by which the Carthaginian army was to march. If they had kept their intentions secret, they might have destroyed Hannibal's army; as it was, their plan having been discovered, they succeeded in inflicting heavy losses on the Carthaginians but suffered no less themselves.

Knowing that the enemy was occupying the commanding points, Hannibal encamped close to the heights, and sent out some Gauls who accompanied him to discover the dispositions and intentions of the enemy. These scouts accomplished their mission and informed Hannibal that the enemy formed up and guarded their positions on the heights carefully by day, but that at night they retired to a neighbouring town. Hannibal then laid his plans in the following manner. He set his army in motion without any attempt at concealment, approached the difficult place, and pitched his camp close to it. At nightfall he lit fires and left the greater part of his army in camp, and having armed detachments of his best troops very lightly, he led them by night through the gorge and occupied the positions on the heights which the enemy had held during the day but abandoned at night in accordance with their custom.

At dawn the enemy observed what had happened, and at first they gave up the idea of opposing Hannibal. But when they saw the mass of pack-animals and horses slowly and laboriously threading their way through the difficult passages, they were encouraged to attack the army while it was on the march. Under their attacks, which they made from above at several points, many Carthaginians and even more horses and pack-animals were killed, not so much as the direct result of enemy action as because of the difficulty of the terrain. The way was not only narrow and uneven, but had a steep drop on one side, down which many animals fell.

It was particularly the wounded animals that caused confusion because, maddened with pain, some turned back on the pack-animals behind them, while others dashed forward and created havoc in the narrow defile in front. Observing this, Hannibal realized that if his convoy were lost, even those men who escaped from this danger would also be lost. He therefore took the troops which he had posted on the heights the night before, and rushed to the rescue of his column in the defile. As in this action Hannibal charged from higher ground onto lower ground, he fell on the enemy from above and inflicted heavy losses on them, but his own army also suffered some, for the tumult in the column increased with the shouting from both ends and the arrival of newcomers on the scene.

Those Allobroges who had survived the onslaught having been put to flight, Hannibal remained master of the field. The horses and pack-animals which remained then wound their way painfully through the difficult passage, and Hannibal went on to capture an enemy town on the other side. This he found deserted, so it was clearly not the Allobroges's town, for Polybius specifically stated that they returned to their homes. But what he did find there was a large number of horses and pack-animals, together with their drivers, in addition to slaughter-animals and wheat enough to supply his army with rations for two or three days. Most important, he instilled such fear among the surrounding tribes that none had the temerity to attack him. He encamped in the town and remained there for one further day before setting off again.

The grassy slopes of the Col de Grimone, the site of the First Battle in the Alps; here Hannibal's infantry could manœuvre without difficulty

The first three days of the march across the Alps were therefore occupied as follows: first day, approach to the pass and occupation of the heights at night; second day, the battle, rout of the enemy and capture of the town; third day, rest in the town. Although Polybius's narrative is so sparing of detail, a number of conclusions can nevertheless be drawn from it. In the first place it is clear that this First Battle was fought over a pass; Hannibal's army had to go up one side to the heights, and as a town of such importance as that which he captured could not have been on such heights, he must have reached it by going down the other side of the pass. Furthermore, there were two special features about this pass; on the approach to it there was a gorge through which the path had a sheer drop on one side; and the pass itself was commanded by heights on which troops could manœuvre and charge downhill. This means that the pass was not through rocky peaks, but through heights of grassy swards, even if steep.

The Col de Grimone satisfies both these conditions. In the approach to it from the valley of the Drôme, there is the little Gorge des Gaz, where the Allobroges must have attacked the convoy from above as it threaded its way through; and the heights on each side of the pass itself are smooth, steep, grassy slopes, over which light infantry could easily manœuvre

The description of the captured town also allows conclusions to be drawn concerning it. A town in which Hannibal could find one hundred and fifty thousand rations of food and fodder was certainly not situated in a high Alpine region, but in a fertile plain. After crossing the Col de Grimone, Hannibal found himself in the valley of the Buëch, a tributary of the Durance which there, in its middle reaches, opens out into a wide fertile basin, the Bassin de Gap, where olive trees grow, a detail not without significance. It is hardly possible to expect that the town which Hannibal captured can be identified, but it is known that near the place where the Buëch flows into the Durance there was, in Gallo-Roman times, the important town of Mons Seleucus, today known as La-Bâtie-Montsaléon, which lies some 30 km. from the Col de Grimone. It is not claimed that this was Hannibal's town, but its existence shows that the region was capable of containing a town large and prosperous enough from the fertility of the surrounding country, to agree with Polybius's description. It lies sufficiently near to the site of the First Battle for Hannibal's vanguard of light troops to reach it on the day of the battle, while the following day, which was spent in this town, was available for the remainder of the army to catch up and rejoin.

THE DURANCE

HAVING DESCRIBED his departure from the captured town, Polybius's account takes Hannibal along for three days without incident, but on the fourth day danger again threatens. Counting from the time when he reached 'the ascent towards the Alps', i.e. the Col de Grimone, this accounts for the fourth, fifth, sixth and seventh days out of the fifteen which he spent over the crossing.

In the corresponding part of Livy's *History*, the additional information is given that after making his way to the territory of the Tricorii, that is the Bassin de Gap, he marched mostly through flat, open country,

The descent from the east side of the Col de Grimone into the valley of the river Buëch, which leads on the right to the middle reaches of the Durance and the Bassin de Gap (the territory of the Tricorii), through which it is known that Hannibal passed

and encountered no difficulties until he came to the river *Druentia,* the Durance. This was an Alpine river, much the most difficult to cross of all the watercourses in Gaul because, although it carries a great mass of water, it is not navigable. It has no well-defined banks, and it runs in many channels which do not remain constant, but change from time to time, making new fording places and new deep pockets of water. These render it difficult to cross on foot because the waters carry with them muddy boulders on which there is no sure foothold. Furthermore, at the time when Hannibal crossed it, it was in spate because of rains, and it led to much disorder in the ranks, caused by the nervousness and shouts of the troops.

This circumstantial description by Livy of the Durance on Hannibal's line of march agrees with the statements made by Timagenes as well as by Livy himself that Hannibal passed through the territory of the Tricorii whose capital was Gap, in the middle reaches of the Durance, as mentioned above. A further point is that Livy's description of the Durance applies to its middle reaches at the time when Hannibal crossed it, and not to the channel (only one out of four) of its lower reaches which flowed into the Rhône near Avignon, crossed by Hannibal one month previously on his way from the crossing-point to 'the Island'. The importance of this becomes apparent when we take into account the time of year when Hannibal made this crossing of the Durance in its middle reaches, and when the physiography of the rivers in this part of Gaul is considered.

The dates of Hannibal's movements can be calculated as follows. When he reached the watershed pass over the main range of the Alps which was about a week later than his crossing of the Durance, both Polybius and Livy state that the Setting of the Pleiades was already at hand. This was the time of year at which the Pleiades can be seen to be just setting in the west when the sun rises in the east, and the date can be determined astronomically. By allowing 35 minutes of arc for the refraction due to the earth's atmosphere, adopting the accepted coordinates (declination and right ascension) for the position of the Pleiades in the heavens, and making allowance for what is called 'nautical twilight', because when the sun has risen above the horizon the brightness of its light makes it impossible actually to see the Pleiades setting, which is possible when the sun is still 12° below the horizon, Sir Terence Morrison-Scott in 1954 arrived at the date 8 December, for latitude 45° North, which is sufficiently accurate for all the Alps between Gaul and Italy. All that is then necessary is to make the corrections for the precession of the equinox between 218 BC and AD 1954, a time-span of 2172 years. This correction works out at 30·6 days. Counting thirty and a half days before 8 December gives 7 November as the day when the Pleiades could be seen setting when the sun rose in 218 BC, the so-called heliacal setting. The date was important to the ancients because it was regarded as the beginning of winter, from which the dates for starting various agricultural tasks were calculated.

The date of 7 November is in good agreement with those calculated for the works of Euctemon (fifth century BC) which also comes out at 7 November, of Callippus (fourth century BC) 8 November, Eudoxus (fourth century BC) 11 November, Pierre Gassend's study of the Roman calendar 11 November, and for the application of Claudius Ptolemy's definition of the 'aspects' of stars with reference to the sun, which J. L. Strachan-Davidson worked out at 9 November. These dates are calculated in accordance with the Gregorian calendar, and are in agreement within a day or two with the Julian calendar when it was instituted in 45 BC, because the discrepancy between it and the solar year in 218 BC was small.

If, when Hannibal was approaching his watershed pass, the date of 7 November was approaching, it is reasonable to conclude that he crossed the Durance in its middle reaches towards the end of October. The importance of this apparently trivial detail is that it confirms the identification of the river which Hannibal crossed as the Durance in its middle reaches, for the following reasons. As already mentioned, there are only two rivers which run all the way from the watershed of the Alps to the Rhône, the Isère and the Durance, and Hannibal must have approached the watershed pass by marching up the one or the other. They differ completely in their annual pattern and time-table of flow. The Isère is mostly glacier-fed, its waters coming from glaciers and snow-fields which give it a maximum rate of flow in the summer months from April to August when the snow and ice are melting, and a minimum flow in the autumn and winter months from September to March, when the precipitations falling as rain or snow are trapped in the snow-fields and glaciers and held there until the following spring. The Isère is near its lowest rate of flow in October, and would not give rise to the difficulties which Hannibal encountered.

The Durance is mostly spring-fed and derives its waters from only a few glaciers and snow-fields which, being situated further south than those of the Isère, are smaller and melt earlier. The result is that the Durance has a spring and summer peak-flow when from April to July its glaciers melt, and an autumn peak-flow from October to

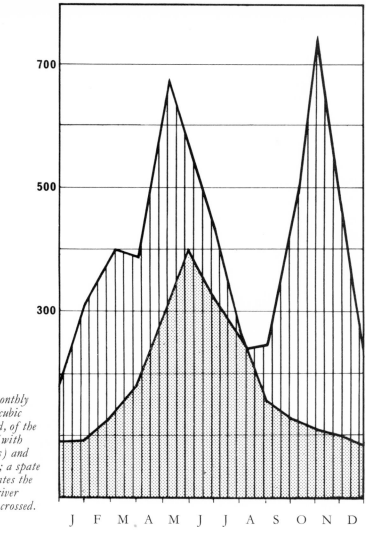

Graphs of the monthly rates of flow, in cubic metres per second, of the rivers Durance (with two peak periods) and Isère (stippled); a spate in October indicates the Durance as the river which Hannibal crossed. After Pardé

December when the rains swell it as they fill the springs and are only to a slight extent trapped and retained by glaciers. In late October, the Durance would therefore be expected to be in spate.

This appeal to natural science to decide whether the river which Hannibal crossed was likely to have been the Isère or the Durance therefore pronounces in favour of the Durance, which agrees with the statements of Livy and Timagenes about the territory of the Tricorii. The diffusion of the falsehood that Polybius and Livy gave the Isère as the line of Hannibal's march is so widespread that it must be nailed as a result of unbiased consideration of all lines of evidence, and there are some more.

Basing himself on Polybius, Strabo gave a list of the passes over the Alps between Gaul and Italy, as follows:

1   the pass through the Ligures
2   the pass to the Taurini which Hannibal crossed
3   the pass through the Salassi
4   the pass through the territory of the Rhaeti.

It will be noticed that these passes are clearly enumerated from south to north in geographical order: *1* is the Corniche road along the shore of the Mediterranean between the Maritime Alps and the sea leading to the heart of Liguria near Genoa; *3* is the Petit Saint-Bernard pass leading to the valley of the Dora Baltea, where the Salassi lived (Aosta); *4* is probably the Grand Saint-Bernard pass, for although Rhaetia proper is in the east of Switzerland, the Roman administration included what is now the Valais (through which the Grand Saint-Bernard pass leads) in the province of Rhaetia. Pass *2* is therefore to be found somewhere north of the Corniche and south of the Petit Saint-Bernard. The only indication given, that it leads to the territory of the Taurini (Turin), suggests that it is a pass out of the Durance basin. The words 'which Hannibal crossed' are not found in all the manuscripts, which has led to the suggestion that they were a later interpolation; while this is possible, they may also have been true, as may be concluded from another list of passes drawn up by Marcus Terentius Varro, which confirms and extends that of Polybius, as quoted by Strabo. Varro's list is as follows:

1   along the sea through the Ligures
2   which Hannibal crossed
3   which Pompey crossed on his way to Spain
4   which Hasdrubal crossed
5   through the Graian Alps.

Of these, *1* is the Corniche route along the Mediterranean; *5* is the Petit Saint-Bernard pass which crosses the Graian Alps; *3* is the Col du Mont-Genèvre, identified by the additional information given by

The valley of the river Ubaye up which Hannibal's army would have had to march to reach the Col de Mary. This route is less probable than the Queyras

Appian and Strabo that it was near the sources of tributaries of the Rhône and the Po, the Durance and the Dora Riparia, and from the letter written to the Senate by Pompey himself, reported by Sallust, in which he said that his pass was different from Hannibal's and more convenient; *4* is presumably the Col du Mont-Cenis, the only practicable pass between the Petit Saint-Bernard to the north and the Mont-Genèvre to the south. There remains *2*, the location of which is narrowed down to a bracket south of the Mont-Genèvre and north of the Mediterranean. As the Mont-Genèvre is the most northerly pass leading out of the Durance basin, this information means that Hannibal's pass also led out of the Durance basin. The importance of this conclusion, which agrees with everything else that is known about Hannibal's pass, derived from textual and scientific studies, is that it puts out of court all the passes leading out of the Isère basin: Petit Saint-Bernard, Mont-Cenis, and Col du Clapier, all of which have been claimed by different commentators as having been Hannibal's pass.

Before leaving the subject of the Durance, there is a further question to consider: why did Hannibal have to cross it? The answer is contained in the statements made by Pompey and by Varro, both respectable witnesses whose evidence cannot be ignored, that the pass which Pompey crossed, the Mont-Genèvre, was not the pass that Hannibal crossed. If he had crossed it, he would not have needed to cross the Durance, for he would have followed it up to its source which is precisely on the Mont-Genèvre, or he could have crossed it high up its course where it is only a rivulet.

The reason why Hannibal was obliged to cross the Durance in its middle reaches in October, when it was a formidable river, was that as he did not follow it up to its source, it lay between him and the watershed over the Alps leading to Italy. Coming as he did from the Rhône valley, north of 'the Island', and therefore north of the mouth of the Durance where it flows into the Rhône, he was all the time to the north-west of the Durance and was obliged to cross it in order to march east.

Arrived at the middle reaches of the Durance, where he was on the sixth day after 'the ascent towards the Alps', Hannibal was presented with two possibilities, for there are two valleys which lead eastwards to the watershed of the Alps. The first of these is the valley of the Ubaye which opens into the Durance valley south of Chorges (its entrance is now drowned by the dam of Serre-Ponçon) and leads to two passes, the Col de Mary immediately south of Monte Viso, and

The entrance at Guillestre to the valley of Queyras through which the gorge of the river Guil leads to the Col de la Traversette; a passage through the mountains here appears possible

the Col de l'Argentière. The second valley is that of the Guil which opens into the Durance valley at Montdauphin, and leads into the region known as the Queyras, from which the Col de la Traversette, immediately north of Monte Viso, leads to the plain of Piedmont down the infant river Po. The rejection of all passes out of the Isère basin and the knowledge that Hannibal did not cross the Mont-Genèvre, leave only the Ubaye and the Queyras as routes by which Hannibal could reach a watershed pass leading out of the Durance basin. The question as to which of these is the more likely will be discussed below.

THE SECOND BATTLE IN THE ALPS

To RETURN TO POLYBIUS'S NARRATIVE: on the seventh day since leaving 'the ascent towards the Alps', Hannibal ran into danger. The tribes who lived near his line of march conspired together to deceive him, and came to him bearing olive branches and wreaths, symbols of friendship, like the caduceus of the Greeks. Olive trees grow in the valley of the Durance, but not in that of the Isère. Very suspicious of this profession of friendship, Hannibal studied the thoughts and intentions of the natives closely. They said that they had learnt of Hannibal's capture of the town, and of the ruin that had befallen all those who had tried to oppose him, and they swore that they had come to him for that very reason. They had no wish to cause or receive any harm, and promised to give hostages.

For some time, Hannibal remained suspicious of them, not wishing to trust them; but he reflected that by accepting their offer of friendship he might make those who had come to him more malleable and conciliatory, whereas if he rebuffed them he would at once make declared enemies of them. He therefore consented to their proposals, and pretended to make friends with them. The barbarians gave hostages and provided an abundance of slaughter-animals, and placed themselves in his power without reservation. Hannibal trusted them so far as to use them as guides through the difficult country that he then had to cross, and placed them in the van of his army, where they continued for two days. But their brethren, having shadowed the march of the army, attacked it when it was making its way through a gorge with an inaccessible cliff on one side and a precipitous drop on the other.

In these circumstances, Hannibal's army might have been destroyed to the last man, had he not to a certain extent feared some such crisis and foreseen what might happen. As a precaution, he had stationed the elephants, the cavalry, and the pack-animals at the head of the column, and the heavy infantry in the rear. As these were on their guard, the damage was reduced, and the shock of the enemy's attack was held. Nevertheless, many men, horses, and pack-animals perished. The enemy occupied the highest positions and attacked everything beneath them, rolling rocks down on some and hurling stones on others, and they caused such confusion that Hannibal was obliged to bivouac with his vanguard on a large bare rock, separated from but covering his convoy

The gorge of the river Guil, looking west. The modern road on the left probably follows the ancient track, precipitous above and below, without possibility of manœuvre

from in front, while it managed with great difficulty to file through the gorge all through the night.

A few more details were supplied by Livy. Hannibal's army found itself on a narrow track, bordered by precipitious rocks, when the enemy sprang from their places of concealment and attacked the column in front and rear. They also attacked from the flank, and succeeded for a time in cutting the column in two and occupying the intervening portion of the track. Next morning, the enemy's attacks had slackened, and the two halves of the convoy were able to remake contact.

That morning was the eighth day of the march across the Alps; the enemy withdrew, and Hannibal, rejoined by his convoy, advanced towards the highest passes in the Alps. He was no longer troubled by general attacks by the barbarians, but was obliged to fight small parties of them here and there, in front and in rear, while they succeeded in capturing some pack-animals in these skirmishes. Hannibal derived great advantage from his elephants in these operations, for when he placed them in front, the enemy, terrified by their strange appearance, dared not attack.

There can be no doubt about the fact that Hannibal's guides were treacherous, and had led his army into a cunningly contrived trap, where the natives could attack it while it was in a very unfavourable position. This was while it entered an increasingly narrow gorge, on a track at mid-height, with a precipice on one side and unscalable rocks on the other, from which the enemy hurled rocks and other missiles down on the column beneath. There was no question here of heights and commanding positions on grassy swards which Hannibal's men could occupy, to charge downhill on the enemy as in the First Battle; everything was rocky and inaccessible.

There were two more features of this gorge worthy of notice. One was that there must have been side valleys, out of which the enemy debouched on the flank of the column. The other was that at the end of the gorge, there was a large bare rock, forming a strong position on which the vanguard of Hannibal's army could bivouac. These and other features indicate (though they do not prove) that the valley through which Hannibal was led was that of Queyras and not Ubaye, for immediately to the east of Montdauphin there is a gorge which answers all these requirements, that of the river Guil. It has precipitous sides, and in antiquity the track through it was at mid-height, as is

The Case déserte on the route of the Col d'Izoard which leads into the valley of Queyras from the north. Hannibal's army was attacked on its flank while negotiating a dangerous gorge

Château-Queyras, the isolated conical rock in the valley of Queyras which was probably 'the bare rock' described by Polybius and Livy as the position on which Hannibal camped with the vanguard of his army while the remainder was passing through the gorge

Château-Queyras, the medieval fortress built on the rock, seen from the east ▶

shown by the Roman inscription found at Les Escoyères, evidence that it was known and used. The inscription itself mentions three tribes, the Quariates who have left their name in that of Queyras, the Briciantes of Briançon, and the Savincates of Savine.

The Quariates were not Celtic Gauls, but Ligurians, like many other tribes which had been pressed back into these out-of-the-way and derelict regions of the Alps by the Gauls in their conquest of Gaul. Hannibal was to meet others on the eastern side of the Alps. The Ligurians were at daggers drawn with the Gauls, and with anybody else who tried to interfere with them, Etruscans, Romans—and now, Carthaginians.

The gorge of the Guil meets the other requirements of the site of the
Second Battle. Near its entrance there emerges into it from the south
the track from the Col de Vars; half way along it, also on the south
side, there is the ravine down which the torrent of Cristillon spills;
near its exit the track from the Col de Bramousse enters from the south,
and that from the Col d'Izoard from the north. Further east, in the
middle of the valley, there rises an enormous isolated rock, which
was bare before the fortress of Château-Queyras was built on its
sugar-loaf top. These are the features, not matched elsewhere, which
make the valley of Queyras the probable route of Hannibal, on his
way to the watershed pass.

HANNIBAL'S PASS: NARRATIVE

ON THE NINTH DAY of his march across the Alps, Hannibal continued up the valley, arrived at the pass over the main watershed, and encamped for two days (the tenth and eleventh) to rest his men and to allow time for stragglers to rejoin the column. Many horses which had taken fright and escaped, and many pack-animals which had thrown their loads, followed the track, came up to the pass, and rejoined the army.

Snow was already piling up on the mountains, for the heliacal setting of the Pleiades was approaching. Seeing that his men were becoming discouraged by the hardships that they had been through, and by the prospect of those which they expected to befall them, Hannibal mustered them, because he now had the unique opportunity of a view over Italy. These mountains are situated in such a way that they present the appearance of a double row of battlements surrounding Italy. So as to restore some confidence in them, Hannibal showed his men the Plain of the Po, the direction in which Rome lay, and he reminded them of the friendly sentiments of all kinds harboured towards them by the Gauls who lived in the plain at their feet.

On the following day (twelfth) he struck camp and began the descent, during which he encountered no enemy other than individuals who slipped through the lines intent on sabotage. But the difficulty of the terrain and the snow inflicted losses on his army almost as heavy as those which had been suffered from enemy action during the ascent. The track was narrow and steep and hidden by snow; any man or animal that accidentally stepped off the track slipped and was lost down the precipice.

But the men, hardened as they were and used to difficulties, persevered. In one place to which they came, however, neither the horses nor the elephants could get by, because the track was so narrow and a landslide had carried it away for about two hundred metres. The men lost heart and began to break ranks. Hannibal looked round for the possibility of circumventing this awkward pitch by another route, but the snow which had fallen made it impossible, and he abandoned the attempt.

The conditions were exceptionally bad. On the surface of the old snow of the previous winter, the newly fallen snow of the current season had piled up. This was easy to tread on because it was soft, had fallen only recently, and was not yet very thick; but when a man's feet penetrated to the old snow beneath, which was dense and frozen into smooth ice, he slipped and slid, as on muddy soil. What then happened was even more distressing, for when the men could not get a foothold on the old frozen snow and tried to get up on hands and knees, they slipped further down the steep slopes. As for the pack-animals, their hoofs were able to break through the old crust but they were then immobilized, unable to get their legs out of the frozen compact snow, and weighed down by their loads. Hannibal therefore gave up this attempt and issued orders for the army to encamp on the pass, which was done after digging away the snow with great difficulty, while pioneers mended the track.

A passage in Livy's description adds a detail which has become famous. It was necessary to remove a rock which was blocking the passage where a landslide had carried away the track. To do this, trees were felled and cut into logs which were piled on to the rock and set alight, making a fire that burned fiercely in the strong wind that was fortunately blowing. The rock was next drenched with vinegar (sour wine) to make it friable, and then attacked with pickaxes to break it up. The track was thus repaired sufficiently to enable the horses and the elephants to pass. The elephants, in particular, had suffered cruelly from hunger, because the bare, snow-covered summits of the Alps provided no sustenance.

Hannibal reassembled the army and continued the descent. He reached the plain on the third day after leaving the pass, the fifteenth since he started to cross the Alps, and rested his men for three days. He had saved 12,000 African infantry, 8,000 Spaniards, 6,000 cavalry, and all his 37 elephants. He had lost as many men from falling down precipices in ravines and difficult places in the mountains as he had suffered from enemy action and in crossing rivers. The Roman Lucius Cincius Alimentus, who was taken prisoner by Hannibal, said that he learnt from Hannibal himself that he had lost 36,000 men since crossing the Rhône; but these figures are very difficult to verify, for, according to Polybius, Hannibal had 38,000 infantry and 8,000 cavalry when he had crossed the Rhône, so that if, after crossing the Alps he had only 26,000 men all told, he must have lost 20,000. The only thing which is clear is that his losses had been very heavy.

According to Livy, there was universal agreement that Hannibal had crossed the Alps by a pass from which he came down into the country of the Taurini, and Polybius describes how he tried to make an alliance with that Ligurian tribe; but they were enemies of the Insubrian Gauls and rejected his offer. Hannibal therefore attacked their town, afterwards Augusta Taurinorum (Turin), and after three days stormed it and killed all those who opposed him, to serve as an example and to strike terror into the neighbouring tribes, who all came to submit and place themselves at his disposal.

So, after marching 1,500 km. from Carthagena in five months, Hannibal had performed the unbelievable feat of bringing his army overland to Italy. He had only 26,000 men left, and even though this strength was soon augmented by Gauls and others who joined him, Rome on Fabius Pictor's estimate could, at a pinch, put three quarters of a million men in the field. Such was the magnitude of the task which Hannibal had set himself, to try conclusions with Rome.

HANNIBAL'S PASS: INTERPRETATION

THE IDENTIFICATION of the actual watershed pass over the Alps which Hannibal crossed has been a sport for two thousand years, but a sport in which the great majority of players have made and broken the rules as they went along. At first, the texts were tampered with to make them fit the editors' ideas. Most of their successors, in blissful ignorance, or apathy, of the false transcription of the name of the *Skaras* have selected a route and a pass on principles that appear to have been based on the regions of the Alps which they knew or lived in, with no regard to the evidence where it did not suit them. The mayor of Guillestre frequently received visits from mayors of other municipalities who asked him (an authority) if Hannibal could not be made to have passed their way because it would be such a tourist attraction and good for trade.

Other players have gone on the principle of first selecting the pass, wherever it was, that seemed to answer best to all the requirements of the classical texts, but without any attempt to consider the evidence for or against the possibility that Hannibal could have taken the route leading to such a pass. Others again have gone into the Alps, to see what they could find, and seldom had any difficulty in making the pass of their choice agree to their satisfaction with their reading of the factitious texts. Henry MacKenzie has related how, in 1775, General Robert Melville went to the Grisons to investigate what he supposed might have been Hannibal's route, a fact which shows in itself how fast and loose he was content to play with the distances given by Polybius, and with the details given by Livy, Silius Italicus, and Timagenes; for a route through the Grisons would add ten thousand stadia

'Hannibal crossing the Alps', by the seventeenth-century artist, Pietro da Cortona. In the background the army is shown struggling through a gorge; on the right, Hannibal pointing out the plain of Piedmont; in the foreground, pioneers working to remove a rock

to Polybius's distances, and would not have brought Hannibal down into the territory of the Taurini. Melville passed another English traveller, who saw him coming back two days later. 'What has turned you back?' he asked. 'I cannot get my elephants over the rock,' answered Melville.

Melville had, at any rate, gone on the principle of exclusion; but others have attempted the converse, and, having selected their pass, they tried to get an elephant to cross it. The species of elephant used did not matter, nor whether or not it had undergone a training march of a thousand kilometres. What is not difficult to estimate is the degree of validity of any conclusions based on whether the elephant had, or had not, succeeded in crossing the pass. If it had, it would not have proved that Hannibal had crossed it; if it had not, it would not have disproved that Hannibal had crossed it, because many paths across passes were deliberately destroyed in Renaissance times on the Italian side, to hinder French invasions, not to speak of the ravages of nature.

The only defensible method of working is, first, to make a critical assessment of the meaning of the texts as read in the oldest extant manuscripts. Without this precaution, any attempt to trace Hannibal's route is nothing but a fancy of imagination. Then, application of principles of natural science to decide on possible alternatives of the route, narrows down the choice by rejecting some alternatives on grounds of physics, meteorology, botany, and other branches of science, which have nothing to do with personal preference. This method must be followed stage by stage along the march, as has been done here, for the point of crossing the Rhône, the location of 'the Island' and of 'the ascent towards the Alps', and of the valley of the Durance in its middle reaches as the line of Hannibal's approach march, and not from the end of the march or the pass backwards. Deductions may be made from three characteristics of the pass itself: the snow on it, hardened into ice from falls of previous winters, gives an indication of its minimum height; the high rate of casualties which the army suffered in crossing it gives information on its difficulty and steepness; and the view over the Plain of Piedmont from the summit narrows the choice greatly.

The pass must have been high enough for snows of previous winters to have persisted through the hot summers of latitude 45° North in southern Europe, and to have lain sufficiently thick, compacted into ice, to cause Hannibal's men and animals the trouble which it did. It cannot have been far beneath the snow-line which in that latitude today is about 3,000 metres. This figure must, of course, be adjusted for any change of climate and temperature that may have set in during the past two thousand years.

There are four independent methods by which it is possible to estimate the climate and past temperature in the region of the Alps in question. The first is based on the study of glaciers, for their extension down their valleys is dependent on world temperature and on precipitation. The limits of their former extensions are shown by the terminal moraines of boulders or hills which they piled up. From the sixteenth to the nineteenth century A D the glaciers advanced much farther than at any other time since the general retreat of the ice at the end of the Ice Age. This means that the present condition of the glaciers of the Alps is not a diminished relic of their extension in the Ice Age, but a relic of their extension during their recent maximum.

Now that the glaciers are once more retreating, they are constantly leaving uncovered trunks of trees from forests which they overran during their recent advance. Some tree-trunks have been found at a

The head of the valley of Queyras, above Château-Queyras, with Monte Viso in the distance, and the track leading to the Col de la Traversette which lies to the left of Monte Viso. This is relatively easy and negotiable Alpine country

height of over 2,250 metres. Even classical authors give a little help, for Strabo quoted Polybius as saying that in the Noric Alps there were gold mines in the territory of the Taurisci which were worked with great profit. This is the region of the High Tauern in Austria, where the Goldberg mines were extensively worked during the Middle Ages. In the seventeenth century A D, however, the advance of the ice covered the adits to some of these mines. It follows, therefore, from the evidence of glaciology that the temperature in 218 B C was at any rate not lower than it is at present.

The second method consists in studying the height above sea level of the tree line, in places where the absence of trees is not attributable to the advance of glaciers, or to the various activities of man, such as the

175

Monte Viso (3,841 metres), the highest and most impressive peak of the Cottian Alps, seen from the approach in the valley of Queyras. The Col de la Traversette is on the left, hidden behind the spruce trees on the rocky spur

pasturing of herds and flocks, or the direct felling of trees for use as fuel. In northern Italy, the tree line is now at least 300 metres lower than it was. Virgil's reference to *Vesulus pinifer*, pine-clad Monte Viso, is very relevant in this respect, for it bears no pine forests today, and Hannibal's pass certainly lay close to it. The inference is that the climate was then warmer.

The third method is based on pollen-analysis, since the stratified sequence of pollen-grains found in peat-bogs and lake beds shows the prevalent vegetation at different times, and each species of plant has a temperature and climatic optimum. These studies indicate that there were temperature maxima in 550 BC and in AD 1200, and between these periods a temperature similar to that of the present day.

The fourth method is based on the study of cores taken from great depths in undisturbed regions of the bed of the Atlantic Ocean. The quantity of calcium carbonate deposited is dependent on the temperature at the surface at the time of deposition, and this time can be ascertained from the level of the specimen studied in the core. At the level corresponding to 550 B C the annual rate of deposit of calcium carbonate was 1 millimetre per square centimetre; today it is 0·9 mm., which means that the world temperature in 550 B C was 1 or 2 degrees higher than at present. This method can be checked by the study of the different species of foraminiferan shells in the deposits because some of them belong to species adapted to live under cold and others under temperate conditions. The values for 218 B C were intermediate between those of 550 B C and today.

It follows from all these investigations that in Hannibal's time the climate was no colder, and the snow-line no lower, than at present; and therefore that the altitude of the pass he crossed must have been considerable. These conclusions narrow down still further the choice of possible passes leading out of the Durance basin; unacceptable are the Col du Mont-Genèvre (1,854 metres), already excluded by the evidence from Pompey and Varro, and the Col de l'Argentière (1,995 metres), also out of the running for a reason about to be given. That leaves the Col de la Traversette (2,950 metres), accessible through the valley of Queyras, and the Col de Mary (2,654 metres), accessible through the valley of Ubaye.

On the question of the difficulty and danger of the pass which were responsible for so many deaths, the Col de l'Argentière (also called Col de Larche) leading from the Ubaye to Cuneo is definitely ruled out, for, as Douglas Freshfield wrote, access to it 'lies over gentle, habitable slopes, cornfields and pleasant pastures'. This total lack of agreement between what Freshfield correctly described and the gorges where the Second Battle was fought, in the texts of Polybius and Livy, did not deter Freshfield from adopting this same Col de l'Argentière as Hannibal's pass, on the grounds that 'Hannibal was sure to rationally choose, not the highest and most difficult, but the lowest and easiest, most southern Alpine pass.' This is a good example of the lengths to which authors of supposedly high repute could go in special pleading for their favourite passes.

There can be little doubt that if the Col de la Traversette was in fact the pass which Hannibal crossed, it was not the one originally intended by him, but was forced on him by the treachery of the guides, as a result of which he lost his way in impasses and culs-de-sac, as Livy stated. As a mountain pass is, by definition, a place where a passage across a range can be made at as low an altitude as possible, most Alpine passes have from their summits no view at all of the plains on either side of them. There are not many passes in the western Alps from which the plain of Piedmont can be seen. One is the Col du Clapier, accessible only from the valley of the Arc, a tributary of the Isère, and therefore excluded because Hannibal did not march up the valley of the Isère. Another pass, out of the Durance basin, the Col de Malaure, is a knife-edge difficult of access, with nothing to be said for it. From the Col de la Traversette, however, the view over the plain of Piedmont has been known for some time. James David Forbes wrote in 1839, 'from the summit the view was superb, stretching away to the hills above Genoa.' This was confirmed by John Ball: 'the view suddenly un-folded at the summit, extending, in clear weather, across the entire plain of Piedmont as far as Milan, is extremely striking.' The Col de Mary, less well known, is also said to allow a view of the plain.

There is a difficulty about the Col de la Traversette, because its summit is narrow and restricted, and could not have accommodated all Han-nibal's army when he pointed out the view. In any case, the men would not all have been available, and they may have seen it in succession, some at a time, or he may have shown it himself only to his officers who then showed it to their men. In spite of this, the Col de la Traver-sette satisfies most of the requirements of Hannibal's pass. It is accessible through a narrow gorge, the Combe de Queyras in the valley of the Guil; it is high enough for permanent snow, and it has a descent on the Italian side difficult enough to account for the casualties which Hannibal's army suffered. The valley of Queyras was in use as a thoroughfare in Roman times, as shown by the inscription at Les Escoyères, and it was sufficiently frequented in the fifteenth century A D for the Marquis de Saluzzo to pierce a tunnel through it, beneath its summit, to facilitate passage. According to the Marquis de Pézay, François I sent his artillery by this pass (then called Col de Viso) when he invaded Italy. Lastly, the Plain of Piedmont at Saluzzo, to which the Col de la Traversette leads down the valley of the infant Po, is 220 km. from the Col de Grimone, which is in fair agreement with the 1,200 stadia or 213 km. given by Polybius for the crossing of the Alps.

If, instead, Hannibal's route was over the Col de Mary, he would have reached it by entering the valley of Ubaye south of Chorges but after Barcelonnette he would not have gone on to the Col de l'Argentière (which might have been his original intention), but would have been misled northwards, through St-Paul-sur-Ubaye to Maljassett and Maurin. Opposite these villages, the Val de Mary debouches by a gorge, and that would have been the site of the Second

Early nineteenth-century engraving showing Hannibal on the summit of his pass over the Alps, pointing out the plain of Piedmont and the direction of Rome

Battle. The large bare rock would have to be found in one of the mounds of gypsum on the northern slopes of the Val de Mary. The Col de Mary leads down into the Val Maira which opens to the plain at Dronero. The inhabitants of these valleys, on the east of Monte Viso, were the Bagienni, a Ligurian tribe, and as Augusta Bagiennorum was described by Ptolemy as situated in the territory of the Taurini, Hannibal would have descended into it whether he had crossed the Col de la Traversette or the Col de Mary. The distances, also, are equivalent. Whichever it was, and the Col de la Traversette has some advantages over its rival, Hannibal's pass was close to the flank of Monte Viso, either to the north or the south.

179

*The descent from the Col de la
Traversette into Italy, showing the
persistence of thick beds of snow in
summer*

*Monte Viso seen from the
Italian side. The Col de la
Traversette is the gap (far right)
on the north side of the peak; the
Col de Mary, not visible, is to the
left of the peak*

The speed of Hannibal's march across the Alps given by Polybius at 1,200 stadia in fifteen days, or 80 stadia a day, is the same as that of 800 stadia in ten days which he said was the rate of marching in the Rhône valley 'along the river'. It has been objected that this speed of 14 km. a day in the valley could not have been kept up in the mountains, especially as no progress was made on five of the fifteen days that the mountain crossing took, so that the effective speed of march of the vanguard must have been about 20 km. a day. Yet this speed bears comparison with that of Julius Caesar's march in 58 BC, when he mobilized five fresh legions in northern Italy and led them from the eastern side of Mont-Genèvre to the frontier of the territory of the Vocontii (the Col de Cabre) in seven days, fighting a battle on the way against the Tricorii. Caesar's itinerary was almost exactly the same in length as Hannibal's, and it is therefore not extravagant to claim that in their forced march across the Alps, Hannibal's professional soldiers proceeded almost as fast as Caesar's new levies.

Finally, there is a point of interest in Livy's description of how Hannibal's pioneers got rid of the rock which barred the way on the descent from the pass. The story of the fire and vinegar used to disintegrate the rock has been ridiculed by many writers, but without any justification. The same story is recounted by Timagenes and by Appian, among classical authors. Pliny confirmed the practice: 'if fire has not disintegrated a rock, the addition of water makes it split'; and, 'flints may be cracked by fire and vinegar'. Vitruvius confirmed it again: 'Stones which chisels and fire cannot break up are split and reduced to powder if they are first heated and then drenched with vinegar.' Metellus captured Eleuthera with the help of traitors who undermined a tower with vinegar, as Dion Cassius related. The tunnel under the Col de la Traversette was pierced with the help of 'iron and vinegar' in AD 1480. In 1956, the Director of the British Museum (Natural History) repeated the experiment himself. Blocks of limestone were covered with logs which were kindled into a hot fire, after which cold water containing ten per cent of acetic acid was thrown on to the stones. There was a cloud of steam and much hissing as the acid attacked the limestone, and when the cloud had cleared the limestone blocks were found to have been split. It is never safe to doubt factual statements of a practical nature by serious classical authors.

The plain of Piedmont with the river Po and Turin. This capital of the Ligurian tribe of the Taurini was stormed and taken by Hannibal immediately after coming down from the Alps

FIRST ROMAN BLOOD ON ITALIAN SOIL

THE ASSAULT AND CAPTURE of the town of the Taurini involved only Ligurians; no Romans had yet felt the weight of Hannibal's hand on Italian soil, and this fact in itself is remarkable. In Cisalpine Gaul, in that same year 218 BC, there had been insurrections of the Boii and of the Insubres, who were in revolt against the establishment of colonies by the Romans at Placentia, Cremona, and Mutina, and the Gauls besieged Mutina. An army under Lucius Manlius marched from Ariminum to relieve it, but was itself ambushed by the Gauls and heavily defeated. The remnants of this Roman army took refuge on a hill until a relief force under Caius Attilius Serranus rescued them, and they then all concentrated in Mutina.

The revolt of the Boii, although premature, helped Hannibal in one sense, because it delayed the departure of Publius Cornelius Scipio from Italy to Spain, and therefore also postponed his return to Italy; but on the other hand, if the Boii had not revolted when they did, Hannibal might have found no Roman armies in the field in north Italy at all. Nevertheless, it is a measure of the utter absence from the Roman mind of the possibility that Hannibal might choose the route across the Alps that not a single Roman outpost, scouting party or intelligence unit was stationed in the Alps.

Rome had two armies in the field in 218 BC. One, under the Consul Publius Cornelius Scipio was destined for Spain and was already on its way when its commander learnt, as it were by accident, that Hannibal had crossed the Rhône. Scipio, as has been seen, sent his army on to Spain and himself returned to Italy to take command of the Roman forces in the north. The second Roman army, under the other

IX   Jacques-Louis David, 'Napoleon crossing the St Bernard Pass' (1800). By including the names of Hannibal and Charlemagne the artist recalls their crossing of the Alps

Consul Tiberius Sempronius Longus, was destined for Africa and still in Sicily, while its commander was dealing with Carthaginian fleets which attempted to surprise Lilybaeum and raided the coast of Bruttium. Sempronius had taken Malta when the news arrived that Hannibal was in Italy, and Sempronius was ordered to return with his army as quickly as possible.

Meanwhile, in the Po valley, Scipio had the double task of opposing Hannibal's army and of restraining the Gauls from spreading their revolt. As was then customary, Scipio harangued his troops to rouse their patriotic fervour, harping on the facts that the Romans had already beaten the Carthaginians in the First Punic War, that after its passage of the Alps Hannibal's army could be nothing but a rabble, decimated, frost-bitten, and lame, that the treachery of the Carthaginians in their attack on Saguntum was beyond dispute, and that there was no other Roman army, or any other Alps, behind them to defend Rome.

Hannibal's oratory to his men was different. He first formed his army into a circle, then had some prisoners brought in, and asked them if they were willing to fight one another, two and two, to the death, the victor thereby gaining his freedom, a horse, and weapons to fight in the Carthaginian ranks. They accepted, and many died in these impromptu gladiatorial fights. Hannibal then addressed his own soldiers, and told them that what they had just witnessed was not an entertainment but an object-lesson of their own position. The prisoners had accepted and fought because there was no other way for them to escape from their predicament than victory or death. This was precisely the situation of the Carthaginians in Italy, without any base, confronted and surrounded by the hated Romans who had treacherously deprived Carthage of her possessions, the islands of Sardinia and Corsica, when she was powerless to prevent it. Hannibal had mastered and practised the technique of psychological warfare, which aims not only to undermine the enemy's will to resist, but also to raise the morale and the determination of one's own side and supporters.

The armies approached one another, on the north side of the Po which Scipio had crossed near Placentia, Hannibal marching down from the site of Turin to encourage the Insubres and the Boii, ravaging the districts of those Gauls who had sided with Rome. There is some doubt exactly where the first encounter took place, but it was near the river

X   The source of the river Po on the north flank of Monte Viso: near this point Hannibal made his descent from the Alps into Italy

Ticinus (Ticino) which flows out of Lacus Verbanus (Lago Maggiore) into the Po from the north. The troops which came into contact were mostly cavalry, six thousand of Hannibal's horsemen against two thousand of Scipio's who also had spearmen with them. These were posted in front of the horses but they broke and fled when Hannibal's heavy cavalry got at them, while his Numidian light cavalry closed in on the Romans' rear. It was not a pitched battle but a skirmish, in which the Romans had much the worst of it, and they might even have lost their general, the Consul Scipio himself, because he fell wounded and would have been captured by the Carthaginians had not his young son, later to become famous as Scipio Africanus, led his squadron straight into the Carthaginian ranks and rescued his father.

So the first blood was to Hannibal. The Romans retreated to the right or south bank of the Po and broke down the bridges behind them, but the troops entrusted with this task and covering the withdrawal were captured by Hannibal. He marched upstream some distance, built a bridge of rafts across the Po, and himself crossed with his army to the south bank, down which he marched towards Placentia, where Scipio had taken up his position.

Hannibal then had two strokes of luck. During one night more than two thousand Gauls, auxiliaries in Scipio's army, massacred the sentries and came over to Hannibal, who welcomed them and sent them to their homes to spread the good word. The other event was even more welcome, because it eased his very difficult supply situation, as nothing had been prepared for his army in advance, and it had brought nothing with it over the Alps. The Romans had collected a store of grain at Clastidium (Casteggio), which Hannibal was preparing to assault when it was betrayed to him for four hundred pieces of gold.

THE TREBIA

A FEW MILES to the west of Placentia, the river Trebia, coming from the Apennines to the south, flows into the Po. Scipio, in Placentia, was on the east of the Trebia, on the opposite side to Hannibal. Meanwhile, Sempronius's army had arrived at Ariminum from Sicily, and was in a position to reinforce Scipio's, which it did, and the two consular armies were concentrated at Placentia. Scipio's wound obliged him to pass the command over to his colleague.

Overriding Scipio's recommendations of caution, Sempronius was all out for giving battle, particularly as Hannibal's light cavalry was devastating the country of those Gauls who were favourable to Rome. Adding insult to injury, Hannibal was able to say to the Gauls that it was to support them and at their request that he had come over the Alps to Italy, and that it was now up to them to support him and to provide him with supplies. At the same time, Hannibal ordered his light cavalry to use the stratagem of feigning defeat and to withdraw when attacked by the Romans, all with a view to drawing Sempronius out, to fight a pitched battle, for Hannibal knew him to be hasty and quick-tempered. Sempronius was only too ready to fall in with this plan. The time for the next election of Consuls was soon due, and a victory over Hannibal would stand well in Sempronius's favour.

The Trebia flowed between high banks covered with scrub and other vegetation which afforded good cover. Hannibal reconnoitred the

The river Trebia, with its high scrub-covered banks. It was following the course of this river that Hannibal won his first major victory on Italian soil against the Romans

ground carefully, and selected a spot for his brother Mago to hide with two thousand men, mounted and foot. He then ordered his Numidian horsemen to cross the Trebia at dawn, to advance towards the Romans, to attack the Roman outposts, and then to withdraw, so as to lure them on, and to recross the river. This was Hannibal's first trap, and Sempronius fell straight into it. The Romans were sent out before they had eaten anything, cold and wet, and when they had crossed the Trebia they were chilled and numbed by the icy cold water. It was winter, bitterly cold, the most unsuitable weather imaginable for Hannibal's main body of troops, who were accustomed to the hot climate of Africa, southern Spain, and the Balearic Islands. But he made his men eat an early morning meal, warm themselves at fires, and rub their bodies with oil, 'and so the southerners from the lands of the sun were able to make use of the rigours of winter to their own advantage.'

As the legionaries advanced, Hannibal's light infantry, slingers from the Balearic Islands, fell back, and a confused battle ensued. The Carthaginian cavalry pressed the Roman horse hard, and the slingers added to their discomfiture. The legionaries held firm against the elephants, which Hannibal immediately transferred to his left wing where they faced the Roman Gallic auxiliaries, who broke and fled. Then Mago and his men made their unexpected appearance and charged straight into the rear of the Romans. The legionaries, though encircled, nevertheless stood their ground and hacked their way through the Carthaginian infantry, back to the river Trebia which they had to cross to reach their camp, but many who had escaped the Carthaginian pursuit were drowned. It was raining so hard that nobody could see. The remnants of the Roman armies returned to Placentia and to Cremona, and those Gauls who had until then remained un-committed flocked to Hannibal in large numbers; more than sixty thousand men—many of them horsemen—are said to have joined him.

The poet Florus compared Hannibal and his army to a thunderbolt which had burst its way through the middle of the Alps and descended upon Italy as if launched from the skies. The first storm broke on the Ticinus and one Consul and his army were defeated. Now, on the Trebia, both Consuls and their armies together had been routed, and the Second Punic War 'wreaked its fury'. Worse was to come.

After this battle, the Numidian horsemen continued to raid, and Hannibal tried to assault and capture a trading post, but in the cavalry battle that ensued, he was wounded, and the action was called off.

188

Another trading post, Victumulae, then attracted his attention; its large Gallic population, which opposed him, was routed and exterminated, as a warning to others. There followed operations in the northern foothills of the Apennines, which Hannibal was anxious to cross so as to win the Etruscans, as he had the Ligurians and Gauls, to his side; but the weather was so bad, infinitely worse than when crossing the Alps, that he desisted. Of those elephants which had survived the battle of the Trebia, he lost seven more.

The Roman Consuls decided that they could not successfully hold the line of the Po, and leaving garrisons in Placentia and Cremona they led their armies into winter quarters, Scipio to Ariminum to bar the road to Rome along the Adriatic, and Sempronius to Lucca and Arretium, to do the same in Etruria. Hannibal wintered in Liguria, and suffering in his army was great. His horses were in very poor condition and developed hunger-mange, but he cured them by bathing them in 'old wine' or vinegar. All the elephants died except one, about which more anon.

LAKE TRASIMENE

THE CONSULS elected for the year 217 BC were Caius Flaminius Nepos and Cnaeus Servilius Geminus. Flaminius was the general who had commanded the army which fought against the Insubrian Gauls in 223 BC without great success, but he had a high reputation as a soldier and no less an opinion of his own prowess, not only in military but in political matters, for he was violently opposed to the Senate and to the aristocratic party. His entry into office was inauspicious. Instead of assuming the Consulship in Rome with the customary ceremonial, visiting the temple of Jupiter, proclaiming the Latin Festival on the Alban Mount, taking the auspices and going to offer prayers on the Capitol, he decided to take over command with his troops in the field, which he did at Arretium, surrounded by a crowd of hangers-on, eager for the spoils which his forthcoming victory could not fail to provide. Meanwhile, his colleague Servilius took over the army at Ariminum.

The reason for the stationing of Flaminius's army at Arretium was to deny to Hannibal the easier passes over the Apennines, from Forli into Etruria, but that was not the route which Hannibal took. After parading his prisoners, making slaves of the Romans and sending the

The Passo della Collina by which Hannibal probably crossed the Apennines from the Po valley to Etruria

Bronze coin from the Chiana valley, c. 217 BC, showing (obverse) a Negro's head, and (reverse) an Indian elephant, perhaps Hannibal's Surus

other Italians home without demanding ransom, for them to dis-
seminate his promise to liberate all their communities from the yoke
of Rome and to emphasize that he was making war only on Rome and
not on Italy, Hannibal left the Po valley in the spring of 217 BC and
crossed the Apennines, perhaps by the Passo Collina which leads
from Bologna to Pistoia; this brought his army down into the valley
of the Arno. That river was so mightily swollen from the melting of
snow on the Apennines and the spring rains, that the low ground was
a marshy swamp, in crossing which the troops suffered great hardships. Livy relates that for four days the army marched through

water, unable to find any dry places to bivouac other than piles of baggage or heaps of dead pack-animals. Many died from drowning or of disease, and Hannibal himself caught an infection and lost the sight of one eye.

He rode the sole remaining elephant, an animal which may have found its way into history, for some years later Cato the Elder recorded that the elephant which fought most bravely in the Second Punic War was called *Surus*. This name means the Syrian, and Syria was where the Ptolemies had captured Indian elephants, some of which they must have given to Carthage. A bronze coin found in the valley of the Clanis (Chiana), on Hannibal's route to Lake Trasimene, bears on the obverse a Negro's head indicating an African connexion, and on the reverse an equally obvious Indian elephant. It is believed to have been minted at just about this time, 217 BC; and as Pyrrhus never came this way with his elephants, the coin probably bears a representation of Hannibal's sole surviving elephant, the Indian *Surus*. The appearance of these animals where they had never been seen before must have created a sensation, for there are other examples of local representations of elephants on coins or in rough statues, connected with Hannibal's passage.

In Hannibal's line of march, the African and Spanish veterans formed the vanguard, followed by the uncertain Gauls who had joined the army, while the rear was brought up by the Carthaginian cavalry. The army emerged from the swamps which covered the stretch of country between Pistoia and Faesolae (Fiesole), and made for the latter town, passing through the most fertile regions of Etruria, rich in grain and cattle. These and the whole countryside, Hannibal proceeded to raid and devastate, under the eyes of Flaminius and his men at Arretium, with the purpose of incensing that general whom Hannibal knew to be arrogant and impetuous. Instead of making for Arretium to attack Flaminius, Hannibal marched past his front, on a more southerly route through the valley of the Chiana to Cortona and Lake Trasimene. The bait was swallowed exactly as expected. Flaminius's staff advised caution and the summoning of the other consular army from Ariminum, but Flaminius would hear nothing of it and gave the order to march in pursuit of Hannibal.

The battle of Lake Trasimene has been the subject of much argument about the site of the battlefield and the positions of the contending armies; but practically all this work has been a waste of time because Giancarlo Susini, in a recent remarkable study of the ground, making use of all techniques, has shown that in Hannibal's day the northern shore of Lake Trasimene was not as it is now. Today, from the north-west corner of the lake at Borghetto to the north-east corner at Passignano, between narrow defiles at each of these places, there is a flat plain about two kilometres wide, separating the shore from the hills. Much of this plain, however, is the result of alluvial deposits from the river Macerone forming a delta, and also of the lowering of the surface level of the lake, which is known to have taken place in AD 1421, when Braccio Fortebraccio built a canal at the south-east corner of the lake to evacuate its waters into the river Nestore.

The popular local name for this plain is 'Navaccia', which means 'pool of water'. The proof of these conclusions is provided by aerial photography. In the first place, this shows the successive additional

Plan of the battlefield of Lake Trasimene (after Susini) ▶

Panoramic view of the north shore of Lake Trasimene, showing the low-lying plain (known locally as Navaccia) where the shore-line has receded

Tuoro

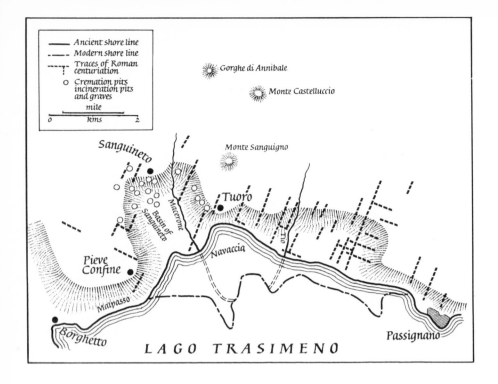

Ancient shore line
Modern shore line
Traces of Roman centuriation
Cremation pits incineration pits and graves

mile
0   kims   2

Gorghe di Annibale

Monte Castelluccio

Monte Sanguigno

Sanguineto

Tuoro

Basin of Sanguineto

Macerone

Pieve Confine

Navaccia

Malpasso

Borghetto

Passignano

LAGO TRASIMENO

Passignano   Malpasso   Borghetto

areas of ground, reclaimed and brought into cultivation, with the sequence of shore-lines, succeeding one another southwards as the delta of the Macerone was built up. Most important is the evidence provided by the traces of the Roman system of land-division (centuriation) into rectangular strips applied to constant areas of 20 *actus* (each *actus* approximately 240 by 120 feet, the century providing one hundred family-plots), separated by tracks and ditches at right angles to each other at standard and constant distances. This system stops at a shore-line which must have been that of Roman times. Furthermore, the longitudinal ditches are all perpendicular to the ancient shore-line, showing that they served for drainage.

The upshot of all this work is that the learned schemes which made the Roman army follow the modern northern shore-line of the lake, to Passignano and even to Montecolognola, in the direction of Perugia, and spread the battlefield over this area, are impossible. Instead, it must be accepted that once past the defile of Borghetto, the 'Malpasso', there was no way of avoiding a little basin, the valley of the Macerone, surrounded by a U-shaped range of wooded hills, running from Pieve Confini on the west, through the village of Sanguineto at the head of the basin, to the little town of Tuoro on the east.

Hannibal passed through the Malpasso and stationed his army partly hidden in the U-shaped range of hills surrounding the basin of Sanguineto, the Gauls and Carthaginian cavalry on the west, and the Balearic slingers on the east, while the encampment of the African and Spanish troops near Tuoro was open to view on the rising ground. Flaminius followed Hannibal. Before the operations began, the narratives recount an extraordinary series of unfortunate omens. On mounting, Flaminius's horse stumbled and threw him; when he gave the order to raise the standards and begin the march, a standard-bearer was unable to lift his standard out of the ground and had to be ordered to dig it out. He arrived with his army at nightfall near the entrance to the defile of Borghetto and encamped.

Next morning the Roman army advanced through the defile of Borghetto, reached the basin of Sanguineto, and saw the Carthaginian camp on the hill facing them. There is a tradition that a fog from the lake hid the dispositions of the Carthaginian army, but this looks suspiciously like a Roman excuse for what was about to happen, namely, that as soon as the Roman army had passed the defile of Borghetto, the Malpasso, and was in the basin of Sanguineto, Hannibal sprang his trap. His men descended from their heights and hiding places, and attacked the Romans in front, in the flank, and in the rear. Their retreat at Malpasso was cut off; the ground was so circumscribed that the legionaries had no room to manœuvre or to fight properly, and in three hours they were killed where they stood to the number of fifteen thousand. Some were drowned in the lake. Hannibal's losses were eighteen hundred, mostly Gauls. The fighting was so fierce that it was said that neither army noticed an earthquake, which shook many Italian towns and deflected some rivers from their courses, at the time of the battle. Flaminius met his end from an Insubrian Gaul, Ducarius, who recognized him as the invader and devastator of his country six years before, and drove his lance through him. In accordance with his custom, Hannibal had a search made for Flaminius's body to give it honourable burial, but it could not be found.

The Roman vanguard of six thousand men who had made uphill, straight for the Carthaginians, managed to hack its way through, in a north-easterly direction, on the south-eastern flank of Monte Castelluccio, towards the river Niccone, a tributary of the Tiber which would have led them to Rome. They were pursued, surrounded, and captured next day by Hannibal's cavalry under Maharbal. The Romans were made prisoner; their allies were released and sent to their homes.

The description of the battlefield and the disposition of the troops of the two armies, given above, is confirmed by two other independent lines of study: archaeology and folklore. Round the basin of Sanguineto, in the form of a U from Pieve Confine on the west, through Sanguineto itself, to Tuoro on the east, there have been found a number of incineration-pits, as much as twenty feet deep, yielding ashes which analysis has shown to contain organic matter. Arrowheads and spear-heads were also found in them. There can be no doubt that these *ustrina* contain the cremated remains of the fifteen thousand corpses of Romans who fell; and as it is impossible to believe that in the speedy disposal of them, which was obviously necessary, the corpses could be carried far, the pits must have been dug near the places where the men died.

South of Sanguineto were more graves, some containing cremated remains of ashes and charred bones, others containing burials, many of the skeletons lacking a limb, and some with their skulls smashed in. All were of adult males, and all had their teeth. There can be no doubt that these graves are also of men who fell in this battle, probably Carthaginians. No arms or equipment were found in the graves, but it is known that Hannibal had all these collected and that he used them to arm and equip his army later. On the battlefield itself, only a bronze helmet, a lance cusp, and arrow-heads have been found.

The contribution which folklore has made to the study of the battle of Lake Trasimene relates to place-names. These can be notoriously unreliable when they perpetuate, not local peasant tradition, but later speculation, and the number of 'Caesar's Camps' which abound in France and England are a salutary warning of the necessity for rigorous analysis and a search for the oldest form of a place-name. There are examples close to the battlefield of Lake Trasimene in the modern names of the villages of Ossaia and Sepoltaglia, very suggestive of carnage in their meanings of 'bones' and 'graves'; but their old names are Ursaria and Speltallia respectively, and they have nothing

Grave containing the skeleton of a casualty from the battle of Lake Trasimene. The Roman dead were cremated in incineration-pits; graves such as this were probably of Hannibal's soldiers who fell in the battle

196

to do with the battle. On the other hand, Giancarlo Susini has found three place-names connected with the battle which are genuinely based on local tradition, free from later falsifications. They are Sanguineto itself and Monte Sanguigno just north of Tuoro, both deriving from the word 'blood'; and the Gorghe di Annibale, a height north of Sanguineto from which the whole battlefield can be surveyed and where presumably Hannibal directed operations from his headquarters.

The disaster of the battle of Lake Trasimene did not drain Rome's cup of bitterness, for more was to follow. The other Consul, Servilius, was advancing with his army from Ariminum to come to the help of his colleague, and he had sent four thousand cavalry forward under Caius Centenius. On hearing of the disaster that had befallen Flaminius, they altered their line of march, but they too were surrounded by the Carthaginian cavalry under Maharbal, and either killed or captured. The place where this occurred is given by Appian as near Lago di Plestia, by the Pass of Colfiorito leading across the Apennines from Foligno eastwards to the country of the Piceni, which was the general direction of Hannibal's line of march, as Umberto Ciotti has emphasized.

STATESMAN AND SOLDIER

HANNIBAL HAD ANNIHILATED organized Roman resistance in the north of Italy, and there were no more formations of Roman troops between him and Rome. The whole of the peninsula was open to him to march wherever he liked, and the direct route to Rome, through Etruria, where the Etruscans had only fairly recently abandoned their independence and accepted Roman supremacy, was unprotected. In these circumstances, with two such magnificent triumphs as the Trebia and Lake Trasimene to his credit, it has often been asked why Hannibal did not immediately march on Rome itself.

Such a question betrays a complete lack of appreciation of what Hannibal's real problem and aim were, of the relation that military operations bear to politics, and of the character of the man himself. The object of his whole expedition was to reduce the political power of Rome so that she should no longer be a constant menace to the prosperity, or even the continued existence, of Carthage. Hannibal knew very well that Roman pride and tenacity would not yield either to terror tactics or to surprise. He could count on no sustained support, or even on any support at all from his home land; he had no base, no seaport, and for so-called allies he had, so far, only the unpredictable and capricious Gauls, from whom to recruit men for his army and to obtain supplies. From these facts he drew two conclusions.

The first was that his main object, and only hope of success, lay in the disruption of the Roman Confederacy, an operation which, if successful, lay in the sphere of politics. Everything that Hannibal did was subject to this principle, and undertaken with this aim, using military means only as an instrument, albeit a very powerful one, to achieve it.

With this in mind, the manner in which he conducted his operations was all-important. His army was small, barely forty thousand men, without a siege-train, in a country where the Romans had garrisons and colonies in many fortified towns, and could eventually mobilize over twenty times his own strength of fighting men. Hannibal's cavalry was supreme, but his horsemen and their horses could not last for ever, and were wasting assets. His best infantry was good, but the Roman was equally good, if not better, as was shown by the manner

Part of the wall of Servius Tullius on the Aventine in Rome. Originally erected to surround and defend the Seven Hills of Rome, the wall was rebuilt in the fourth century BC

in which some of the legionaries hacked their way through the Carthaginian ranks at the Trebia and Lake Trasimene.

It would have been courting certain and ignominious failure for Hannibal to have tried to assault Rome. It was defended by its substantial walls, built between 378 and 325 BC, in addition to which the Romans were not people to subscribe to the fatally erroneous view that walls defend men, but maintained on the contrary that men defend walls. Skilled in warfare and military history as Hannibal undoubtedly was, he also had before him the warning of what happened to Demetrius Poliorcetes when he attempted to assault the citadel of Rhodes in 305 BC. In spite of all his equipment of assault-towers, battering-rams, catapults, Demetrius was unable to overcome the Rhodians' resistance because they were kept supplied by sea. Hannibal, without any siege equipment, would have been confronted with the same difficulty, for Rome could be supplied from Ostia, and he would have been powerless to stop this flow because he had no fleet.

Where Hannibal excelled, and he knew it, was in generalship. Whence followed his second principle, that the war must be conducted in such a manner that the Romans should never know what to expect next, should be unable to plan to meet the next blow, and should make mistakes. He must never abandon the initiative, and with it the precious element of surprise. By this means he could enlist the war of nerves as an ally to the war of arms.

The prosecution of such a method of war meant, necessarily, that it was in a supreme degree a war of movement. A static war of position would not only afford his military skill no scope, but lose time and endanger his army by allowing larger Roman forces to concentrate against him. Tricks, even treachery, and every other combination of ruse would be put to use. At the same time, with the major political aim in view, a war of movement would be a direct attack on the Roman Confederacy, for he would ravage and devastate the territories of Rome's allies, and they would see for themselves that Rome was powerless to protect them. From that situation, the next step would be for the confederate cities to shake off allegiance to Rome and make an alliance with Hannibal.

If that is understood, it becomes easier to see why a less gifted general like Pyrrhus might try to march on Rome, but a genius like Hannibal would not. During the fifteen years that Hannibal was in Italy, there were two occasions when the Romans thought that he might assault Rome, of which this was one; but he refrained. On the other occasion, he did march on Rome, not to assault it, but as a desperate measure to influence the plan of campaign of the Roman commanders by making them fear that this was his aim. As will be seen, it failed.

While fighting was going on in the north of Italy the Gauls became restive at the destruction of their country; but it was not to save it from being a theatre of war that Hannibal moved south. After his victory at Lake Trasimene he marched past Perusia (Perugia). There is a questionable tradition that he attempted to assault Spoletium (Spoleto) and failed; it was not on his line of march, which lay through Umbria where he devastated the Roman colonists' homesteads, across the Apennines to the Adriatic coast, during which he ravaged the country of the Piceni, and down the eastern side of the Apennines into Apulia, near Luceria where he rested his army.

He was now in a fertile countryside, very different from the rugged Alps which had so severely tried his men. Foraging parties were sent out and collected plentiful victuals for the winter. There, Hannibal not only rested his men, but proceeded to take steps which showed what a master of tactics he was. Isolated in enemy territory, he re-organized his infantry so as to incorporate into their drill the best features of Roman tactics and training, which he was quick to observe and admire, and he re-armed his men with Roman weapons, of which he had captured more than enough. Moreover, he was now in the neighbourhood of Italic tribes whose loyalty to Rome was of most recent date, and he hoped to make an impression on them. So far, he had made none, for not a single town had opened its gates to him. Hannibal had won one skirmish and two resounding victories, and destroyed a consular army; but Rome could already make one all-important claim: no Latin colony or community had joined him.

FABIUS CUNCTATOR

ROME MADE NO ATTEMPT to minimize the military disasters which had befallen her. 'We have been beaten in a great battle', the Praetor, Marcus Pomponius, frankly admitted to the multitudes who crowded round the Senate House, waiting for news. A Dictator was appointed, Quintus Fabius Maximus, to defend the city, repair the walls, and break down the bridges over the Tiber.

XI   Fragment of a wall-painting probably depicting the meeting of a Samnite leader and Quintus Fabius Rullianus (cf. page 74), great-grandfather of Quintus Fabius Maximus

Fabius was an aristocrat, a sound soldier, and the very reverse of the demagogic Flaminius, who had omitted the customary ceremonies on taking office, and had spurned the omens in the field. It is possible, as Giancarlo Susini has suggested, that the misdeeds of Flaminius were exaggerated in the narratives, as a result of anti-democratic feeling and pressure exerted by the Senate, and some of the stories are suspect. But the effect on Fabius Maximus was marked. All the neglects of religious ceremonies must be expiated, and he began by ordering the Sibylline Books to be consulted. They revealed that the sacrifice to Mars had been incorrectly performed, insufficient, and must be repeated. A

Roman Republican denarius with obverse showing the head of Venus Erycina, and reverse showing the Temple of Venus at Eryx. The denarius was introduced by Rome c. 187 BC to curb the inflation caused by the war against Hannibal

vow must be taken to hold games in honour of Jupiter; a shrine must be dedicated to Venus Erycina and to Mens; public prayer must be instituted; a *lectisternum,* 'strewing of couches' with a banquet, must be offered to the images of the gods on their couches, one each for Jupiter and Juno, Neptune and Minerva, Mars and Venus, Apollo and Diana, Vulcan and Vesta, Mercury and Ceres. A vow must be taken to make an offering to the gods of Sacred Spring if, in the forthcoming spring, the fortunes of war favoured Rome.

XII   The river Vulturnus near Venafrum; in 217 BC this valley featured prominently in Hannibal's operations against Rome

When these steps had been taken, Fabius Maximus addressed himself to military matters. On taking up his command, he had under him the army which Servilius had brought down from Ariminum to the neighbourhood of Rome, and he ordered the raising of two new legions, so that his army was more powerful than Hannibal's, except in cavalry. To meet Hannibal's expected march on Rome, orders had been given for a scorched-earth policy to be carried out, burning crops, destroying bridges, and withdrawing populations behind the fortifications of strongly held towns. Hannibal had in fact no intention of undertaking a march on Rome; instead, he continued his activities in Apulia.

Although no ally of Rome had as yet given any indication of wishing to defect, the Romans could not afford to leave Hannibal unmolested on his own, in the midst of their allies, without a Roman army near by, to show the eagles. Fabius accordingly marched out along the Via Appia, through Campania, Beneventum, and the mountains of Samnium to Apulia; but his strategy and his tactics were the reverse of those of his predecessor, and a radical departure from what had previously been the Roman method of making war, which was to attack the enemy. After the disasters which the Roman army had just suffered at his hands, Fabius saw that Hannibal must not be given the chance to do what he most wanted, which was to fight pitched battles in open country. Fabius therefore kept his men in the foothills of the Apennines, where Hannibal's cavalry could not get at them, while he harassed Hannibal's foraging parties by guerilla warfare. Hannibal tried every stratagem to taunt or coax Fabius into giving battle, laid ambushes, marched away and marched back again; but the old Roman stuck to his principles for which reason the Romans gave him the additional name of Cunctator, the Delayer.

Seeing that he was making no progress and acquiring no deserters from the Roman Confederacy, Hannibal left Apulia, passed by Fabius's flank, and marched through the mountains of Samnium and the country of the Hirpini, past Beneventum which closed its gates to him, into Campania, practically along the same route as that followed by Fabius on his way to Apulia. There were many reasons why Hannibal came to Campania. It was the most fertile district of Italy, the fruits of which he wanted to enjoy for his army and to deny to the Romans. Campania had good seaports, such as Cumae and Neapolis, of which he needed one for his communications with Carthage. In Campania was the great city of Capua (on the site of what is now Santa Maria Capua Vetere), the most important of all Rome's allies.

Map of Italy showing principal sites in Hannibal's successful campaigns against Rome (218–216 BC)

Hannibal knew from his spies that the population of Capua contained a powerful section which was very discontented with the oppression that they suffered from Rome, and ready, if given the chance, to desert Rome and strike up alliance with him. Finally, Hannibal hoped that by threatening Capua he would bring Fabius into the Campanian plain where he could fight him.

Beyond Beneventum Hannibal went down the river Calor, captured Telesia together with an enormous store of grain, and went up the river Vulturnus which he crossed near Allifae. Next, he threaded his way through a pass across a mountain which Polybius called Eribanus and Livy Mons Callicula (probably near Borgo S. Antonio) and descended into the plain of Campania. He established a fortified camp on the northern bank of the Vulturnus near Casilinum (site of the rebuilt city of Capua), and from there his Numidian cavalry ravaged the countryside while the Roman soldiers were obliged to look on, prevented from stopping it by orders of Fabius.

In the ranks of the Roman army, as in the ruling circles in Rome, Fabius's policy of delay was meeting growing opposition. Hannibal, of course, knew this, and it suited his book for if the Romans reverted to the practice of offering battle, he could beat them. He therefore fanned the flame of this opposition by carefully avoiding doing any damage to Fabius's own property in the raids that constantly went on. This was known to the Romans, and led to the belief held in some quarters that Fabius was in collusion with Hannibal, and therefore a traitor. Nor did it help Fabius's cause that, when he made a convention with Hannibal for an exchange of prisoners, 247 more Romans than Carthaginians were exchanged; for these Fabius proposed that the Senate should pay ransom, but the Senate refused, and Fabius paid it himself, by selling the estates which Hannibal had not destroyed, thereby providing the enemy with money.

Nevertheless, Fabius was still Dictator, and he continued unruffled to conduct his campaign as he thought best. He followed Hannibal to Campania, encamped athwart the road to Rome near Falernus Ager, in the foothills of Mons Massicus, where he was safe from assault and could threaten the pass through which Hannibal had come from Allifae. It could not be claimed that this was a threat to Hannibal's rear, for he had no rear, and this was Fabius's chief strategic difficulty. But the political difficulty of refraining from risking a battle while Hannibal continued to raid and devastate the countryside of Rome's allies, whom she was supposed to defend, continued to increase. So the wily old Fabius, in his turn, laid a trap for Hannibal.

The plain into which Hannibal had led his army was bounded on the south by the river Vulturnus, which was unfordable and spanned by only one bridge at Casilinum which was held by its Roman garrison. On the west was the sea. To the north, the Via Appia was held by Fabius's army; the Via Latina was blocked by the Latin colony at Teanum. To the east there were hills, and the pass by which Hannibal had come. In this pass, probably near Borgo S. Antonio, Fabius stationed four thousand men, at the same time strengthening the garrison of Casilinum, and moving his main army further eastwards to threaten Hannibal's escape, which he thought would be eastwards. The trap was extremely clever, for each of the detachments of the Roman army was assured of its supplies, from Latium in the north, Campania in the south, and Beneventum in the east, and there was no necessity to move in order to forage, which would have given Hannibal an opportunity to do damage. The Delayer could afford to wait.

Hannibal was well aware of what had happened. He calculated that as the pass leading to Allifae was difficult, and as he had come by that route and had the reputation of never going by the same route twice, the Romans would least expect him to go that way, in spite of the precautions which they had taken to block the pass. Accordingly, that was the route which Hannibal decided to take, with his now immense stock of stores and booty. He began operations by sending out his Numidian cavalry to make a demonstration against Fabius's army on the Via Appia, in order to dispel the idea that he intended to march eastwards by the pass to Allifae. Fabius sent Hostilius Mancinus out to meet the Numidians who retreated as pre-arranged, with the Romans pursuing them; whereupon the whole body of Carthaginian cavalry fell on the Romans, cut them down and killed Hostilius. Still Fabius refused battle, which Hannibal offered him in front of his camp near Teanum, for he was determined to fight Hannibal only if he was in movement, and to attack him in the flank or in the rear.

Hannibal then had recourse to unorthodox methods which, for ingenuity, would have done honour to Odysseus. From the herds that he had collected, he selected two thousand vigorous head of cattle and had faggots of dry branches and pitch-pine fastened to their horns. In the middle of the night these torches were lighted, and the terrified beasts were driven up the slopes of the hills forming the sides of the pass. Mad with pain and fear, the animals rushed up the hills and through the woods, leading the Romans to believe that the Carthaginians were escaping by climbing the heights themselves, and not trying to force a way through the pass. The Roman defenders of that

Remains of the Sanctuary of Hercules Curinus at Sulmo (Sulmona) also called the Villa of Ovid, whose birthplace Sulmo was

Hill near Gerunium which has been identified as Mons Calenus, which Hannibal's army occupied during the campaign in Apulia

pass, hearing the noise and confusion on the heights, imagined that their own position was being turned, and they left their position to oppose what they thought was the enemy. This was just what Hannibal had expected and waited for. To attack the pass he sent some light infantry who found it practically undefended, and the road was then open. Fabius drew up his army near his camp, but was afraid to attack in case he fell into one of Hannibal's dreaded ambushes, so his clever plan was ruined and Hannibal got clean away, with his army, his baggage-train, his stores and his booty, and encamped at Allifae.

Hannibal then proceeded up the valley of the Vulturnus to Venafrum whence a road led through eastern Latium to Rome. Thereby he hoped to increase Fabius's nervousness on that score, whereas in fact he marched through Samnium, crossed the Apennines to Sulmo (birth-place of Ovid), passing through the territories of the Samnites, Peligni, and Frentani, all of which he pillaged, to Gerunium in Apulia (north of Luceria), where a large Roman store of grain had been collected. Unable to persuade the inhabitants of Gerunium to open their gates to him, he stormed the town, razed it to the ground except for the granaries, killed the inhabitants, and set up a strongly fortified camp near by. Back again in Apulia with its plains so favourable for the activity of his cavalry, he took advantage of its being harvest time to forage and prepare for the winter. But he was by this time a disappointed man. He had kept the initiative throughout the year and gone where he wanted. He had promised Rome's allies independence from Rome, and shown that he could either ruin or help them. But still not one town had come over to him, and the Roman Confederacy was as solid as ever.

Fabius's failure to catch Hannibal in his trap added still further to the discontent at his policy of delaying tactics. He followed Hannibal cautiously and encamped at the foot of Mons Calenus, near Larinum. From there he had to return to Rome on public business, and the command of the army devolved on his Master of the Horse, Marcus Minutius Rufus, who had long been losing patience and wanting to throw Fabius's policy overboard and attack Hannibal. Taking advantage of his superior's absence, Minutius advanced towards Gerunium and encamped a short distance away. Knowing all about Minutius's character, Hannibal had expected this, and he now sent forward a small force to occupy a hill, as an implied threat to the Roman camp. Minutius attacked it with a stronger force, drove it back, and then established his own camp in the same place.

In spite of his professed opinions, Minutius pursued Fabian tactics by refusing to be drawn into battle, and Hannibal adopted the technique of resuming his foraging raids, which necessarily reduced the number of his own troops in camp. Minutius sent out cavalry to intercept Hannibal's foragers, and himself attacked Hannibal's depleted camp, but was driven off. He had, however, shown fight, and Rome promoted him to rank equally with Fabius, who now returned to the army. There were then two dictators, and they decided that each should command two of the four legions of the army. Minutius withdrew his and encamped in a position further forward in the plain. In front of Minutius's camp was a hill which Hannibal sent a small force to occupy by night, with orders to demonstrate and draw the Romans on. Meanwhile Hannibal posted strong forces, hidden in uneven ground on Minutius's left flank. Again the trap worked. Minutius attacked the hill which Hannibal reinforced with driblets of men, and eventually Minutius brought out his legions in full force. Hannibal threw in his heavy cavalry, and the battle was properly joined. At nightfall, when the Carthaginians hidden behind Minutius's left flank suddenly came into action, Minutius's legions panicked, fled, and were pursued by the enemy. But Fabius was there. With his legions he advanced and saved Minutius's army from destruction.

Hannibal's comment on this event is recorded for us by Livy: 'At last the cloud that hovered on the crests of the mountains has come down in a storm of rain.' Afterwards Minutius apologized to Fabius for his failure.

Hannibal went into winter quarters where he was, the Roman army in the camp at the foot of Mons Calenus. Fabius's term of office as Dictator came to an end, and the command devolved on the Consul Servilius, and on Marcus Atilius Regulus who had succeeded the defunct Flaminius as Consul until the new elections were held.

CANNAE

FOR THE YEAR 216 BC, there could be no question of repeating the highly unpopular expedient of appointing a dictator in Rome, with all the vexation, frustration, and bad feeling that it had involved. Until the election of new Consuls, the outgoing Consuls Atilius Regulus and Servilius Geminus took over the armies previously commanded by Fabius and Minutius respectively. In Rome, the elections were bitterly contested. A popular candidate appeared in the person of a son of a butcher, Caius Terentius Varro, enemy of the Senate and the aristocrats. A coarse man with no attainments except in demagogy, he was elected Consul as the people's champion. The Patricians put forward Lucius Aemilius Paullus, a good soldier who had conducted the Illyrian War in 219 BC with success, and a friend of Fabius. He also was elected Consul. The Senate decided that the army should be raised to the unprecedented strength of eight legions to oppose Hannibal, besides which a ninth legion was sent under Lucius Postumius Albinus to Cisalpine Gaul, with the object of disheartening the Gauls who had taken service in Hannibal's army, and, if possible, of drawing them off.

The two Consuls took command on alternate days, in accordance with custom. This absurd system was repeated two thousand years later by Marlborough and Max of Baden, before the battle of Blenheim. But whereas Max did nothing, Marlborough could always act brilliantly on the days when he was in command. With Varro and Aemilius Paullus the position was reversed, for it was Varro who was all for action, but devoid of military skill.

Varro began his term of office by making violent and arrogant speeches, in which he accused the Senate and the conservative party of deliberately prolonging the war, whereas he promised to finish it with his first offensive battle against Hannibal. Fabius prophesied a second and more calamitous Lake Trasimene. Nobody could have been more happy than Hannibal at the measures which Rome had taken. He was now to be confronted by an army of which one half would be raw recruits, commanded by two generals at loggerheads over military matters and politics. But his problem was supplies, for his winter stock was nearly exhausted. He started operations by leaving Gerunium and marched southwards, past Luceria, crossed the river Aufidus (Ofante) and captured the town of Cannae which contained one of the Roman magazines. Ruins of this Apulian town have recently been excavated.

A skirmish turned out to the advantage of the Romans, which whetted further Varro's determination to take the offensive. But Aemilius Paullus, who was in command that day, checked the pursuit for fear of falling into a trap. Varro was furious and accused his colleague of throwing away a golden chance of victory and of ending the war. The two Consuls hurled much invective at one another. Against Varro's recklessness, Aemilius Paullus instanced the fate of Sempronius and of Flaminius, to which Varro retorted by pointing out the disastrous results of Fabius's policy of caution and delay.

Hannibal then laid another of his snares. He led his army out of camp carrying only weapons; all baggage, riches and treasure were left in full view in open tents, without sentries but with fires burning. He hoped to make the Romans think that he wanted to get right away, while he hid his army behind a few hills, waiting to pounce on the enemy when they entered his camp and started to plunder. At dawn the Romans reconnoitred the camp and suspected a deliberate trap; but the soldiers threatened to mutiny unless an assault was ordered, and Varro was only too ready to oblige them. He was restrained, however, by a bad omen: the Sacred Chickens in their golden cage had refused to eat their food. This augury was confirmed by two escaped prisoners who reported that Hannibal was hiding in the hills with his army, and waiting only for the Romans to advance. So Hannibal's bait was not taken.

Although the battle which was about to be fought was one of the most important in history, the greatest uncertainty still prevails regarding its site. The recent discovery by M. Gervasio of a cemetery near Cannae itself appeared to provide an answer to the problem, and the human remains were attributed by General D. Ludovico to Hannibal's battle; but the careful archaeological studies of Fernanda

Bertocchi, and Giuseppe Genna's examination of some 170 skeletons, show conclusively that the cemetery was mediaeval. It contained no weapons at all, but Byzantine ear-rings of the tenth century A D, coins of Romanus II Junior and of John I Zimisces, who spanned the dates A D 959 to 976. Furthermore, the skeletons were those of all ages, children, boys and girls, young, middle-aged, and old, men and women. There is no reason to be surprised at the coincidence of a big cemetery in the neighbourhood of the great battlefield, for Cannae is the key to Apulia and the scene of a number of battles: here in A D 861 the Lombards fought the Salernese, and ten years later the Saracens; in 1018 the Byzantines defeated the Normans, who took their revenge in 1041; and in 1083 Robert Guiscard captured and destroyed Cannae.

From the classical texts it is not even clear whether Hannibal's battle was fought on the left bank or the right bank of the Aufidus; but Nevio Degrassi has pointed out that this problem is probably insoluble, because the river constantly changes its course (it did so markedly during the six years that he studied the site). His opinion is that as the battle immediately took the name of the town of Cannae,

Air view of the hill of Cannae on which stand the ruins of the town; in the surrounding plain can be seen (foreground) the cemetery which recent research has shown to be medieval and to have nothing to do with Hannibal's battle

212

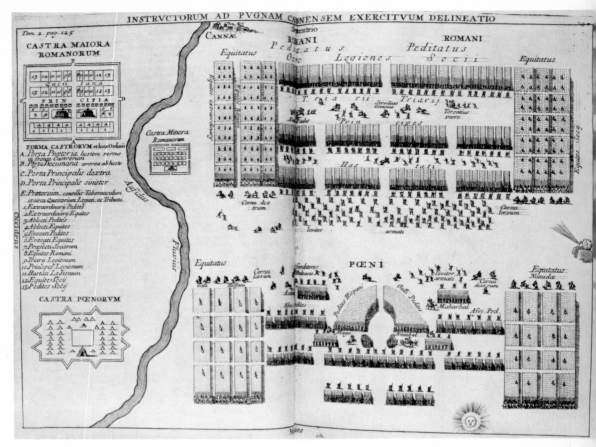

A seventeenth-century plan of the battle of Cannae, drawn to illustrate an edition of Livy's History. *It shows the relative positions and the formations of the two armies*

◄ *The river Aufidus (Ofante) with the monument to the battle of Cannae, an ancient column re-erected in recent times, inscribed with a quotation from Livy (xxii, 54, 10): 'No other nation could have suffered such tremendous disasters and not been destroyed'*

it was fought close to it; otherwise it would have borne the name of the river, in this instance the Aufidus, as was the case with so many other Carthaginian battlefields: Ticinus, Trebia, Metaurus. Polybius stated that the Roman army, facing south, had its right flank on the river, while Hannibal's army faced north. This suggests that the battle was fought on the left bank of the Aufidus, whatever its course then, and the description which follows is based on that supposition.

In front of Cannae, the Romans established two camps, one on each side of the Aufidus, that on the right bank near Canusium. Aemilius

213

Paullus's day of command passed with little activity except a skirmish, but on the morrow Varro soon got things going. The Roman army crossed to the north bank of the Aufidus and drew up in line, facing and parallel to it. Hannibal followed, crossed the river and drew up his army facing the Romans with his back to the river, his two wings resting on it, for his numbers were only about forty thousand men, whereas the Romans had twice that number, and this disposition prevented Hannibal's flanks from being turned. Hannibal's men had the sun and the south-east wind behind them, whereas the Romans had both, and the dust, in their faces. The Roman infantry was in the centre, the Roman cavalry on the right, under Aemilius Paullus, the allied cavalry on the left, under Varro. Hannibal posted the Gallic and Spanish cavalry on his left under Hasdrubal (not Hannibal's brother), and the Numidian cavalry on the right, under Maharbal. Of the Carthaginian infantry, the Gauls and the Spaniards were in the centre, with African troops on each side of them under the direct control of Hannibal and his brother Mago. One further change which Hannibal made in the disposition of his army was to advance his centre of Gauls and Spaniards, so as to form a wedge, projecting towards the Romans.

Before the battle, there was the usual oratory from the commander on each side, in which connexion Plutarch relates an anecdote about Hannibal. Riding in front of the army and looking at the Romans with their greatly superior numbers, Gisgo, one of the Carthaginian commanders, like Westmorland at Agincourt, regretted the disparity. Hannibal answered, 'There is one thing, Gisgo, that you have not noticed.' 'What is that, Sir?' 'In all that great number of men opposite, there is not a single one whose name is Gisgo.' They both immediately broke into roars of laughter, which acted as a tonic to the rank and file of the Carthaginian army.

The battle began with a head-on collision between the cavalry on Hannibal's left and the Roman right, Hasdrubal's eight thousand against Aemilius Paullus's two thousand, with the result that the Roman horsemen, many of whom dismounted as there was no room to fight, hemmed in between the river and the infantry, were crushed. Hasdrubal's squadrons were then able to ride round behind the Roman infantry and help the Numidians on Hannibal's right; they had been skirmishing with the Roman allied cavalry, which now fled.

Meanwhile, the Roman infantry centre had attacked the Gauls and Spaniards in Hannibal's projecting centre, and driven it in. This operation was controlled by Hannibal in person, and by design, as his centre withdrew the Romans were drawn on. Varro had made the tactical blunder of concentrating his infantry in the centre by diminishing the intervals and gaps between the units, with a view to striking a harder blow at the Carthaginian army. By so doing, he had deprived the legion of one of its most valuable tactical assets, its flexibility and manœuvrability. The further the Roman centre advanced, the more troops Varro poured into it. The result was that from having been a convex line, Hannibal's front became concave, then V-shaped, and finally U-shaped, the two wings where he had purposely placed his African veterans forming parallel lines facing each other, with the Romans sandwiched in between. The legionaries were packed so tightly together that they were unable to make proper use of their weapons, let alone manœuvre, since the Carthaginians held them as in the jaws of a vice, and bore in on them from both sides. Finally, Maharbal with his heavy cavalry, which had completed its task of driving the Roman cavalry from the field, charged the Roman infantry, the battle became a massacre and the Romans were butchered where they stood without chance of escape. Two double consular armies, eight legions strong, had been utterly destroyed.

The losses are difficult to estimate. Hannibal is said to have lost six thousand men, the Romans seventy thousand, including the unfortunate Consul Aemilius Paullus. Seeing him wounded and bleeding, Lentulus, a military tribune, offered him his horse on which to escape and spare Rome the additional calamity of a Consul's death. But Aemilius Paullus refused, and requested Lentulus to hasten to Rome, to urge the Senate to fortify the city, and to tell Fabius that he had never been unmindful of his advice. As for Varro, he fled from the field with the allied cavalry and made for Venusia. The garrisons of the two Roman camps near Cannae managed to assemble at Canusium, about fourteen thousand men, galvanized into further resistance by young Publius Cornelius Scipio. This represented all that was left of Roman armies in the field, for as if to fill the Romans' cup of bitterness to the brim, Lucius Postumius, in the north of Italy, fell into an ambush. As the Romans were marching through a wood, they were trapped by trees bordering the road, which the Boii had earlier half sawn through and now caused to fall. Postumius, Consul-elect, was killed and his legion destroyed.

Hannibal's army was busied for some time collecting spoils from the battlefield. It is said that Hannibal sent to Carthage three bushels of gold rings, taken from the fingers of fallen Roman knights. Aemilius Paullus's body was found and given ceremonial burial. The three thousand infantry and fifteen hundred cavalry prisoners were paraded before Hannibal, who sent the non-Romans to their homes and fixed a ransom tariff for the Romans: 500 denarii for a cavalryman, 300 for a foot-soldier, and 100 for a slave. He then sent ten of them on a delegation to Rome to report to the Senate and demand the ransom, but the Senate refused, saying that it had no use for such poor soldiers. The survivors from the battle were afterwards punished by being sent to serve in Sicily without pay; but when Varro arrived at the gates of Rome he was met by the dignitaries of the city who congratulated him on not having despaired of the republic.

In its dark hour, the determination of the Roman government was grim. Weeping and wailing were prohibited, wearing of mourning was restricted, silence was imposed, the spreading of rumours was forbidden, and nobody was allowed to leave the city. There remained the gods to be propitiated. Orders were given for the Sibylline Books to be consulted, and Quintus Fabius Pictor was sent to the Oracle at Delphi to discover what special prayers must be offered up and rites performed to placate the wrath of heaven. Recruiting was speeded up, debtors and criminals were released from prison, armed, and incorporated in the army. Eight thousand healthy slaves were bought from their owners at public expense and likewise pressed into service under arms, workshops were set up to make weapons, Marcus Junius Pera was appointed Dictator, with Tiberius Sempronius Gracchus as his Master of Horse, and the Praetor, Marcus Claudius Marcellus, who was a veteran of the Gallic War, was placed in command of the forces at Canusium.

The disaster which Roman arms had suffered at Cannae had one further result, of all the greater importance to Hannibal because it was political; for the first time a crack appeared in the hitherto solid front presented by the Roman Confederacy. A number of towns and peoples joined Hannibal: Arpi, Salapia, Herdonia, and Uzentum in Apulia, most of the towns in Lucania, all those in Bruttium (other than the Greek cities), the Picentes who had been transplanted to the region of Salernum, the Hirpini, most of the Samnites except the Pentri, and, soon, the city of Capua in Campania, most important of Rome's confederates.

Not one of these represented a Latin community. The Latin colonies of Venusia, Luceria, Canusium, Brundisium, Poseidonium (Paestum), Cosa, and Cales (Calvi), however dangerously exposed, all kept firm in the Roman allegiance, as did the Greek cities of Neapolis, Rhegium, Thurii, and Tarentum, not only because they were enemies of the

Air view of the site and harbour of Cosa (Ansedonia), one of the Roman colonies which remained unswervingly loyal to Rome after the disaster at Cannae when many towns sided with Hannibal

Lucanian and Bruttian tribes that had sided with Hannibal, but also because of the deep-rooted hatred of Greeks for Carthaginians. With these exceptions, practically all the south of Italy below a line running from the river Vulturnus to Mons Garganus on the Adriatic coast was in Hannibal's hands.

CAPUA

IT WAS not only allies in Italy that Hannibal needed, but a seaport and support in men, money, grain, and animals from Carthage. To Carthage he sent his brother Mago to report on the progress made, and to press immediately for assistance, to make good the losses which the Carthaginian army had suffered, to hold the ground gained, and to extend it by beating the Romans in the field and thereby persuading more states of the Roman Confederacy to defect.

But Hannibal had an enemy in the Senate of Carthage, of the name of Hanno (not his brother), the gist of whose arguments ran as follows: Hannibal says that he has destroyed whole Roman armies, but asks for reinforcements; what would he have asked for if he had been beaten? He claims to have captured two Roman camps full of supplies, but asks for money and grain; what would he have asked for if his own camp had been plundered? He has annihilated the Roman power at Cannae, but has any Roman or any Latin member of the Confederacy come over to Carthage? No. The war aims have not been advanced by one inch since it started and Hannibal set foot in Italy. Besides, in Spain, Hamilcar had made war self-supporting; why cannot Hannibal do the same in Italy?

In spite of all this cold water, Carthage did decide to send to Hannibal a small amount of aid: four thousand Numidians and forty elephants. It also intended to send him twenty thousand men from Spain, but these never came, because in Spain the two Roman generals, Publius Cornelius Scipio and his brother Cnaeus, defeated Hasdrubal Barca (Hannibal's brother) and one of the Hannos, and drove them south of the Ebro. A contributory factor which blinded Carthage to a true appreciation of where its strategic interests lay was the fact that Spain was Carthage's chief source of supply of silver. Solicitude for the treasury stood in the way of recognition that where Hannibal was, there was the best hope of victory. The military failure in Spain made Carthage all the more parsimonious in its support for Hannibal, and it was to Spain that most aid was sent. Yet a unique opportunity for reducing Rome and saving Carthage had been presented. Sardinia had revolted against Rome and might have been seized, together with Corsica, by resolute action; the Boii had revolted and might have inflamed all the Gauls in Italy, and induced Etruscans and Umbrians to desert Rome. A treaty had been made between Carthage and Philip V of Macedon, who hoped to recover Epirus and to land an army in Italy. The opportunity was missed.

A fifteenth-century representation of Hannibal in Capua. On the right he is shown dining with Pacuvius Calavius, a rich Capuan who had played a prominent part in diverting Capua from its allegiance to Rome and inviting Hannibal. In the left background, Pacuvius's son attempts to assassinate Hannibal to preserve the Roman alliance

From Cannae, Hannibal made his way into Samnium, took possession of Compsa which joined his side, and entered Campania, with the intention of attacking Neapolis and providing himself with his sorely needed seaport. But he desisted when he saw the strength of its walls, and instead marched towards Capua. In that opulent and corrupt city, there were two parties, one determined to remain loyal to the Roman alliance, the other keen to renounce it and join Hannibal. For the Capuans the situation was extremely awkward. A delegation of Capuans was sent to Varro, who was still at Venusia, and he impressed on them their duty to help Rome in her plight with all that they had, which was plenty of money, grain, and an army of thirty thousand foot-soldiers and four thousand cavalry, which could easily be raised in Campania. This was not the way to endear Rome to Capua, particularly when a Hannibal stood outside the walls of Capua with an army. Capua therefore expelled its Roman garrison, and made a treaty with Hannibal. No Carthaginian official was to have any authority over Campania, no Campanian was to serve in the Carthaginian army except as a volunteer, Capua's laws and magistrature were to remain inviolate, and Hannibal was to hand over three hundred Roman prisoners which Capua could exchange for a similar number of Capuans in the Roman army, who had been sent to serve in Sicily as hostages for Capua's loyalty. Hannibal was received in Capua and treated to a sumptuous banquet.

The defection from Rome of Capua was the most important result which Hannibal had yet achieved, and it was political. It immediately entailed the similar defection of two neighbouring Oscan towns, Calatia and Atella, the latter publicizing its new alliance by depicting an African elephant on its coins. It almost looked as if Hannibal's dream might come true.

Bronze uncia of Atella, a town which defected from Rome to Hannibal with Capua: obverse, head of Sol; reverse, an African elephant

Another town with a popular party in favour of Hannibal was Nola, east of Neapolis, and some of its citizens offered to open its gates to Hannibal; but it had a Roman garrison and Marcellus heard of the intention just in time to march into the city. Hannibal now actually made an attack on Neapolis, but when this failed, he proceeded to capture Nuceria Alfaterna (Nocera de' Pagani), and appeared before Nola. There he suffered his first check at the hands of Marcellus.

Imagining that he was having trouble with the popular party in the town, Hannibal ordered his army to approach the walls with a view to an assault, but a well-timed and well-led sortie by Marcellus forced him to retire.

Hannibal then turned his attention to Casilinum, the position of which with the only bridge over the lower Vulturnus was of importance to him. An attempted assault was unsuccessful, and Hannibal resorted to blockade; this resulted in the surrender of the town, but not before supplies in casks floating down the river were stopped. The garrison was ransomed at seven ounces of gold per man and allowed to march away to Cumae. Hannibal gave Casilinum to the Capuans but placed a Carthaginian garrison in it, after which he retired to winter quarters in Capua.

It has repeatedly been alleged that the soft luxuriance of life in Capua undermined the moral fibre of Hannibal and his army, and that this was the reason for his failure to win any more sensational victories. The old bogey of his avoidance of a march on Rome after Cannae is also raised in this connexion. Livy relates that, following that triumph, Maharbal asked to be allowed to make for Rome without delay, saying to Hannibal that in five days he would be having dinner on the Capitol. On being refused, Maharbal is said to have replied, with the bombast of a cavalry officer who has had a great success but knows little about sieges, 'Hannibal, you know how to win a battle, but not how to exploit it.'

The myth of a lost opportunity for a march on Rome has also been associated with an alleged sentimental weakness for women on the part of Hannibal, presumably based on a remark of Appian who said that Hannibal 'abandoned himself to unaccustomed luxury and the delights of love', to which, in any case, a Roman would have been more unaccustomed than a Carthaginian; and this gives further point to the direct contradiction by Justin, who recorded as a matter of surprise that Hannibal's behaviour towards women was of such perfect propriety as to make it difficult to believe that he had been born in Africa. Appian's remark was Roman propaganda.

The year 216 BC marked the zenith of Hannibal's success, both military and political, and thereafter his fortunes suffered a slow decline. For this there were many reasons. The first was that after two full terrible years of hard marching and even harder fighting, over thousands of miles, the old core of veterans from Africa and Spain in Hannibal's army was shrinking, from casualties and wastage, and it was not being made good. Instead, he filled his ranks with inferior military material, Gauls and Italians, which his genius welded into soldiers, but of nothing like the same calibre.

Next, while Hannibal was raining blows on the Romans, he was also teaching their generals by the hard way how to plan a campaign and to fight it. He himself had not been slow to learn the superiority of the Roman legion over his own infantry, and to copy it in training and equipment. In the same way, the Roman generals were his pupils in the art of war.

Then, while the Romans were defending their own country with ardent patriotism, Hannibal's men, most of them, had no country of their own to defend. They were not citizen soldiers like the Romans but mercenaries from Africa, Spain, the Balearic Islands, Gaul, Liguria, Italy, and Greece, owing allegiance only to Hannibal himself. It is an astonishing tribute to his powers of leadership that during the fifteen unbroken years that his army fought in Italy, far from their homes, they never murmured, let alone mutinied against him, or showed dissensions between themselves. On two occasions only, small units deserted.

Finally, Hannibal was sadly let down by Carthage, which grudged him what little support it sent. The wonder is that in spite of all these difficulties, he maintained the offensive for so long.

Ruins of the Acropolis at Cumae. From Cumae Greek culture diffused into Italy, and the Cumaean Sibyl (cf. page 277) sold the Sibylline Books to Tarquin the Proud

V Rome Recovers

BAFFLED HOPES

FOR TWELVE MORE WEARY YEARS, Hannibal was to continue moving about Italy, winning a number of successes in the field, but no triumphs such as he had previously won, suffering some checks but none to cause serious damage to his army. His star, and that of Carthage, was waning slowly all the time and time was not on his side. It is a matter of some difficulty to discern a pattern in the yearly succession of military operations and retirements into winter quarters. The twelve years, can, however, be divided into two periods: the first, of five years, devoted to Hannibal's attempt to defend Capua, and the second, of seven, when there was really no hope left for Carthage.

Of the Consuls Rome had appointed for 215 BC, Lucius Postumius had been killed fighting the Boii, and Marcus Claudius Marcellus was chosen to succeed him, but he declined owing to some omens which he considered to be unfavourable. The two Consuls were therefore old Quintus Fabius Maximus, the ex-Dictator, and Tiberius Sempronius Gracchus. Marcellus was Pro-Consul.

Rome now had to fight not only Hannibal but Capua as well; it is therefore not surprising that the main theatre of operations was Campania. Fabius commanded the two legions that had been stationed at Teanum and which were now at Cales (Calvi); Gracchus assembled his army at Sinuessa when he advanced to Liternum, to protect Cumae and Neapolis; Marcellus commanded his two legions behind Suessula, from which he could cover and protect Nola. There were therefore three Roman armies in Campania, while a fourth under Marcus Valerius was stationed in Apulia to protect Tarentum and Brundisium; for Hannibal still needed a seaport and might cast his eyes on them.

With this same aim in view, far away to the south in Bruttium, a Carthaginian army under Himilco had laid siege to the little Greek town of Petelia (Strongoli), which resisted for eight months, but it fell, and with it the other Greek colonies of Cosentia, Locri, and after a fierce resistance, Crotona. Hannibal at last had a seaport, and at Locri Bomilcar landed the long-awaited reinforcements from Carthage, Numidians and forty elephants. These were particularly welcome because Hannibal was now confronted by eight Roman legions, and although he had recruited men in Samnium and in Capua, the strength of his army was numerically much inferior to that of the Roman forces opposing him.

The other theatres of war almost conspired to prevent Hannibal from receiving further support or from benefiting from the dispersal of

Silver shekel minted at Carthagena, 218–209 BC. The obverse shows a head believed to represent Hasdrubal Barca, Hannibal's brother, and the reverse the prow of a warship

Roman forces. Mago, his brother, was ready to leave Carthage with a respectable force of twelve thousand foot, fifteen hundred horse, twenty elephants and a thousand talents of silver. But the Sardinians appealed to Carthage for help, and it could not resist allowing that irrelevant island to deflect it from its true strategic interests. At the same time, the Scipio brothers in Spain had pressed south from the Ebro to the Guadalquivir, and won two battles against Hasdrubal and the Carthaginians. The result was that Mago's force was sent to Spain, and some troops from Spain were sent to Sardinia, where they were promptly routed by Titus Manlius Torquatus with his two legions there. At sea, Titus Otacillus defeated a Carthaginian fleet, but did not prevent Bomilcar's reinforcements from reaching Locri. This was, however, more than offset by the fact that the Macedonian ambassadors, on their way home after making a treaty with Hannibal, were captured by a Roman vessel and taken to Rome, which let the cat out of the bag. The Romans promptly sent a fleet under Marcus Valerius Laevinus to Brundisium to oppose a landing by Philip V of Macedon. There remained Sicily. After the death of Hiero, who for so many years had been an ally of Rome, Syracuse had a new king, his young grandson Hieronymus, who now made a treaty with Carthage and provided Carthage with yet another direction in which to fritter away resources and deny them to Hannibal.

The policy of the Roman generals was now one of attrition, to surround Hannibal's army without fighting major engagements and to wear him down. He nevertheless maintained the initiative, from a camp which he had established on Mons Tifata, some few miles north of Capua. The Capuans made an attempt to capture Cumae, but Gracchus foiled it with great loss to them, and occupied Cumae himself. Hannibal then moved to blockade Cumae, but was obliged to retire without accomplishing anything. Meanwhile, Fabius, Gracchus and Marcellus concentrated their armies and retook a number of towns which had sided with Hannibal. Marcellus raided the lands of the Lucanians, Samnites, and Hirpini, who naturally appealed to Hannibal for help. In order to draw off Marcellus, Hannibal marched again to Nola and made a second attempt to capture it. Recourse to treachery failed, and after a subsequent battle was drawn, Hannibal returned to his camp on Mons Tifata.

In Lucania, Hannibal's lieutenant, Hanno son of Bomilcar, was soundly beaten by one of Marcellus's generals, the Legate Sempronius Longus, and driven back into Bruttium. Shortly afterwards there occurred one of the two known desertions from Hannibal's army, when twelve hundred Numidian and Spanish horsemen went over to the Romans.

Denied most of the plain of Campania by the Roman armies, and always solicitous for his supplies, Hannibal left Mons Tifata and made for Apulia where he wintered at Arpi; and so came to an end a dismal year during which the Romans began to recover lost ground. The curious thing was that although they had now had experience of how to prevent Hannibal from winning pitched battles, they never interfered with him when he was on the march, but only followed and tried to prevent him from ravaging too much territory. This was the pattern for the rest of the war in Italy.

Map of southern Italy and Sicily to illustrate Hannibal's later campaigns (215–204 BC) before he was driven back to the African mainland by Scipio

ALTHOUGH HIS ALLIANCE with Capua was the biggest political feather in Hannibal's cap, as it was the only major sign of success in his endeavour to disrupt the Roman Confederacy, militarily it was a millstone; for the Capuans were inefficient, quite unable by themselves to withstand the might of Rome which had a score to settle with them, and they consequently bombarded Hannibal with constant appeals for help, which, again for political reasons, he could not refuse. This naturally interfered with his exercise of initiative, tied him down, and obliged him to do something that he had never done before, namely, to resort for the most part to a defensive role.

In 214 BC the Consuls were Fabius and Marcellus, and the policy of Rome remained, as in the previous year, patience, pressure, and avoidance of risk, with the addition of preparations for besieging Capua. The strength of the army was raised to no less than twenty Roman legions, nearly a quarter of a million men including allies. Of these, two under Lucius Cornelius Lentulus were in Sicily, two under Quintus Mucius in Sardinia, two under Manius Pomponius in Cisalpine Gaul, in case Hasdrubal should come out of Spain and cross the Alps, one under Varro in Picenum as a reserve to those in Cisalpine Gaul, two under the Scipios in Spain, and two in garrison in Rome. This still left nine legions to contain Hannibal, two under Fabius at Cales, two under Marcellus at Suessula, two under Gracchus at Luceria, two under young Fabius (son of the Consul) near Venusia, and one at Brundisium for use also against Philip of Macedon if he should come. In addition, there were the garrisons of the various colonies and towns loyal to Rome.

The appeal for help from Capua brought Hannibal away from Arpi. He had received no help from Macedon, Spain, or Carthage except for the derisorily small reinforcements received in the previous year. At the same time, it was vitally important for him to encourage his Capuan and other allies. He passed round Gracchus's flank at Luceria, and, by way of Beneventum, Telesia, and Caiatia, returned to his old camp on Mons Tifata. None of the Roman armies dared to attack him. Once more in Campania, he saw that the Roman preparations for the siege of Capua were not advanced, and so, in order to make a diversion

Roman amphitheatre at Capua (Capua Vetere) showing the plain of Campania surrounded by hills across which Hannibal passed; the amphitheatre was built in the reign of Augustus

The commanding site of Luceria (Lucera), the 'key to Apulia', where a Latin colony was established in 314 BC. The castle is that of Frederick II Barbarossa

Beneventum, which became a Latin colony in 268 BC; situated on the Via Appia, it ▶ commanded the approaches to Apulia from Campania

and if possible to gain his much-wanted seaport, he marched on Puteoli (Pozzuoli) and encamped on Lake Arvernus. But Puteoli would have necessitated a regular siege, as would Cumae or Neapolis, and sieges were not in Hannibal's line. Instead, he had a third try at taking Nola, but again Marcellus had wind of his intention, hurried up from Suessula, and thwarted Hannibal once more.

Meanwhile, after Hannibal had left Apulia, Fabius had ordered Gracchus to advance from Luceria to Beneventum, and his son to take Gracchus's place at Luceria. These moves had important consequences, because Hannibal ordered Hanno to advance from Bruttium, where no Roman army opposed him, to Campania to join him. There were only two roads by which Hanno could come; one, by Nola, was barred by Marcellus; the other, by Beneventum, was now barred by Gracchus. Hanno marched by the Beneventum road and reached it at about the same time as Gracchus, but as the town had a Roman garrison, Gracchus entered it and Hanno could not get by without fighting a battle. His army consisted mostly of Bruttian and Lucanian levies, with a small force of African cavalry. Gracchus's legions were

largely composed of slaves who had been promised their freedom if in their first fight they comported themselves well and won, which they did; Hanno's army was almost completely destroyed, although he escaped. The Romans considered, however, that some of Gracchus's men had not fought as well as they should, and they were punished by being forbidden to sit down for their evening meal for the rest of the campaign. Rome was not soft.

This was the worst disaster which Carthaginian arms had yet suffered in Italy, and Hannibal made an effort to retrieve his fortunes in Campania, by making yet another attempt on Nola. But again Marcellus was there; and although the battle was drawn, Hannibal was balked of his objective. He had at least prevented the Romans from investing Capua and had enabled the Capuans to gather their harvest. Disappointed in his attempts to provide himself with a seaport in Campania, he left that province with an eye on Tarentum, but Valerius had just reinforced that city from Brundisium. Hannibal therefore marched northwards and took up winter quarters at Salapia, on the Adriatic. As soon as he had left Campania, Fabius and Marcellus felt free to undertake the blockade of Casilinum, the former from the north bank and the latter from the south bank of the Vulturnus. Its fall was foredoomed, and the garrison capitulated to Fabius, on the understanding that it would be allowed to retire to Capua. It was, however, obliged to march out on the south side of the town, and Marcellus, repudiating these terms, fell on the wretched column and killed or captured all but fifty men.

Hannibal's departure from Campania, and the consequent capture of Casilinum, were the results of Gracchus's victory over Hanno at Beneventum, which also had further effects; for Fabius was now free to enter Samnium and make contact with his son in Apulia and with Gracchus in Lucania; together they ravaged the territories of towns

Site of Heraclea Minoa, on Capo Bianco in Sicily; near here Himilco landed a Carthaginian army in 214 BC

which had sided with Hannibal, and recapture a number of them. Trebula, Saticula, Telesia, Compsa, Melae, Fulfulae, and Orbitanum in Samnium, Blanda in Lucania, and Aecae (Troja) in Apulia, were made to pay heavily for their defection.

The war had taken on a very different complexion, and fortune was turning strongly in favour of Rome. A further blow to Hannibal fell when Valerius sailed from Brundisium to Apollonia where Philip of Macedon had assembled an army, defeated it, and burnt the Macedonian fleet. This was the start of the First Macedonian War.

Meanwhile, events had come to a head in Sicily, that hoary bone of contention between Carthage and Rome which had been the cause or the pretext for the First Punic War, and to the loss of which Carthage could not become reconciled. In Syracuse, the young king Hieronymus had been murdered, and in the ensuing confusion, hostilities had broken out between Syracusans and Roman troops bordering on Syracusan territory. By devious methods, two of Hannibal's envoys, Hippocrates and Epicydes, saw to it that Syracuse lined up on his side. A Roman guard-post near Leontini (Lentini) was overrun by some Syracusan deserters, suitably incited by Hippocrates. Rome, as determined to retain possession of her province of Sicily as Carthage was to regain it, sent Marcellus to Sicily with two legions, and the war against Syracuse, which Marcellus besieged by land and sea, began.

In the centre of the island, several towns had gone over to Carthage, after slaughtering their Roman garrisons. In one town, Enna, it was the garrison that murdered the townspeople in order to avoid being massacred themselves. Then, Himilco landed from Carthage at Heraclea Minoa (on Capo Bianco) with an army of twenty-five thousand infantry, three thousand cavalry, and twelve elephants, all of which would have been worth their weight in gold to Hannibal in Italy. Himilco captured Agrigentum and marched towards Syracuse, hoping to intercept a Roman legion that had landed at Panormus, but was prevented by Marcellus; Himilco returned to Agrigentum while Marcellus continued to besiege Syracuse.

In Spain, fortune favoured the Scipios who pressed the Carthaginians hard, and might have captured their camp near Munda, had Cnaeus not been wounded in the thigh by a javelin; this unsettled the legionaries. Finally, the Romans took the town of Saguntum which had been the cause of the outbreak of war when Hannibal had captured it five years previously. All this affected Hannibal because Carthage felt obliged to support her armies in Spain, and Hasdrubal could not leave that country to bring him help.

TARENTUM WON

THE CONSULS for 213 BC were Tiberius Sempronius Gracchus and the younger Quintus Fabius Maximus, and the number of troops raised was increased to twenty-two legions. Of these, eight surrounded Hannibal in his winter quarters at Salapia: Fabius had two at Herdonia (Ordone), Aemilius Lepidus two at Luceria, Cnaeus Fulvius Flaccus two near Capua, and Gracchus two near Venusia to prevent Hannibal and Hanno, in Bruttium, from joining forces. Fabius began the campaign by capturing Arpi, where a thousand Spaniards deserted to Rome, but the Carthaginian troops fought with such gallantry that Fabius allowed them to rejoin Hannibal at Salapia.

Hannibal's position became increasingly difficult, and his only hope was for reinforcements. He marched southwards along the coast to the neighbourhood of Tarentum, where he spent the summer in comparative inactivity. In Bruttium, there were signs of some of the towns wishing to go over to Rome, and some did; but the cruelties inflicted by a Roman commander in devastating part of the country reversed this tendency. This brutality on the part of the Romans was to cause them further trouble.

In order to secure their hold on the Greek city of Tarentum and on Thurii, the Romans had taken hostages from among the population which was suspected of wanting to revolt. A few of these escaped, but were recaptured and executed with such cruelty that the Greeks became more resentful than ever. Philemenus of Tarentum, with a dozen confederates, left the town on the pretext of a hunting expedition. As intended, they were arrested by Hannibal's sentries and taken to him. On their explaining their position, Hannibal promised his support in obtaining independence for Tarentum, and gave them some cattle to round up and take back to the town, which provided verisimilitude for their story of having gone out for a raid. This technique was repeated many times, particularly at night, always resulting in a present of booty to the Roman Prefect and the Guard Commander. Eventually, the gate was opened for Philemenus merely on his whistle-call.

Hannibal knew that the time was ripe for him to act. He had pretended to be ill, to account for his protracted and abnormal inactivity. With ten thousand men and a handful of Numidian cavalry, he secretly approached Tarentum and encamped. The Numidians raided the countryside, which confirmed the Roman commander in his opinion that Hannibal was still inactive in camp and gathering supplies. At dead of night, Hannibal moved his men up to the walls of the city, and after exchanging a pre-arranged signal with Philemenus and his friends, he approached a gate. The confederates slew the Roman sentries and opened the gate, and Hannibal passed some of his infantry into the city. Meanwhile Philemenus came up from outside to the gate which he normally used, whistled, and said that the boar they had caught was too heavy for them to carry. The sentries came out to help and were promptly dispatched, and the Carthaginians poured in. In the city, in the dark, the Carthaginians fell on the Romans who had no notion of what had happened; but at dawn they realized, and made for the citadel. Hannibal assembled the townspeople and told them all to go home and write their names on their doors. The Carthaginians then plundered all the houses without names.

Reverse of a coin of Tarentum showing Taras riding on a dolphin, and holding a bow and arrow; beneath is an Indian elephant commemorating Pyrrhus

An eighteenth-century engraving of a map of Tarentum, showing the entrance to the Inner Harbour (Mar Pesco) commanded by the citadel

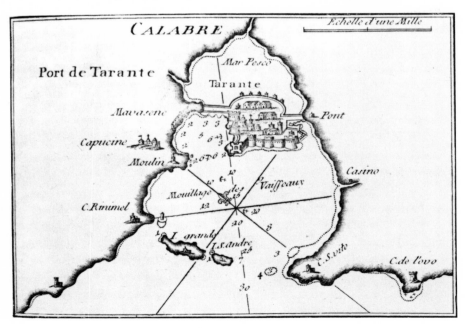

The citadel, Hannibal saw, was almost impregnable, so he built an earthwork to prevent the Romans from issuing in a sortie to attack the Tarentines; but this was just what the Romans did, and they succeeded in destroying the fortifications. Hannibal then realized that a blockade was the only way to reduce the garrison, but this was all the more difficult because the citadel, on a promontory commanding the entrance to the inner harbour, where the Tarentine ships were, not only immobilized these ships, but could receive supplies by sea. Carthaginian ships were not to be counted on to stop this, and the Tarentine ships were all bottled up in the inner harbour. Hannibal solved this problem by getting the Tarentines to draw their ships out of the inner harbour on land, drag them through the streets of Tarentum on wheels with mules and men, the streets having been freshly paved to make it easier to get the loaded waggons along, and launch the ships in the outer harbour, where they were able to blockade the entrance and the citadel with its garrison of Romans.

After this exploit, Hannibal, whose unmistakable signature it bore, got possession of two more Greek towns. Metapontum went over to him as soon as the Romans had removed their garrison there to reinforce the citadel of Tarentum, and Thurii presented another version of how to take a town by treachery. The Romans in these Greek colonies which had either allied themselves to, or been taken by Rome, armed and equipped the inhabitants who, the Romans hoped, would remain loyal to them because the hatred between Greeks and Carthaginians had been so great. Outside Thurii was a Carthaginian army in Bruttium under Hanno and Mago, with whom the Thurians made an arrangement that if that army were brought close to the town, they would double-cross the Romans. The Carthaginians came and offered battle which the Romans accepted, the Carthaginians retiring to draw the Romans away from the walls. When the Carthaginians counter-attacked, the Thurians, who had been resting on their arms, fled back into the town, and shut the gates behind them on the pretext that if they did not do so the Carthaginians would get in. Thus the defeated Romans were left outside, not the Carthaginians.

Events in Spain introduced two picturesque figures who were destined to play important parts later on in the story. As a result of the recent successes of the Roman armies in Spain, Syphax, a Numidian king, whose capital was Siga (at the mouth of the river Tafna, west of Oran in Algeria), was persuaded by the Scipios that it was to his advantage to join the Roman cause. This not only weakened Carthage in Spain, where she relied so much on Numidians who now deserted the Carthaginian ranks and went over to the Romans, but also in Africa because of Syphax's influence there. Syphax admitted to the Romans that his forces were trained only as cavalry and that his foot-soldiers lacked both training and equipment, which the Romans promised to provide.

On learning of this action on the part of Syphax, Carthage hastened to approach Gaia, king of the Maesulian part of Numidia and father of Masinissa, a young prince of great ability, on the Carthaginian side. Gaia's capital was Cirta (Constantine) in eastern Algeria. The Carthaginian envoys had no difficulty in persuading Gaia that Syphax had joined the Romans only to increase his own influence in Numidia, which would be at the expense of Gaia. Hasdrubal Barca with his army was recalled from Spain, and, together with Gaia's army under Masinissa, they inflicted a crushing defeat on Syphax, who is said to have lost thirty thousand men killed. Syphax escaped to the Marusian Numidians in Morocco, where he recruited another army with which to cross the strait to Spain. But Masinissa defeated him again, and Hasdrubal was able to return to Spain with his army. Nevertheless, the Scipios were able to score an important point by alienating Syphax from Carthage, and also by capturing the fortress of Tarraco, Tarragona, future capital of Roman Spain.

SYRACUSE LOST

THE MOST IMPORTANT EVENT of the year 212 BC was the siege of Syracuse and the tragedy that it involved. The late king Hiero had sent one of his townsmen, Archimedes, to Alexandria, where Euclid was teaching, and Archimedes acquired a knowledge of Greek science and mathematics such as to be an honour to the world. This knowledge he brought back to Syracuse and developed by his own discoveries to a state of proficiency which enabled the Syracusans to thwart the success of Marcellus and his besieging forces for many months. Archimedes's mechanics and ballistics enabled the Syracusan catapults to throw heavier stones for longer distances with greater accuracy; he increased the fire-power of darts and other missiles so enabling the Syracusans to foil the Romans' attempts to approach the city walls with pent-houses and towers, to mine underneath them or batter them down from above. By means of compound pulleys which he invented, and grapnels suspended from beams balanced with counter-weights

237

on the sea-walls, Roman ships which came close were hooked and up-ended from stem or stern, and then let down suddenly back into the sea, where they sank or capsized. He is credited with having devised a system of concave mirrors or 'burning-glasses' which he is said to have trained on Roman ships so as to concentrate the sun's rays on them and set them on fire.

Taking advantage of a feast in honour of Artemis when the Syracusans were dead drunk, Marcellus scaled the walls of part of the town and eventually captured the Euryalus fortress which protected it on the land side. He was then attacked by the Carthaginian army under Himilco and the Sicilians under Hippocrates, while the Syracusans made a sortie from the main part of the city, the Achradina, and the Carthaginian fleet, anchored off the city, threatened to impede the movements of Roman reinforcements. Marcellus repelled all these attacks, but a plague then broke out, which affected both armies. The Carthaginians were the worse hit, and Himilco and Hippocrates fell victims to it and died, and their armies dispersed. The Roman army, under cover in the part of Syracuse which it had captured, suffered less severely. After an act of treachery by a Spanish officer in the garrison called Moericus, Marcellus stormed the remainder of the city, and gave it over to his troops to pillage, but not without strict orders to spare Archimedes. But when a Roman soldier shouted at him as he was working out a theorem with his finger in the dust, he paid no attention and was killed.

A century and a half later, Archimedes's tomb was found by none other than Cicero when he was Quaestor in Sicily. It was near one of the gates of Syracuse, neglected, overgrown and forgotten, surmounted by a column with a representation of a sphere inscribed in a cylinder, recalling Archimedes's discovery of the mathematical relation between these geometrical forms.

While allowing his army to plunder Syracuse, Marcellus had taken care to safeguard the royal treasure, and this he sent to Rome, with statues and paintings which abounded in the city. According to Livy, this act of despoliation was the first introduction of Greek art to the Romans, and the origin of their admiration for Hellenic culture.

The siege of Syracuse, showing Archimedes's invention to destroy Roman warships by means of balanced beams with counter-weights from which grapnels were hung to hook the ships and capsize them; from an eighteenth-century engraving

The Euryalus Fortress, Syracuse, built by Dionysius I between 402 and 397 BC, captured by Marcellus in 212 BC. Standing on high ground, it was the key to the city's land defences

Most of the towns in Sicily tried to make their peace with Marcellus, but there were still Carthaginian forces in the island, near Agrigentum, under Hanno and Epicydes. These were joined by an African emissary of Hannibal's, Muttines, who commanded some Numidian cavalry, with which he raced about Sicily and had some success in maintaining the loyalty of some towns to Carthage. Emboldened by his exploits, Hanno and Epicydes left their fortress of Agrigentum and advanced to the river Himera, where Muttines had already had a successful engagement with Roman outposts. But when Marcellus arrived and gave battle, the Carthaginians became a rabble fleeing back to Agrigentum, and all resistance to the Romans ceased. From Hannibal's point of view, the campaign in Sicily had been more than useless, for not only had it accomplished nothing, but if the Carthaginian troops so recklessly squandered there had been entrusted to him instead, he would certainly have put them to better use.

As it was, Hannibal was confronted by the two Consuls, Quintus Fulvius Flaccus and Appius Claudius covering the north of Apulia. Gracchus meanwhile watched Lucania, and Caius Claudius Nero at Suessula barred the approach to Capua from the south. The Romans had now begun the siege of Capua, and soon there came the usual appeals to Hannibal for help, particularly as the Romans controlled the plain of Campania and the Capuans were unable to sow their crops or bring in their harvest.

Hannibal was unwilling to leave the neighbourhood of Tarentum, so he ordered Hanno to advance from Bruttium towards Beneventum for the purpose of supplying Capua with food. Hanno skilfully evaded the armies of Gracchus on his front and Nero on his flank, and set up a fortified camp where he collected a store of grain and told the Capuans to come and fetch it with all the wheeled traffic on which they could lay hands. Lax, indolent, and feeble of purpose, the Capuans sent only four hundred waggons, to Hanno's disgust as he had undertaken a dangerous operation to get near them. He sent the Capuans back for more transport and they returned with two thousand waggons; but by this time the Romans had discovered what was going on. Fulvius Flaccus marched up while Hanno was out of camp foraging, and in the ensuing battle the Carthaginians in camp were overwhelmed and the Capuans and their waggons were captured. Hanno with his foraging party got safely back to Bruttium but the city of Capua received no supplies.

To remedy this situation, Hannibal had to take action himself. Though four Roman armies were posted between Tarentum and Capua, covering the roads by which he might march into Campania, he managed to send two thousand Numidian horsemen who evaded the Roman cordons and entered Capua. In a sortie they scored a success over the Romans and killed fifteen hundred of them. Then, unexpectedly, fortune turned still further in favour of the Carthaginians. Flavus, a Lucanian hitherto loyal to Rome, approached Gracchus and invited him to meet other Lucanian magistrates who, he said, were anxious to cut loose from Carthage now that Hannibal's star was on the wane, and revert to their alliance with Rome. Gracchus fell into the trap and accompanied Flavus with only a squadron of cavalry. On the way, Flavus's men fell on the Romans, and Gracchus was killed. His body was given ceremonial burial by Hannibal.

Hannibal then astounded his enemies by appearing with his army at his old camp on Mons Tifata. Next, he entered Capua itself in spite of the fact that two consular armies were besieging it. A battle took place outside the city, and Hannibal's cavalry was beginning to turn the struggle in his favour, when an unidentified body of cavalry appeared on the flank of the two armies, which caused alarm on both sides. Hannibal withdrew into Capua.

So long as Hannibal was in or near Capua, the Roman commanders feared that he would play on them some trick in the open country of Campania, to their great disadvantage. They therefore resorted to a Hannibalic ruse to lure him away. Fulvius Flaccus marched his army towards Cumae, and Appius towards Lucania, from which he could threaten Hannibal's hard-won gains along the south coast of Italy. Hannibal therefore followed Appius, but that general gave him the slip and returned to Capua, as did his colleague Fulvius Flaccus, and the siege was resumed.

Hannibal decided to return to Tarentum, as he could do nothing more for Capua. On his way, he found Marcus Sentenius Penula with his army drawn up to obstruct his passage. That general, having put himself at the head of his troops, was soon killed by the Carthaginians, and the Roman army, now thrown into dismay by the death of its commander, and completely surrounded by Hannibal's cavalry, was all but annihilated.

Instead of making straight for Tarentum, Hannibal turned to the north-east, to Herdonia which the Praetor Cnaeus Fulvius was besieging. In the ensuing battle, Hannibal sent Mago with the Numidian cavalry to occupy the roads in Fulvius's rear, and also prepared an ambush on his right flank. The result was a massacre of Romans, and Fulvius fled; scarcely two thousand of his army escaped.

La Torra de los Esciones, the reputed tomb of Publius Cornelius Scipio the Elder and of his brother Cnaeus, near Tarragona, Spain. Both were killed at the head of their armies by the Carthaginians in 212 BC; from a nineteenth-century engraving

Fulvius was accused of cowardice, and exiled himself to Tarquinia; the survivors of his men were punished by being forbidden to take up winter quarters within a distance of ten miles from any town.

Two Roman armies had been destroyed, and two Roman generals killed; Hannibal had shown that he was still a force to be reckoned with. He had strengthened his hold on southern Italy, with its seaports which he must keep to receive reinforcements; but his main problem was no nearer solution, Roman political power over the Confederacy was still unshaken, and the outlook for Capua very precarious. He made a further but unsuccessful attempt to assault the citadel in

242

Tarentum which the Romans had succeeded in reinforcing, and he also made an attempt to capture Brundisium; but he had no friendly party in that city, which had been a Latin colony since 244 BC, and he failed.

While the Romans had triumphed in Sicily, and were gradually recovering their position in Italy, in Spain they met with disaster. Publius Cornelius Scipio (the Elder) faced Carthaginian armies commanded by Hasdrubal son of Gisgo, Mago, and Masinissa; the Roman army was all but destroyed, and Publius was killed. His brother Cnaeus, whose army was separated from that of Publius, confronted Hasdrubal Barca who had bribed the Celtiberians highly to defect from the Roman side. In a battle near Amtorgis, the Romans were defeated and Cnaeus too was killed. The year 212 BC was a black one for the house of Scipio. The Carthaginians returned north to the line of the Ebro; but in their carelessness after the destruction of the Scipios' armies, they were held in check by the brilliant exploits of a young Roman commander, Lucius Marcius, who assembled a scratch-force, and inflicted heavy losses on the Carthaginians.

CAPUA LOST

CAPUA WAS NOW BESIEGED by three armies of two legions each, commanded by Appius Claudius, Quintus Fulvius Flaccus, and Caius Claudius Nero. The Consuls for the year 211 BC, Publicius Sulpicius Galba and Cnaeus Fulvius Centumalus, were themselves to confront Hannibal and keep him where he was, on the south coast. The disaster of the previous year in Spain made it all the more necessary to station an army in Cisalpine Gaul, under Publius Sempronius, in case reinforcements should try to reach Hannibal over the Alps, and for the same purpose another army under Marcus Junius was stationed in Etruria. Counting the armies in Italy, Spain, Sicily, Sardinia, and the fleets under Otacilius and Valerius, Rome had mobilized twenty-three legions.

The Capuans made sorties with the Numidian cavalry which Hannibal had sent them, and the Romans experienced so much trouble from them that they instituted a new type of tactical formation, by mounting their light infantry behind their cavalrymen on their horses, and by this means the Capuans were contained. The city of Capua was now surrounded by Roman fortifications, as strong as they knew how to

Air view of Capua (Capua Vetere). The Roman amphitheatre (cf. page 229) is on the right, and in the centre the rectangular town-planning system of the original Etruscan city of Vulturnum (see page 44), continued by the Romans, can be discerned

build them, but no attempt was made at assault; the siege was a blockade and the city was to be reduced by hunger.

The inevitable appeals for succour were sent to Hannibal, who this time left Tarentum with thirty thousand of his best troops, and thirty-three elephants which had been brought by Hanno. Hannibal, after marching past Venusia and Beneventum, seized the town of Caiatia, and reappeared behind his old camp on Mons Tifata. A plan was concerted with the Capuans, by which they were to make a sortie at the same time as Hannibal attacked the Roman entrenchments from the north. The fight was furious. Hannibal's Spanish infantry broke through the Roman lines, and if they had been more numerous they would have pierced the defences, but they were cut off, surrounded, and killed. The Capuans in their sortie were repulsed; Hannibal withdrew and the combined operation failed.

Alba Fucens, a Latin colony founded in 303 BC on the Via Valeria, past which Hannibal marched to Rome in 211 BC in an attempt to lure the Romans away from Capua. View looking across the forum to the base of the basilica, with Monte Velino in the background

Seeing that he had neither the quantity nor quality of troops required to shake the Roman hold on Capua and lift the siege, Hannibal had recourse to one last stratagem which, in its way, was the counterpart of the one the Romans had used against him the year before. He attempted to lure them away by marching off himself and placing his army nearer to Rome than they were. In a similar way, two thousand years later, Napoleon attempted to draw the Allies away from Paris by marching towards Germany.

There now ensued Hannibal's march on Rome, undertaken not to assault the city, but to induce the legions to move away from Capua by the fear that he might assault Rome. In order to leave the Roman commanders in uncertainty about his movements, he took a circuitous route. Marching through Samnium to Sulmo, and then through regions hostile to Rome, Hannibal passed by Alba Fucens where his

Rough stone carving of an elephant from Alba Fucens; the elephant, obviously African from the size of its ears, reflects Hannibal's march past the town in 211 BC

Reverse of a coin from Capua showing an Indian elephant, which reflects Pyrrhus's passage; the inscription, however, is in Oscan which suggests that it was struck during the defection of Capua from Rome, 216–211 BC

passage is reflected in two roughly-carved stone elephants, unmistakably African from the large size of their ears. Passing on through Amiternum, Reate, and Eretum, the Numidians ravaging as they went, he debouched on the right bank of the river Anio, in full view of Rome and encamped only six miles from the city. There, the cry went up, *Hannibal ad portas,* and for a time panic reigned, for some Numidian cavalry in Roman service in the garrison were mistaken for Hannibal's, and the rumour went round that he had already entered the city. But the inhabitants were quickly galvanized into fresh energy and sterner resistance.

Publius Cornelius Asina was for abandoning the siege of Capua, but Fabius Maximus saw through Hannibal's manœuvre, and instead of summoning every Roman soldier back for the defence of the city, the matter was left to the Pro-Consuls to decide. Leaving fifty thousand men for the siege of Capua, Quintus Fulvius, his colleague Appius Claudius being wounded, marched to Rome with fifteen thousand men, where the garrison was already forty thousand strong.

The land on which Hannibal's camp was situated happened to be up for sale at the time, but in spite of Hannibal's occupation of it, it was sold without any reduction in price, such was public confidence in the future.

Hannibal marched up the right bank of the Anio, crossed it higher up on its course, came down the left bank and encamped nearer to the city, which he reconnoitred in person, up to the Porta Collina. Next day, the Roman army was drawn up in battle array, facing his; but a downpour of rain and hail of such violence came on that both armies went back to their camps. The same thing happened on the following day, and this was regarded as of such bad omen that Hannibal decided not to give or accept battle. Besides, he had learnt that the Romans had not abandoned the siege of Capua. His stratagem to lure the Romans away from it had failed, and Capua's fall could only be a short question of time, and there was nothing more that he could do for the luckless city. His grand design to disrupt the Roman Confederacy was shattered, and the important thing for him to do was to safeguard his own position on the south coast of Italy.

Hannibal left Rome and went back by the Valerian Way, the Romans harassing his rearguard. Near Tibur (Tivoli) they captured part of his baggage and booty, but he returned on his tracks, made a night attack on the Roman camp, and inflicted such a beating on them that they retreated hastily. He went on through the territory of the Peligni, and turning south through Samnium, by Aesernia, Bovianum, and Herdonia, he reached Apulia and continued his march to Tarentum. The inhabitants of Capua on learning what had happened gave way to anger and despair. The Consuls promulgated a decree of the Roman Senate to the effect that any citizen of Capua who surrendered to Rome would have his life spared and suffer no harm. The Capuans dared not trust this promise, and many killed themselves with poison or their swords. The commanders found themselves obliged from hunger to make an unconditional surrender, and the Romans, having marched in and occupied the city, wreaked terrible vengeance on the luckless inhabitants who had been responsible for the secession from Rome.

247

Masters of Campania, the Romans could now progress at will into Apulia and Lucania. It was no longer possible for Hannibal to keep garrisons in the numerous little towns which he had previously occupied, not only for political reasons but for supply of forage. His space for manœuvre was practically reduced to the south coast of Italy and Bruttium, yet he continued to hope that if only he could receive adequate reinforcements from Carthage or from his brothers in Spain, he might yet wear down Roman resistance. He was to remain in Italy for seven more years, his armies growing weaker all the time; but he never gave up, and he still had some hard shots in his locker.

Agrigentum in Sicily, seen from the east, showing the plateau on which the Greek temples stand. This was the last Carthaginian stronghold in the island to fall to Rome

CARTHAGENA LOST

THE PRICE of carrying on the long war was making itself felt in Rome, where discontent was general at the unceasing increase in taxation. Furthermore, there was inequality in its imposition. Valerius Laevinus protested against this state of affairs in the Senate and urged that the senators should set an example of their patriotism and confidence in the future of the State by handing over to the treasury all the jewels, gold, and silver that they possessed, keeping only what was in use by their wives and daughters, and on their tables. The measure was adopted, and the Forum was soon filled with citizens and their slaves, heavily burdened with riches which they deposited in the State coffers. The example was widely followed, and the sinews of war were provided, but this was not the last sacrifice to be called for.

The Consuls for 210 BC were Marcellus, who had returned from Sicily to Italy, and Marcus Valerius Laevinus who had had success against Philip of Macedon in Greece. Before he left that country, he had concluded an alliance with the Aetolian League of Greek States, and with the State of Pergamum, against Philip, who thus had enough to do without thinking of mounting an expedition to invade Italy and help Hannibal.

The Roman plan was to continue to recapture as many towns which had gone over to Hannibal as possible, so as to restrict his freedom of movement still further, and to reduce the areas from which he could derive supplies and forage. For this purpose, Marcellus commanded two legions in Samnium, the Pro-Consul Cnaeus Fulvius Centumalus two in Apulia, and Quintus Fulvius two at Capua.

In Apulia, the town of Salapia, where Hannibal had wintered four years before, reverted to the Roman allegiance, and Marcellus captured the towns of Narronea and Meles in Samnium. Fulvius Centumalus was encamped before Herdonia, and in communication with persons inside the town with a view to its reversion to Rome. Hannibal learnt of this while in Bruttium. With thirty thousand foot-soldiers and six thousand horse, he advanced so swiftly that he arrived at Herdonia before the Romans knew that he had moved. In the battle that followed, Hannibal followed his usual practice of sending part of his cavalry against the Romans' camp and another part to attack their infantry in the rear, while his infantry held the legionaries in front. The result was a Roman disaster: Fulvius Centumalus was killed, while barely three thousand of his army escaped to join Marcellus in Samnium. It was no wonder that the Romans continued to take all precautions when confronted by their old foe, weakened though he had been.

The inhabitants of Herdonia were no longer to be trusted, so Hannibal burned the town to the ground, executed those inhabitants who had tried to treat with Fulvius, and sent the remainder to Metapontum and Thurii. He then returned to Lucania and encamped near Numistro, in the hope of luring Marcellus towards him and bringing him to battle. Marcellus came, and a battle was fought which failed to bring any decisive result. After much marching and counter-marching, Hannibal returned to Tarentum without succeeding in catching Marcellus off balance, while Marcellus went into winter quarters at Venusia.

Ruins of Herdonia (Ordone), a town which had joined Hannibal; close by in 210 BC Hannibal destroyed a Roman army, and afterwards burnt the town to the ground

The storming and capture of Carthagena by Publius Cornelius Scipio the Younger in 209 BC, by J. van der Straet. Roman soldiers are shown scaling the fortifications, while others prepare an assault tower

In Spain, the disaster of the previous year, when the two elder Scipios were killed, had led Rome to send Caius Claudius Nero there, to prevent Hasdrubal from leaving Spain for Italy. Nero succeeded in confining Hasdrubal to the mountains between Iliturgi and Nentissa, but in the negotiations which followed, Hasdrubal completely outwitted Nero and escaped with his army. Rome then replaced Nero by young Publius Cornelius Scipio. He was the boy who had rescued his father the Consul at the first battle against Hannibal in Italy, on the river Ticinus. He was still only twenty-four years old and had never yet held high rank. His appointment to the command in Spain showed that Rome continued to find it necessary to take untried measures.

Young Scipio soon showed his mettle by the decision which he took, worthy of an opponent of Hannibal, to capture nothing less than the city of Carthagena, Hannibal's original base in Spain, the finest Spanish harbour on the Mediterranean, the centre of Carthaginian power, of wealth, and of stores in the Iberian peninsula. With twenty-five thousand foot-soldiers and two thousand five hundred horsemen, he practically denuded the north of Spain of Roman troops, crossed the Ebro, and marched south along the coast, nobody knowing anything of his destination except his naval commander Caius Laelius, whom he ordered to approach Carthagena but not to enter the harbour.

The Romans arrived in front of Carthagena and took up a position north of the town. Hasdrubal Barca with his army was near the source of the Tagus, Hasdrubal Gisgo near its mouth, and Mago was at Gades; all of them many days' march from Carthagena. The Carthaginian garrison was commanded by another Mago.

The vast defences and high walls of the city were manned; Scipio ordered an assault with ladders, but he learnt from fishermen that at low tide it was possible to enter the city easily from the lagoon. While the Roman fleet made a feint attack from another direction, Scipio led a party of five hundred men at low tide, with a north wind blowing which reduced the level of the water still further. Nevertheless, the men had to wade waist-deep until they reached the low wall which they found undefended. They entered the city and forced the gates from inside. The Carthaginian garrison surrendered, the butchery started, and plundering began. The stores captured were immense: gold, silver, grain, arms, catapults, timber and rope. The booty included eighteen ships which were added to the Roman fleet, and sixty-three merchant ships.

This was the occasion of the famous episode of the beautiful captive. Hostages and prisoners were being paraded, when a young girl of such surpassing beauty was brought forward that she attracted everybody's attention. Scipio asked her where she came from, and learnt that she was betrothed to a young Celtiberian chief. He and the girl's parents were sent for, and Scipio addressed them. He said that he took pride in the care with which the young man's bride had been treated by his troops, which was characteristic of the Roman people, and he gave her to him freely, only asking in return that he should become and remain a friend of Rome. The girl's parents had brought with them a sum of gold for her ransom, and when they learnt that no ransom was demanded, they begged Scipio to accept it as a gift. He agreed to accept it, and immediately told the young man to take the gold as a wedding present from him. This exercise in psychological warfare on the part of Scipio was very profitable, for a few days later the young chief returned to Scipio with a force of cavalry, fourteen hundred strong, to support his army.

After training and parading the troops, and sending the prisoners off to Rome with Laelius to report the victory, Scipio left a garrison in Carthagena and marched north with his army to Tarraco.

In Sicily, the whole of the island was in Roman hands, now that the Carthaginian resistance in Agrigentum had been stamped out. This made possible a development which was to show the shape of things to come. A Roman fleet of fifty ships under Valerius Messalla set sail from Lilybaeum to raid the Carthaginian coast of Africa and to obtain information about the enemy's intentions. A landing was made near Utica, a large tract of country was raided, and many prisoners were taken before the Romans got safely back to their ships and set sail for Sicily. What the prisoners had to say was of supreme importance,

Coin showing (obverse) Masinissa, king of Maesulian Numidia (Algeria), and (reverse) a Numidian horse. First a valuable ally of Carthage because of his Numidian cavalry, Masinissa changed sides, joined the Romans and played an important part in the victory of Zama

particularly as it confirmed what was said by those sent to Rome from Spain by Scipio. An army of five thousand Numidians under Masinissa was at Carthage, and other mercenaries were being recruited, to send to Hasdrubal Barca in Spain as soon as possible, so

254

that he should command a numerous army with which to cross the Alps and join Hannibal in Italy. Furthermore, a large fleet of ships was being built for the reconquest of Sicily. That Carthage was still able to mount expeditions was shown by the raids which the Carthaginian fleet had carried out at Olbia and Caralis in Sardinia.

The Senate at Rome was profoundly disturbed by this intelligence and determined to resort to the expedient of appointing a Dictator. The rules of the constitution however caused difficulties, for a Dictator could only be appointed by a Consul, and Valerius Laevinus who was in Rome wanted to appoint Valerius Messalla who was in Sicily. The Senate insisted that a Dictator could not be appointed outside Roman territory. Valerius Laevinus, unwilling to carry out the Senate's wishes, slipped away to Sicily, and the Senate was obliged to send for the other Consul, Marcellus, to come to Rome and carry out the prescribed duties. He came and nominated Quintus Fulvius Flaccus as Dictator, until the elections were held.

'The Continence of Scipio', by François Lemoyne (1688–1737). Scipio had captured Carthagena, and hostages and prisoners were being paraded, including a strikingly beautiful girl, whom he returned to her betrothed Celtiberian chieftain together with the gold which her parents had brought for her ransom

IN 209 BC there occurred an event which showed in unmistakable terms how hard Hannibal had hit the Roman Confederacy, and what a tragedy it was for him that he had not been supported and reinforced in time to save Capua from recapture by the Romans. So long as Hannibal held the initiative, the Romans were obliged to spread their forces all over Italy, Sicily, Sardinia, and Spain; but Carthage might have concentrated hers under Hannibal, had her rulers had any strategic insight at all. What happened was that twelve of the old members of the Roman Confederacy, Latin communities, informed Rome that they were unable to continue contributing men, money, and supplies. They were Ardea, Nepete, Sutrium, Alba, Carseoli, Sora, Suessa, Circeii, Setia, Cales, Narnia, and Interamna. Inflation had raised the price of grain to three times what it had been before the war began; if supplies had not been obtained from Egypt, and if Sicily had not again become a granary for Rome, there would have been famine. The complaining communities said that they had been bled white, and they had probably also suffered from the attentions of Hannibal's Numidian horsemen. It was not a rebellion, but it was an act of disunion, and if Capua had still been on Hannibal's side, this tendency might have spread. It showed that some of Rome's allies were more than weary of the war.

There was also a social aspect of the case. The legions which Rome had sent to Sicily were largely composed of Latin citizens, and these colonies and communities protested that service in the legions was more like exile, which, for many of their men, had lasted for nine years; whereas a prisoner of war captured by the Carthaginians was often repatriated without any ransom being demanded. If the experienced soldiers were not allowed to come home, and young men were continuously recruited, there would very soon be no men left behind to work the farms.

Rome made inquiries about the feelings of other members of the Confederacy, and was relieved to find that they were staunch in her support. There were eighteen of them: Signia, Norba, Saticula, Fregellae, Luceria, Venusia, Brundisium, Hadria, Firmum, Ariminum, Pontiae, Paestum, Cosa, Beneventum, Aesernia, Spoletium, Placentia, and Cremona. It is noticeable that these included many that were under danger from Hannibal. The twelve defaulting communities were left alone for the time being; but money had to be found, and it was found by dipping into secret funds in the temples.

The Consuls for 209 BC were old Fabius Maximus and Quintus Fulvius Flaccus. Their task was to confront Hannibal and to recapture the city of Tarentum, in which the Roman garrison in the citadel was still holding out. The importance of wresting the harbour of Tarentum from Hannibal was all the greater since it was now known that Carthage intended to reinforce him, and if this was to be by sea, the harbour of Tarentum would be of great value to him. It also served him for his communications with Philip of Macedon. It was vital for Rome to recapture Tarentum.

Quintus Fabius Maximus, nicknamed Cunctator, 'the Delayer'; from a seventeenth-century engraving

To assist Fabius in his operations, two other Roman armies were in the field. One under Fulvius Flaccus was to reduce more towns in Samnium and Lucania which still adhered to Hannibal but were wavering in their loyalty to him; the other, under Marcellus, near Venusia, had the task of making diversions so as to draw Hannibal if possible towards northern Apulia, and distract his attention from what was about to happen. Meanwhile, Roman forces from Sicily were to besiege Caulon and deprive Hannibal of another harbour.
From the fact that Hannibal had recently shown reticence in accepting battle when it was offered to him, the Roman commanders were led to believe that his own powers, and the fighting capacity of his army,

had begun to sink. Accordingly, Marcellus advanced towards him from Venusia and approached Canusium. Hannibal gave ground, crossed the river Aufidus of Cannae fame, and made for the plain at Ausculum, between Aquilonia and Herdonia, where a hard-fought battle took place. After desperate fighting, Marcellus managed to disengage his army, and renewed the attack on the next day. The elephants, thrown into action by the Carthaginians, began to make havoc in the Roman lines, until they were turned back, when they did equal damage to the Carthaginians who were obliged to return to camp. But Marcellus's army had been mauled so severely that he withdrew to Venusia, and from there to Sinuessa in Campania, and took no further part in that year's fighting. Hannibal marched to Bruttium, raised the siege of Caulon, and forced the besiegers to surrender.

Fulvius Flaccus, having no Carthaginian army to contend with, proceeded to raid Samnium, where all the towns which had sided with Hannibal surrendered without resistance, since they had no hope of further support from the Carthaginians. Meanwhile, Fabius began his operations against Tarentum, which he conducted alone. Before attacking Tarentum he captured Manduria with its Carthaginian garrison, and thereby secured his rear. Among the Tarentine commanders was a Bruttian who was desperately in love with a woman who had a brother serving in Fabius's army, and who also no doubt sensed which way the wind was blowing. He got in touch with Fabius and agreed to leave unguarded a portion of the city wall. Following a demonstration by the Romans along the whole line of the fortifications, the Carthaginian commanders in Tarentum were thrown into confusion, under cover of which, in darkness, the Romans climbed the unguarded portion of the wall and entered the city, the gates of which they opened. It was given over to plunder and the inhabitants were enslaved.

One of the few archaeological relics of Hannibal is a stone bearing a Latin inscription in honour of a great man who had covered himself with military glory by the capture of a city that had sided with Hannibal. The inscription, which was recently found at Brundisium (Brindisi), is damaged and incomplete; Giovanni Vitucci has shown, however, that the city referred to must be Tarentum, and the great man who captured it Fabius Maximus.

Hannibal knew that Fabius was intending to attack Tarentum; he had hurried up from Caulon, and was only three miles away when the city fell. One of his asides on hearing the bad news has been preserved:

'So the Romans also have a Hannibal. They have taken Tarentum as we did,' that is, by treachery. He continued to forage in the south of Italy and provision his army, without the Romans doing anything to prevent him, and took up winter quarters at Metapontum.

In Spain, young Scipio, having no further enemies to fear at sea, beached his fleet at Tarraco and incorporated the crews in his army, with which he marched south to Carthagena, engaging Hasdrubal Barca in battle at Baecula, near the river Baetis (Guadalquivir). Hasdrubal was beaten, but he made good his retreat to the north, beyond the Tagus, which was the first stage on his march to Italy. As more and more of the Celtiberian tribes turned to Rome, there seemed

Latin inscription found at Brundisium (Brindisi), containing the only known contemporary mention of Hannibal by name; the extant portion reads 'PRIMVS SENATVM LEGIT ET COMITI . . . BARBVLA COS CIRCVM SEDIT VI . . . DIVMQVE HANNIBALIS ET PRAE . . . MILITARIBVS PRAECIPVAM GLOR . . .' It commemorates Fabius' capture of Tarentum

259

to be no prospect of keeping the country for Carthage. Hasdrubal Gisgo retreated into Lusitania, Masinissa southwards to protect Gades, and Mago went to the Balearic Islands to recruit more men to send to Italy.

DEATH OF MARCELLUS

IF EVER there was a year, since Hannibal had arrived in Italy, when his chances of securing victory, military or political, seemed to have dwindled to the most slender dimensions, it was 208 BC. He had lost Tarentum with its magnificent harbours; he had lost all the towns which he had formerly held in Samnium, to say nothing of Capua and Campania; and his chances of disrupting the Roman Confederacy had vanished into thin air. Carthage had lost Sicily irremediably, and in Spain most of the tribes had turned against Carthage. Nevertheless Hannibal hung on, always hoping for reinforcements, from Carthage, or Spain, or Macedon, and he refused to leave Italy unless peremptorily recalled or beaten. After all, he had not returned to square one, because he had arrived and still was in Italy, fighting the Romans, and Hasdrubal his brother might still come. The year was to provide surprises.

The Consuls for 208 BC were Marcellus and Titus Quintus Crispinus, each with an army of two legions facing Hannibal in Lucania and Apulia. Fabius's army in Tarentum was commanded by Claudius Flaminius. Crispinus began by besieging Locri, one of Hannibal's last ports in the south. When Hannibal marched towards it, the Romans raised the siege and marched away without a fight, because Crispinus was afraid of being bottled up in the extreme end of Bruttium, the 'toe' of Italy. He joined Marcellus near Venusia. Hannibal kept in touch with them and advanced towards Bantia, where he had the two consular armies in his front, and the two legions in Tarentum on his right flank. While there, Hannibal learnt that a Roman force had been sent from Sicily to resume the siege of Locri, and that one legion from Tarentum had been ordered to join them. On this legion Hannibal pounced, from an ambush near Petelia, killed two thousand, captured twelve hundred, and sent the remainder flying back to Tarentum. The Carthaginians then returned to their camp near Bantia.

Meanwhile, Marcellus wanted to get Hannibal to fight a general battle, all the more so because he seemed to be shunning such an engagement.

Remains of Roman monuments at the Latin colony of Venusia (Venosa), near the hill where the Roman general Marcus Claudius Marcellus was killed by Numidian cavalry in an ambush set by Hannibal in 208 BC

Between the Roman and the Carthaginian camps was a wooded hill, in which Hannibal hid a force of Numidians. The Consuls considered that this hill would be an admirable position for their own camp, and set out with a small cavalry escort to reconnoitre it. The Numidians fell on them, killed Marcellus, and wounded Crispinus, who managed to escape, with Marcellus's son. So died Marcus Claudius Marcellus, Hannibal's most dangerous foe, of whom, according to Livy, Hannibal said after the first day of their last battle at Asculum, 'How very curious; we have to deal with an enemy who seems to be incapable of enduring success or failure; if he wins he cannot leave those whom he has beaten alone; if he loses, he again fights the army that beat him.' Another remark of Hannibal's about Marcellus was: 'He is the only general who, when victorious, allows us no rest, and when we beat him takes none himself.' He had Marcellus's body ceremonially cremated and sent the ashes to Marcellus's son in a silver urn.

Both at Lake Trasimene and at Cannae, Hannibal had killed one of the Consuls in office, and since then he had killed many Roman generals.

262

Ruins of Salapia in Apulia, where Hannibal spent several winters. After Marcellus's death, Hannibal tried by a trick to regain possession of Salapia, but failed

◄ *Statue of Marcus Claudius Marcellus, the Roman general of whom Hannibal said, 'He is the only general who, when victorious, allows us no rest, and when we beat him takes none himself'*

Now, when Crispinus died of his wounds, it meant that he had killed both Consuls for the year. But his cause was not thereby advanced in the least; it availed him nothing unless it was conducive to political advantage, which it was not; and it was but another example of the fact that by itself, military victory led nowhere.

With the death of Marcellus, Hannibal had come into possession of his seal-ring. Aware of this fact, the Romans sent the information to all the principal towns loyal to them, to warn them to beware of anything that looked like a ruse on the part of the wily Carthaginian. He did, in fact, make an attempt to use the ring to regain possession of Salapia in northern Apulia, which he wanted to secure in case his brother Hasdrubal reached Italy and marched down its east coast. Hannibal's ruse took the form of a letter, written in Marcellus's name, to the garrison commander at Salapia saying that Marcellus would arrive on the following night. When Hannibal reached the town he sent forward an advance party of Roman deserters, armed with Roman weapons, who called in Latin to the guards at the gate to open it as the Consul was coming. But the warning had reached Salapia just in time. The guards raised the portcullis just enough to let some of the deserters in, and then dropped it in Hannibal's face. He had been foiled. He left Salapia, turned south, and marched once more on Locri where he again raised the siege. His possession of the extreme south of Italy was undisputed, but of nowhere else. He wintered at Metapontum.

In Spain, Scipio had already defeated Hasdrubal Barca; but had failed in his chief object, which was to keep Hasdrubal in Spain and prevent him from marching to Italy. Late in the year, Scipio learnt from Massalia that Hadrubal had crossed the Tagus, turned the head-waters of the Ebro, and, passing round the western end of the Pyrenees, had entered Gaul where he spent the winter of 208–207 BC, waiting for the snow to melt in the Alps.

THE METAURUS

THE ROUTE taken by Hasdrubal Barca to lead his army from Gaul to Italy is more problematical than that taken by Hannibal, because no details are known, and the accounts of classical writers are contra-dictory. Marcus Terentius Varro, the Roman historian who has already been quoted, placed Hasdrubal's pass quite distinct from Hannibal's, with Pompey's pass in between them. If, as is probable though not certain, Hannibal's pass was close by Monte Viso (Col de la Traversette or Col de Mary), Pompey's was the next to the north, the Col du Mont-Genèvre, and Hasdrubal's would have been the pass beyond that, the Col du Mont-Cenis, for in Varro's list it comes below the pass 'through the Graian Alps', which can only have been the Petit Saint-Bernard. As Hasdrubal had come from the western end of the Pyrenees, and had crossed the country of the Arverni, Auvergne, in the centre of Gaul, it would have been normal for him to follow the route of the Isère, and the Mont-Cenis pass leads out of the basin of that river.

But two other authors, Livy and Appian, stated that Hasdrubal crossed the same pass as his brother Hannibal. It is possible that they

XIII   The death of Archimedes in 212 BC (cf. page 239) as depicted in a Roman mosaic, probably third century AD

were speaking figuratively, meaning that in leading his army from Gaul to Italy over the Alps, Hasdrubal was following in Hannibal's footsteps, without implying an exactly identical itinerary. Whichever pass it was that Hasdrubal crossed, he entered the plain of the Po.

The Consuls for 207 BC were Caius Claudius Nero and Marcus Livius Salinator. Each had an army of two legions, the former near Venusia facing southwards confronting Hannibal, the latter at Senagallica on the Adriatic facing northwards, waiting for Hasdrubal, to prevent him from joining his brother. Supporting Nero was Fulvius's army in Bruttium and that of Quintus Claudius. Opposing Hannibal there were thus no fewer than three armies. In the north, Livius's army was supported by two others, one under Lucius Porcius Licinius in Cisalpine Gaul, and the other under Varro in Etruria. In all, Rome mobilized twenty-five legions.

The timing between the two Carthaginian brothers was not good. Hasdrubal met less opposition in his crossing of the Alps than Hannibal had done, and debouched into Italy sooner than expected, but the precious time thus gained he then wasted by besieging Placentia, without success. He next decided to wait until some new reinforcements of Gauls and Ligurians reached him, mindless of the fact that by this time the Romans knew that he had arrived, and could mobilize and concentrate far more men than he could hope to recruit in any given time. But the Romans knew even more than this, for with unbelievable carelessness Hasdrubal wrote a letter to Hannibal in plain Punic, telling him that he was raising the siege of Placentia and would march down the Via Flaminia, along the Adriatic coast, and hoped to meet him on that route. This letter Hasdrubal entrusted to four Gallic and two Numidian horsemen, who made their way southwards through the whole length of Italy; but instead of going to Metapontum which was in Hannibal's hands, they went to Tarentum and were promptly captured. Hasdrubal's plan of campaign was revealed to the Romans, and Hannibal did not know that the Romans knew it.

From Metapontum, Hannibal moved northwards to Grumentum in Lucania, hoping to receive news from his brother, for he did not even know what the Romans knew. Nero moved down from Venusia to confront him, but Hannibal was disinclined to risk a general engagement until he could do it in conjunction with Hasdrubal. Nero forced an action, making use of one of Hannibal's own tricks of an

XIV   Monument to a Numidian prince near Dugga, Tunisia, an outstanding example of Punic masonry of the third or second century BC

ambush on the flank, and Hannibal was obliged to withdraw. There followed a series of marches and counter-marches, by which Hannibal tried to establish his position as far north as possible in Apulia with the object of approaching his brother and of drawing the Roman armies away from his path. But Nero dogged his footsteps and headed him off from the north.

With the help of his invaluable intelligence, Nero planned the Roman campaign. He left the bulk of his army facing Hannibal, and marched secretly with picked troops to join Livius and block Hasdrubal's way. The plan was risky, for he had left a depleted army to oppose Hannibal, and Hasdrubal, who had already outwitted him in Spain three years previously, might do so again. In seven days, Nero's flying column of six thousand legionaries and one thousand horse, marching light without baggage, but making use of locally provided transport, covered the four hundred kilometres and joined Livius. The junction of the two armies was also kept secret by the doubling-up of troops in camp, which remained no larger than that of a single Consular army. Hasdrubal had advanced to the river Sena, but when his scouts informed him that two trumpets, not one, were blown in the Roman camp, which meant that both Consuls and two Consular armies were there, and that they now wanted him to know this, he became hesitant, and retreated to the line of the next river to the north, the Metaurus. The retreat was badly conducted, and the Roman vanguard attacked the rear of Hasdrubal's army. He drew it up as well as he could, on rising ground, the African and Spanish troops on his right, the Ligurians and ten elephants in the centre, and the Gauls on his left. The Romans were drawn up with Livius's army on their left, Nero's on the right, and between them Porcius's army from Cisalpine Gaul.

The battle was fought desperately hard, and at first the Romans made little progress against the Carthaginians, while the elephants did as much damage to friend as to foe, 'racing about to and fro between the armies like ships without steering oars'. Presently, Nero, seeing that the obstacles in his front which protected the Gauls, would also prevent the Gauls from advancing, took most of his army back, round the rear and the left of the Roman lines, and fell on the right and rear of Hasdrubal's lines. The result was the complete destruction of Hasdrubal's army, a Cannae in reverse. The exact site of the battlefield has been identified by N. Alfieri, who even found among the remains of bones a cup with an Iberian inscription of the third century BC. To the oracle at Delphi the Romans presented a golden crown and silver figures from the booty which they captured.

Hasdrubal had now paid the price for his delay in leaving Spain, his delay in Gaul, his delay before Placentia, his waiting for reinforcements (of doubtful value), his abominable carelessness in sending Hannibal a message *en clair* to the wrong address, and for the grievous mistake of trying to reinforce Hannibal by land instead of by sea. Hasdrubal died fighting, sword in hand. The Roman generals did not share Hannibal's respect for the bodies of dead enemy commanders. Nero had Hasdrubal's head cut off, and when he had marched his

267

army back with all speed to Apulia, in six days this time, he had the head thrown into Hannibal's camp. This was the first and only information which Hannibal received of his brother Hasdrubal's fate. With it evaporated all hope of being reinforced by his army. He is reported to have said, when he saw his brother's head, 'I see there the fate of Carthage.'

In this desperate campaign, Nero showed himself to be a general infinitely better than Hasdrubal, and even better than Hannibal, for his bold manœuvre was faultless. The day of the battle of the Metaurus was described by Horace as the first on which victory smiled on the Romans since that day when the terrible Carthaginians had crashed through Italy like a fire through a pine-forest. Rome was at last safe, though the war was not over. The effect of the victory on the Romans and on the Confederacy was delirious. The Consuls were accorded a well-earned triumph.

Hannibal withdrew all his garrisons in Metapontum and in Lucania, and retired into Bruttium, unmolested. Meanwhile, in Spain, fortune had continued to attend Scipio's operations. Armies under Mago and Hanno were defeated in Baetica (Andalusia), and the latter was captured. The remaining Carthaginians in Spain shut themselves up in Gades. The curtain was coming down.

SPAIN LOST

THE CONSULS for 206 BC, Quintus Caecilius Metellus and Lucius Veturius Philo, whose duty it was to carry on the war against Hannibal, had a period of office which differed from that of all their predecessors over twelve years, because during this year there were no offensive operations against Hannibal's army at all. He was confined to Bruttium with an army now of very poor quality, and the Romans were happy to leave him along for the time being, so long as he left them alone. Except for a short raid on Cosentia in Bruttium, where the Romans, having ravaged the countryside, were attacked with their booty in a pass by Bruttians with some Numidians but got away, there was little fighting in Italy.

In Spain, Scipio fought a general action against the Carthaginians under Hasdrubal Gisgo and Mago at Baecula. Copying Hannibal's practice at the Trebia of giving his men an early meal before the battle, which the Carthaginian commanders had not done, Scipio won a decisive victory, which he followed up with further attacks against Hasdrubal, who escaped by sea to Gades and from there to Carthage. Almost all the Celtiberian tribes had abandoned the Carthaginian cause, but some mopping-up remained to be done, the revolt of Mandonius and Indibilis had to be put down, and the towns of Iliturgi and Castulo, which had behaved treacherously when Scipio's father and uncle had been killed, were destroyed. A mutiny in part of Scipio's army, over pay and conditions, while he was thought to be ill, had to be suppressed, but Rome was now in undisputed possession of all Spain, and the Celtiberians even offered to make Scipio their king. For Rome, Spain was a bonus.

Coin showing (obverse) head of Syphax, king of Numidia, who when he became the husband of Sophonisba, daughter of Hasdrubal Gisgo, made an alliance with Carthage; (reverse) a Numidian horseman

The war in Spain being at an end, Scipio already began to make preparation for its inevitable sequel, which was a war in Africa. With this end in view, he entered into negotiations with Syphax, and took the remarkable step of crossing over to Africa to visit him. As he entered the African harbour with his two quinqueremes, who should arrive in the same harbour but Hasdrubal Gisgo, also on a visit to Syphax. The two old enemies, the Roman and the Carthaginian, were now both in Syphax's territory, and no hostility of any kind was shown between them as they went to call on the king. Syphax was not unnaturally honoured that such senior generals of two of the world's leading powers should visit him on the same day, to ask for his friendship. He invited them to be his guests, and to eat dinner with him. Scipio won Syphax over completely with his charm and eloquence.

He even played on Hasdrubal's feelings, although the Carthaginian saw that Scipio's visit could only portend a Roman invasion of Africa, for which Syphax's help was being invited. Hasdrubal was correct in his surmise, and Syphax made a treaty with Scipio.

There remained Masinissa, whose brilliant leadership of his Numidian cavalry had long been a thorn in the side of Rome. Masinissa was in Gades, where he persuaded Mago to allow him to cross to the Spanish mainland—as he said, to exercise his horses which were in bad condition from having been confined in the island, in fact to meet Scipio at a pre-arranged place. There he also fell under the spell of Scipio's charm, and made a treaty with him.

There was nothing left for Mago to do but to sail from Gades to the Balearic Islands to recruit more men, and Gades, the oldest colony planted by Tyre nine hundred years before, admitted the Romans. Mago sailed to Ebusus (Ibiza) where he was well received and replenished his crews and equipment, before going on to Majorca. There he was repulsed, and sailed to Minorca, taking possession of the town near the harbour, where he recruited men and passed the winter. Scipio on his return to Rome was not accorded a triumph because, although he had held a command in the field, he had never yet held a high magistracy. His entry into Rome was nevertheless triumphant, preceded by his contribution of 14,342 pounds of silver to the treasury, without counting the silver bullion.

PREPARATIONS FOR AFRICA

AT THE ELECTIONS in 205 BC Scipio was made Consul and his colleague was Publius Licinius Crassus. On the Capitol, Scipio sacrificed the hundred oxen to Jupiter which he had vowed to do while fighting in Spain; he also fulfilled his vow, made when part of his army mutinied in Spain, to celebrate games, and a decree was passed enabling him to defray their cost from the treasure which he had brought.

The province allotted to Scipio was Sicily, and it was common knowledge among friend and foe that the next step would be to carry the war into Africa. The war in Sicily had been ended by Marcellus, that in Greece by Publius Sulpicius, that in Spain by Scipio himself; only in Italy did war still smoulder against Hannibal in Bruttium. Africa was the obvious place in which to open up a second front. and Sicily the obvious stepping-stone to it. Scipio began his preparations.

Twenty quinqueremes and ten quadriremes were built in forty-five days.

Crassus was given Bruttium as his theatre of war, and Hannibal as his responsibility. This provided an opportunity for old Fabius Maximus to oppose in the Senate the proposed campaign in Africa, on the grounds that Hannibal was still formidable in Italy, where no general dared to attack him, but that he would be still more formidable if he went back to Africa, his home country, where Rome would have to rely on the untrustworthy support of the fickle Syphax, and the Roman army would be divided between Scipio's and Crassus's commands. It would be better, said Fabius, for the army to be concentrated in Italy to deal Hannibal a death-blow. After much argument and political in-fighting, Scipio got his way, and his preparations in Sicily went ahead.

Mago Barca had passed the winter in Minorca where he had raised twelve thousand foot soldiers and two thousand horsemen. With these, in defiance of all sense and notwithstanding the fact that he had to risk Roman supremacy at sea, Mago sailed to Genua (Genoa), in the heart of the Ligurian country, landed his army and occupied the town. Marching westwards (and therefore, away from Hannibal) he took Savo (Savona), where he deposited his plunder. Some Ligurian tribes joined him, principally the Albingauni (from the vicinity of Albenga), but the Gauls fought shy of bringing down on themselves more trouble from the two Roman armies in Cisalpine Gaul. Incredible as it may seem, at this late hour Carthage found it possible to send to Mago, and not to Hannibal, a reinforcement of seven thousand men, seven elephants, twenty-five ships, and money, with the fatuous directive to march on Rome and draw near to Hannibal. Never was there a worse example of too little being sent too late to the wrong place. The two Roman armies, one under Marcus Valerius Laevinus at Ariminum and the other under Marcus Livius at Arretium, not only blocked the roads by which Mago could ever hope to reach the south of Italy and Hannibal, but also prevented the Gauls from going to Mago's aid.

In Bruttium, the war had degenerated into a series of forays, carried out by both sides. The only operation of importance was Scipio's attack on Locri. With the help of some Locrian exiles in Sicily, and some Locrian prisoners taken by the Romans and ransomed by the exiles, Scipio got into communication with one of the garrisons in Locri, and set on foot a conspiracy to hand it over to the Romans. Three thousand men were sent from Rhegium under Quintus Pleminius. As

The Strait of Messina, looking from Rhegium (Reggio) towards Messana (Messina), across which Scipio came with a part of his army from Sicily to deprive Hannibal of the port of Locri

Ruins of Locri, the Greek city founded about 680 BC. One of Hannibal's last remaining ▶
mainland seaports, it was recaptured by Scipio

soon as Hannibal heard of this, he marched towards Locri and ordered the Carthaginian garrison, which still held one of the two citadels, to make a vigorous sortie at the same time as he attacked the town and the other citadel which had fallen into the hands of the Romans. But Scipio, at Messana, in his turn learnt of Hannibal's movements, and came with a fleet to Locri where he disembarked a force which he hid in the town. The result was that when Hannibal attacked, Scipio and his men suddenly streamed out of one of the gates and took the Carthaginians in flank and rear. Hannibal's troops, now of very poor quality, were demoralized and had to be withdrawn to camp. Hannibal then marched away, more hemmed in than ever, now that he had lost Locri, for he had previously abandoned Thurii. It was during this period that he placed in the temple of Hera Lacinia on Promontorium

Lacinium (Capo Colonne) an inscription in Punic and in Greek, recording the strength of his army after he had crossed the Alps thirteen years before: twelve thousand Africans, eight thousand Spaniards, and six thousand horsemen. This is known on no less authority than that of Polybius himself, who wrote: 'I found near Lacinium, the bronze tablet on which Hannibal had recorded this list when he was in this part of Italy.' The tablet was on an altar dedicated by Hannibal in this temple, which is an additional sign that he worshipped Greek gods, as is shown by those whom he invoked in his treaty with Philip of Macedon.

A further disappointment for Hannibal was the peace which Philip of Macedon had made with Rome. The war in Illyria had been desultory, and an event had occurred in the eastern Mediterranean which provided

273

Philip with more profitable troubled waters in which to fish than supporting Hannibal would do. Ptolemy IV Philopater of Egypt had died, and his successor Ptolemy V Epiphanes was a minor. To Philip, and to Antiochus III of Syria, this seemed a golden opportunity for seizing all Egypt's possessions outside Africa. Philip was to have the Aegean islands and the cities in Thrace that belonged to Egypt, while Antiochus's cut would be Phoenicia, Palestine, and Cyprus. This was the start of a situation which was ultimately to have important personal consequences for Hannibal.

THE BEST MAN

IT IS ONE of the lasting mysteries of the Roman character that it combined flint-hard rationalism with extreme superstition. Throughout the long war, whenever anything extraordinary was reported, falls of stones, births of monstrous calves, the Consuls had ordered the Sibylline Books to be consulted, so as to come to some conclusion about what steps should or should not be taken, and omens were studied, and almost constantly followed. Before a campaign, generals took the auspices on the Capitol; in the field or at sea they took Sacred Chickens with them in golden cages to see if they ate.

In 204 BC there had been unusually numerous falls of stones, and a prophecy was found in the Sibylline Books saying that a foreign invader of Italy could be defeated provided that the image of Cybele, Mother of the gods, was transported from Pessinus in Phrygia to Rome.

King Attalus of Pergamum was favourably disposed towards Rome, because both were confronting the same enemy, Philip of Macedon. A formidable deputation was therefore sent from Rome to Attalus, including Marcus Valerius Laevinus, Marcus Caecilius Metellus, Servicius Sulpicius Galba, and others, all of whom had played important parts in the war. On the way, the ambassadors consulted the oracle at Delphi and received an encouraging answer. Attalus received the deputation kindly and escorted them to Pessinus where he handed to them the sacred image of Cybele to take to Rome.

Doric column of the Temple of Hera Lacinia on Promontorium Lacinium (Cape Colonne), where Hannibal placed an inscription recording the strength and losses of his army during his passage of the Alps

The oracle at Delphi had stipulated that it was of the greatest importance that the image should be welcomed in Rome by the best man in the city. By some method of selection which is not clear, the Senate decided that the best man was Publius Cornelius Scipio Nasica, son of the Cnaeus Scipio who had been killed in Spain, and therefore first cousin of the young Scipio who was preparing to invade Africa. The best man sailed out of the mouth of the Tiber and out to sea to meet the returning fleet. He received the image of the goddess from the priests and carried it ashore. There, he handed it to the leading married women of Rome, who passed it on from hand to hand. A procession was then formed, and the image was borne into the city to the accompaniment of prayers and burning incense, and deposited in the Temple of Victory on the Palatine.

The more objective aspect of the Roman character showed itself when the Senate decreed that the twelve Latin communities, which had refused to furnish their allotted contingents of men and money five

The Magna Mater, a bronze group of Cybele enthroned on a chariot drawn by lions. The Sibylline Books predicted that fortune would favour Rome if the image of Cybele were brought from Pessinus in Phrygia to Rome

The Grotto of the Sibyl at Cumae (cf. page 223), described by Virgil thus, 'a vast cavern, ▶
a hundred entrances and a hundred tunnels lead into it, through which the Sibyl's oracle emerges in a hundred streams of sound'

years before, were now required to furnish twice the previously stipulated number of foot-soldiers, one hundred and twenty horsemen each, and to pay a special tax. Another measure, more liberal in its effects by contrast, provided that the sums of money which had been voluntarily contributed to the treasury by Senators and others, six years before, should be refunded to them.

Scipio was not elected Consul for 204 B C, but as Pro-Consul he retained his command in Sicily. The Consuls were Publius Sempronius Tuditanus who watched over Bruttium and Hannibal, and Marcus Cornelius Cethegus who did the same over Etruria and Mago.

In Bruttium operations had reached a very low ebb. Sempronius Tuditanus, eager for battle, marched towards Hannibal and met his army near Crotona, which was practically his last foothold in Italy. In the ensuing battle the Romans had the worst of it, but summoning up the Pro-Consul Publius Licinius Crassus with his army the Consul tried conclusions against Hannibal again. The Romans had four of their own and four allied legions, against which Hannibal can have been able to put into the field only half that strength. Nevertheless, he accepted battle outside Crotona, but had to retreat into the town. The Romans also retired; they took the town of Clampetia by storm, while Cosentia and Pandosia submitted voluntarily.

The centre of interest shortly shifted to Africa, where a rough-and-tumble of incredible complexity took place. While Masinissa was still in Spain, his father Gala had died, and the succession to the throne of the Maesulian Numidian kingdom was caught up in a civil war, in which Masinissa's uncle (who had inherited the throne) and cousin were killed at the hands of a brigand, Mazaetullus, who roused the people and placed on the throne a boy, Lacumazes, while he himself as guardian retained all power. He then married the old king's widow, who was the daughter of Hannibal's sister, and by that means sought to ingratiate himself with Carthage.

Masinissa left Spain and came to Morocco, whence he entered what was really his kingdom with a few Numidians who had joined him. After a successful fight against Mazaetullus's puppet king who was on his way to visit Syphax, numerous Numidians joined Masinissa who then confronted Mazaetullus's army which had been strongly rein-forced by Syphax. Masinissa was successful and recovered his king-dom, but he soon saw that he had not finished with his deadly enemy Syphax.

Goaded on by Hasdrubal, Syphax attacked Masinissa and defeated him so thoroughly that he was driven to take refuge in mountainous country and to live by raiding the adjoining Carthaginian lands. Syphax sent troops to attack Masinissa again, and the latter barely escaped with his life, hiding in a cave, nursing his wounds, with only two companions. He had been reported to Syphax as dead, but as soon as his wounds were sufficiently healed, he returned to his kingdom, announced his identity, and was immediately joined by supporters who constituted a new army with which he provoked Syphax to war. Between Cirta (Constantine) and Hippo Regius (Bône) a savage battle was fought in which Syphax won a complete victory. Masinissa just managed to escape with sixty horsemen to the shores of Syrtis Minor (Gulf of Gabès) where he remained in hiding.

From Sicily, Scipio had sent a fleet under Caius Laelius to obtain information about Carthaginian intentions. On learning of Laelius's arrival, Masinissa hurried to Hippo Zarytus (Bizerta) to meet him, and complained bitterly that Scipio had been so dilatory in invading Africa, while Carthage was already so deeply shaken, adding that Syphax was fully engaged in troubles of his own and would never give loyal support to Rome if he was given time to settle his own affairs. This was duly reported to Scipio on Laelius's return to Sicily. Meanwhile, Hasdrubal Gisgo had been sent by Carthage to Syphax, of whose pact with Scipio he knew, to win back Syphax to the alliance with Carthage. He succeeded in doing so by marrying Syphax hurriedly to his beautiful daughter Sophonisba. To strengthen this bond 'before his passion had had time to cool', Hasdrubal urged and Sophonisba persuaded Syphax to send envoys to Scipio warning him not to cross over to Africa and carry on the war there. His reasons were that he, Syphax, was now tied to Carthage by his marriage and by a treaty. Rome might fight Carthage as long as she liked away from African shores, but if she invaded Africa, Syphax would be obliged to take sides, and his side could only be that of Carthage, to defend a land which was also his, and to support his wife's native city and gods.

The news of this deputation got about in Sicily among Roman military circles, and the troops began to show nervousness at the prospect of having to fight not only the Carthaginians but Syphax's army as well. Scipio countered this development by the most brazen propaganda, and 'filling his men with lies', as Livy said. He pretended that just as Masinissa had been worried at the delay by Rome in invading Africa, now Syphax was actuated by the same anxiety, and wanted either immediate invasion, or to be informed of the change of plans, if any. Enthusiasm for battle in Africa was rekindled in the legionaries' hearts, especially as Scipio had remedied the grievance under which they had suffered for twelve years; for most of them had fought at Cannae and had been punished by being sent to serve in Sicily without pay. He restored their self-esteem, most important before a campaign.

SCIPIO IN AFRICA

IN THE SPRING of 204 BC, Scipio set sail from Lilybaeum with thirty thousand men and landed near Utica at Promontorium Pulchrum west of Cap Bon. In order to have the use of a town and a harbour, he moved to besiege Utica. Carthage was terror-stricken, and with better reason than Rome had been when Hannibal invaded Italy, for Carthage now had no proper army to hand and no great general at home. Masinissa had joined Scipio, all the more readily as he had been Syphax's rival for the hand of Sophonisba, and, as Livy remarked, 'Numidians surpass all other barbarian peoples in the violence of their appetites.'

Carthage expected a contingent of troops from Philip of Macedon, which was all that he could send, and some Celtiberian mercenaries were awaited from Spain. A small force of cavalry under Hanno Barca was ordered to observe the operations of the Roman army. Scipio sent out Masinissa with his Numidians to deal with it, and crushed it completely. Hanno was killed. If ever there was justification for censuring Hannibal because he did not march on Rome when he could, there is even more for questioning why Scipio did not immediately march on Carthage, now utterly powerless and in complete confusion. Even if he did not storm it, he could have blockaded it at once. Scipio would have run no danger whatever, for Carthage had no Confederacy like Rome, and there was no Carthaginian army in Carthage. But Hasdrubal Gisgo soon raised one, together with his ally Syphax, although only a rabble of miserable quality, quite unable to stand up to veteran Roman legionaries. Nevertheless Hasdrubal marched towards Scipio, who raised the siege of Utica and established a defensive camp on the peninsula of Promontorium Pulchrum, the Castra Corneliana, where he went into winter quarters.

The elections for 203 BC appointed as Consuls Cnaeus Servilius Caepio and Caius Servilius Geminus; Scipio was confirmed in his command

XV   Cap Bon, north-east of Carthage (cf. illustration, p. 37), the point on the north coast of Africa nearest to Sicily

A bath and its drainage system in the Carthaginian town of Dar Essafi near the Cap Bon peninsula. Fourth to third century BC

XVI Stele and other remains of Punic Carthage; little of the city survived the destruction by Roman forces in 146 BC

in Africa until the end of the war. He had used his time to acquire intelligence about the Carthaginian army. Pretending to start negotiations for peace, although he had no senatorial authority to do so, he sent out envoys accompanied by experienced centurions disguised as servants, who soon nosed out every secret in the Carthaginian camp; they found discipline lax and the camp badly guarded. Throwing off all semblance of negotiations, Scipio sent a small body of troops towards Utica with a siege train, to make the Carthaginians believe that he was about to resume the siege, and this occupied the attention of Hasdrubal and Syphax when Scipio made a night attack on their army in camp. Syphax's troops were in reed huts, and these Masinissa and Laelius soon set on fire. Syphax's men, thinking that the fire was an accident, rushed out unarmed and were cut down. Hasdrubal's men in their wooden huts were equally alarmed at the fire and rushed out of camp, only to meet the same fate. In this manner, the Carthaginian army was destroyed.

Astonishing as it may seem, Hasdrubal and Syphax then set about and succeeded in collecting another rabble of an army, in which the only reliable fighters were the Celtiberian mercenaries from Spain and the contingent of Greeks from Macedonia. With this army of scarecrows they again confronted Scipio, and he again destroyed the rabble with great slaughter. Hasdrubal took refuge in Carthage and Syphax in Cirta (Constantine) which was Masinissa's capital in Numidia.

Scipio then entrusted the blockade of Utica to his fleet while he marched with the larger part of his army, at last, against Carthage, ravaging the country as he went. He also sent a column under Laelius and Masinissa to pursue Syphax. That worthy tried another battle, in which he was not only wounded but captured. Cirta, and Sophonisba, fell into the hands of the Romans.

Cirta had been the capital of Masinissa's father Gaia, and Masinissa was as pleased to recover his kingdom as his subjects were to receive him. On entering the palace he was met by Sophonisba who pleaded with him to save her from the only possible fate which the Romans could have in store for her. Masinissa fell head over heels in love with her, promised to grant her request, and married her that very same day so that she should be recognized as the wife of a Numidian king, and not be a prisoner of the Romans to adorn Scipio's triumph. Laelius on arriving at the palace was, of course, furious, and insisted on sending Sophonisba with Syphax and all the other prisoners to Scipio, but Masinissa persuaded him to leave to Scipio's decision the question of what should happen to Sophonisba.

Brought before Scipio, Syphax, mad with jealousy against Masinissa, pleaded that he had been blinded by the daughter of Carthage, who had enslaved him with her love, and poisoned him with her irresistible passion; his only consolation was to see that his bitter enemy Masinissa was now entangled in the same coils. Masinissa then arrived and Scipio, while congratulating him on his military prowess, reproached him bitterly for his inability to resist the temptations of sensuality, a field in which he, Scipio, had never failed. Syphax was a prisoner of

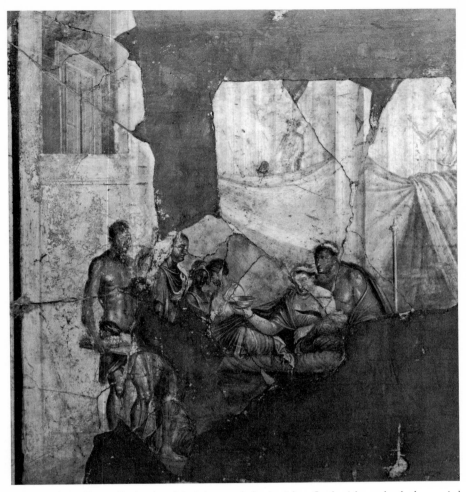

Fresco from Pompeii showing Masinissa and Sophonisba. Sophonisba, who had married Syphax, subsequently fell in love with Masinissa

Rome, and Sophonisba, who was also Syphax's wife, was likewise a prisoner and must be sent to Rome.

Masinissa, very ashamed, admitted to Scipio that he had promised Sophonisba not to hand her over to the Romans. In his tent, Masinissa ordered a trusted servant, who had charge of the poison 'which all kings keep against the changes and chances of fortune', to mix a cup of it and take it to Sophonisba at Cirta, with the injunction to remember that her father was Hasdrubal Gisgo, the Carthaginian. Sophonisba took the hint and drank the poison.

Meanwhile, the war went on in Italy. With a tardiness that beggars belief, Carthage then sent orders to Hannibal and to Mago to return to Carthage with their forces. An attempt to destroy the Roman fleet and to relieve Utica failed, the defeat and capture of Syphax robbed Carthage of any hope of successful resistance, and, a peace party having gained power in the Carthaginian Senate, overtures were made to Scipio to beg for an armistice. The terms of the treaty proposed by Scipio were: all Carthaginian troops to be withdrawn from Italy (which of course meant Hannibal and Mago), all fugitives, prisoners and deserters to be returned to Rome, Masinissa to be confirmed in the possession of his kingdom, the cession to Rome of Spain and all Mediterranean islands, the surrender of all ships except twenty, the supply of a million gallons of wheat and six hundred thousand of barley, and the payment of a war indemnity of five thousand talents. To these terms Carthage agreed, and they were sent to Rome for ratification. The Roman Senate and Assembly authorized Scipio to act as he thought best, and he confirmed the treaty.

In Liguria, Mago had advanced into the territory of the Insubres in Cisalpine Gaul, where he had engaged an army under the Pro-Consul Marcus Cornelius, but was decisively defeated, and himself seriously wounded. The remnants of his army re-embarked, but he died on the journey back to Africa and Hannibal lost his last brother.

Hannibal had foreseen his own recall and taken some steps to prepare for it. He embarked at Crotona, but as Carthage had neglected to send him any transport ships to bring his army home, and he had none in which to transport his wonderful horses, he was obliged to kill them. Their loss was to be crippling for Carthage in the next and last battle to be fought. He left Italy with twenty-four thousand men, but how many of these could have been survivors of the twenty-six thousand veterans with which he had entered Italy fifteen years previously it is easy to guess. Sailing in the autumn of 203 BC, he landed with the remnants of his army at Leptis and wintered at Hadrumetum (Sousse). Italy was at last free from the bogy-man on her soil, and Rome breathed freely. It has been estimated that Hannibal's presence in Italy cost Rome and her allies the lives of three hundred thousand men. The Senate and the Assembly acknowledged the debt which the State owed to the man who had saved it in its hour of greatest danger, Quintus Fabius Maximus, the shield of Rome as he was called, and the decoration of a wreath was bestowed on him. Shortly after this, he died. The other hero of the war in Italy, Marcus Claudius Marcellus, who had been called the sword of Rome, was already dead.

If Rome was elated at Hannibal's departure, Carthage was also elated at his arrival. With their great man, so long under-estimated among them, the Carthaginians took the disastrous step of denouncing the treaty with Scipio. Realizing at last his magical achievements in Italy, with his veterans and his horsemen, they thought that he could repeat the miracle in Africa without the indispensable instrument for making successful war, a tried and trained army. The Carthaginians captured some Roman ships with supplies for Scipio which had been blown by a storm into the harbour of Carthage. Not content with that, they manhandled the Roman envoys whom Scipio had sent to demand satisfaction. The gloves were off for the last bout.

ZAMA

Scipio and Hannibal had never met, either in private, or in battle except for the encounter at the beginning of the war, on the Ticinus, when Scipio saved the life of his father the Consul. Both Scipio and Hannibal now realized that the confrontation was between the two of them; there was no one else on either side fit for the leadership; and yet an attempt was made by a Roman to deprive Scipio of his. The Consul Cnaeus Servilius Caepio thought that the honour of bringing down Carthage and securing lasting peace for Rome should belong to him, as he was Consul when Hannibal left Italian soil. He went to Sicily with the obvious intention of going on to Africa where his rank would place him above Scipio. The Roman Senate got over the difficulty by the appointment of Publius Sulpicius as Dictator, who, with his higher rank, was in a position to order the Consul to go back to Rome. From Hadrumetum, Hannibal heard only sinister reports. Scipio was marching up the valley of the Bagrades (Medjerda) river, devastating the country, which could not fail to be fatal to Carthage. Worse still, Masinissa had joined Scipio with six thousand foot-soldiers and four thousand Numidian horsemen of a quality which Hannibal knew only too well. He accordingly advanced with his army inland, to Zama Regia, not far from Sicca (Kaf, near Ras O Dschaber) and asked Scipio for a personal interview. Scipio agreed to this, and the two generals met, between their respective armies, each accompanied by a single interpreter.

What exactly happened at this interview, which, like that between Napoleon and Alexander I of Russia two thousand years later, was of

such great importance for the history of the world, is not known for certain. In Livy's words, 'mutual admiration struck them dumb, and they looked at each other in silence.' Hannibal then said that he had come to sue for peace, and was glad that Scipio should be the man to whom he had come to ask for it. He admitted that he had been the aggressor, and that Carthage had recently forfeited her credibility by violating the truce; but a sure peace was better and safer than an uncertain hope of victory; by granting peace now, Scipio would crown all his victories, while to bank on a continued favour from fortune might bring his reputation to the ground.

Scipio replied that although Carthage did not deserve conditions for peace more lenient than those that he had proposed in the terms of the treaty which she had now violated, Hannibal was asking to have them bettered, because, from the terms previously offered he had omitted all those not already in the possession of Rome. Even now, if Carthage offered compensation for the violation of the treaty, he would have something to lay before the Senate in Rome, but surrender must be unconditional; if not, there was nothing for it but a trial of strength by force of arms. So it was.

Hannibal's army now consisted of some fifty thousand men, made up of Africans, Ligurians, Gauls, and Italians, some Macedonians sent by Philip, Balearic Islanders, a small force of Numidian horsemen, and eighty elephants. Scipio's army consisted of two Roman and two allied legions, numbering about twenty thousand, light troops amounting to fourteen thousand, nearly three thousand Roman cavalry, and Masinissa's six thousand Numidian horsemen.

Hannibal drew up his army in three lines; in front the Ligurians, Gauls, Balearians, and Moors, troops on which he placed little reliance. In the second line were Africans, Carthaginians, and Macedonians, recently raised and untried. The third line consisted of the troops which Hannibal had brought back from Italy with him, mostly Italians from Bruttium. The eighty elephants were placed in front of the first line, covering the front of the army.

Scipio's army was drawn up in the standard Roman pattern, except that the maniples of the legions, instead of being stationed chequer-wise from front to rear, were placed one behind the other leaving intervals all the way through the lines, in which light troops were

Gobelins tapestry (after Giulio Romano), depicting the meeting between Hannibal and Scipio before the battle of Zama, the first occasion on which they met

Bronze bust of Publius Cornelius Scipio Africanus (286–183 BC), victor of the battle of Zama

posted for the purpose of attacking the elephants, or alternatively, if the elephants attacked, of getting out of the way so that the intervals served as safety valves for the animals which could pass harmlessly through them. Masinissa's Numidians were on the right, Laelius with the Roman cavalry on the left.

Hannibal's elephants were driven forwards, but they were untrained and they stampeded, bringing confusion into the Carthaginian ranks, particularly on the left where Hannibal's few Numidian horsemen were brought into disarray. Masinissa saw his opportunity and launched his own Numidians at them, and broke them up. At the same time, Laelius fell on the African cavalry facing him and drove it from the field. Hannibal now had no cavalry at all on either flank, and no more elephants. Scipio took advantage of the latter fact to make a tactical change in his formations, by closing the gaps between the maniples and forming a solid line, with which he charged Hannibal's first line. The Ligurians and Gauls were no match for the legionaries, and as the Africans and Carthaginians of the second line were slow in coming up in support the Ligurians and Gauls, imagining that they were being deserted, started to attack the Africans and Carthaginians behind them, at the same time as they were assaulted by the Romans in front. Hannibal then had his first line fighting his second.

The second line was steadied by Hannibal, while the remnants of the first disappeared round the flanks. But the legionaries continued their pressure, and the front of the Africans and Carthaginians was broken and pushed back in disorder. There remained only Hannibal's third line, behind which he had no reserves. The fighting became desperate, and Laelius and Masinissa, having driven the Carthaginian cavalry from the field, now came back and charged into the flanks and rear of the wreck of Hannibal's army. The battle was irretrievably lost. Hannibal left the field and, with a small escort, made for Hadrumetum.

Scipio then advanced with the legions on Carthage, and the question arose whether to lay siege to the cursed city with a view to destroying it. But Scipio decided against this, and to the supplicant Carthaginian envoys he dictated the conditions of peace. All deserters, prisoners and slaves were to be handed over; all elephants to be surrendered and no more to be trained; all warships to be surrendered except ten triremes; no war to be made on anyone either in or outside Africa without Rome's permission; restitution of his kingdom to be made to Masinissa; grain and money to be supplied for the allied armies; ten thousand talents of silver to be paid to Rome in fifty yearly instalments, and one hundred hostages, chosen by Scipio, to be handed over to

Rome. In return, Carthaginians would be allowed to live as free men in the cities and territories which they had previously held in Africa, under their own laws.

When these terms were read before the Carthaginian Senate, a senator rose to speak against them, but Hannibal pulled him down with his own hands. The terms were accepted, and envoys were sent to Rome for ratification. They were given a chilly reception by the Roman Senate, and when the proposal was put forward that Rome should make peace with Carthage, the Consul Cnaeus Cornelius Lentulus interposed a veto. He wanted to be credited with an easy victory if the war should continue, or the honour of bringing the war to an end in his Consulship. The question was then put before the people, who voted that peace should be granted to Carthage, and that the man to make that peace and bring the army home should be Scipio.

The envoys returned to Carthage, and Scipio made peace, just forty years after the peace which had ended the First Punic War. Its provisions were carried out, prisoners handed over, ships burnt. Then Carthage was presented with the problem of finding the first instalment of the reparations payments, and faces in the Carthaginian Senate were long, when Hannibal scandalized them all by bursting into laughter. Rebuked for laughing when everyone else was weeping, Hannibal replied that the time for weeping was when their arms and ships were taken from them. Now, public misfortune had begun to be felt only when it impinged on private interests. While Carthage was being disarmed, nobody raised a groan; now that contributions had to be wrung from private purses, they were behaving like mourners; yet this was the least of the troubles which they would have to put up with. Masinissa was reinstated in his kingdom, now under Roman protection; Scipio embarked the army and returned to his triumph in Rome. He had earned his title of Scipio Africanus.

HANNIBAL IN CARTHAGE

AFTER ALL THAT ROME had suffered from Hannibal, the fact that she did not insist in the peace treaty on the surrender of his person, or his inclusion among the hostages, must be ascribed to the intervention of Scipio, who had conceived a genuine admiration for his opponent. It was also probably realized by Rome that without Hannibal, Carthage would go completely to pieces, and Rome would get no reparation

Hannibal being crowned as head of the government in Carthage, after the surrender to Rome, from a fifteenth-century MS. Head of the government Hannibal was, in the office of chief magistrate, but never crowned

payments at all. Returned to civilian life, Hannibal now had the opportunity to use his great powers of statesmanship, no longer hidden by his prestigious military skill. There was plenty of scope for it, in his politically ruined country.

One of his first tasks, after his appointment as Chief Magistrate, was to have an investigation made of the resources still left to Carthage. The situation was better than could have been expected. The city was on the way to recovering its commercial prosperity; but before long, a scandal broke out. The first instalment of the reparation payments due to Rome under the peace treaty was paid in 199 BC, but the Quaestors in Rome who examined it found that the silver was one quarter below standard. It would be interesting to know by what exact method the Roman assayers established the fact, because it was only a dozen years since Archimedes, the man who discovered the method by specific gravity, had been killed at Syracuse.

In looking into the scandal, Hannibal soon found himself up against the Board of Judges of the Carthaginian Senate, a self-perpetuating body of aristocrats appointed for life, from whose negative decisions he had for so long had to suffer, when fighting, unsupported, in Italy. He obtained a revision of the constitution, and the Board was made subject to annual elections. By eradicating corruption and embezzlement, and collecting arrears of unpaid taxes, Hannibal showed how the reparation payments could be made without increasing taxation.

The financial situation of Rome, on the other hand, was very bad. The strain of the long war against Hannibal had led to a rapid and prolonged inflation, which was not brought under control until fifteen years after the end of the war, when, in 187 BC, the *denarius* system was introduced, with a coinage of three silver denominations and seven of struck bronze. Shortly after the start of the Second Punic War the metal content of the cast *aes grave* was reduced, and it continued to fall until pieces one twelfth of their original weight were struck.

Hannibal had another and more difficult problem with which to deal. When Mago's army left Genua, an officer with the hackneyed name of Hamilcar stayed behind and put himself at the head of a number of malcontent Ligurian and Gallic tribes in Cisalpine Gaul, where revolt still smouldered. Placentia and Cremona were attacked. The Roman Senate naturally complained to Carthage, demanding the recall and surrender of this freebooter, whose activities were a breach of the peace treaty. Suspicion, naturally, was laid on Hannibal of having taken some part in these operations; but the Carthaginian Senate replied that it had no power to do anything beyond exiling this Hamilcar and confiscating his property.

Meanwhile, in 200 BC the Second Macedonian War had begun. Since 205 BC when Ptolemy V Epiphanes acceded to the throne of the Pharaohs, and Philip of Macedon and Antiochus of Syria had hatched their plan of helping themselves to the Pharaoh's dominions outside Egypt, alarm was great in many States of Asia Minor and the Aegean. Rhodes in particular, with its active commerce, did not relish the prospect of the Dardanelles and the Bosphorus falling into the hands of a more powerful Philip of Macedon. Eumenes, king of Pergamum, had the same horror of a still more powerful neighbour in Antiochus of Syria. Moreover, the Egyptians had placed their young Pharaoh under the protection of Rome. Nor had Rome forgiven Philip for the reinforcements of troops which he had sent to Carthage for the battle of Zama, despite the treaty which Macedon had made with her in 205 BC.

It was a turning-point in Roman history when, in 200 BC, she declared war on Philip of Macedon. During the Hannibalic War, Rome could justifiably claim that she had acted defensively against aggression. The wars in Italy, and even the First Punic War in Sicily, could be regarded as establishing a ring-fence round Rome. Now, she was embarking deliberately on a war undertaken at a distance from Italy. Secondly, while Rome had been engaged in strengthening her position in Italy she had kept her attention almost entirely in the west, in Sicily, Sardinia, Spain, and Carthage. Now she was turning east, adventuring beyond Illyria and what she had previously done in

Obverse of coins of Ptolemy IV Philopater (244–205 BC) and his successor, the young Ptolemy V Epiphanes (210–180 BC), who was placed under the guardianship of Rome

Greece, and was now allied to Rhodes, Pergamum, and the Aetolian League of Greek States. Rome's great empire was already in the making.

For the first two years, the results obtained by Rome against Philip were not particularly successful, but in 197 BC, the young Consul Titus Quinctius Flamininus was put in command, and the situation changed rapidly. Proclaiming that he had come to liberate all Greece from the yoke of Philip of Macedon, he succeeded in deflecting the States of the Achaean League from their alliance with Philip, and he defeated his army decisively at the battle of Cynoscephalae. Philip was forced to give up all his possessions in Greece, to hand over his fleet,

293

and to pay a heavy war indemnity. Macedon's power was broken. In the ensuing year, 196 BC, there followed a master-stroke of Roman policy. At the Isthmian Games in Corinth, Flamininus proclaimed that Rome meant what she said when she came to liberate Greece; he solemnly declared all Greek States to be independent, and that they would pay no tribute to Rome and would not have to support any Roman garrisons. The proclamation was received with immense enthusiasm by the Greeks, but in fact it served two corner-stones of Roman policy. First, it attached the Greek States to Rome by links of gratitude and admiration, and at the same time deprived Antiochus of the possibility of claiming that he was coming to liberate the Greek States from Rome. Second, the policy ensured that Rome's neighbours in Greece would be a large number of small, weak States, far preferable to a centralized powerful State such as would be there if Antiochus gained control of Greece. It was a subtle expression of the policy of *divide et impera*.

Bust of Antiochus III of Syria (223–187 BC), with whom Hannibal continued to fight the Romans

There remained Antiochus, who, meanwhile, had helped himself to Phoenicia, Palestine, Cyprus, and the other Egyptian possessions in Asia Minor. He had not only let Philip down badly, by not coming to his help against Rome, but took advantage of Philip's discomfiture by himself annexing the Dardanelles and some Greek cities in Thrace. His ambition was nothing less than to re-create for himself the old empire of Alexander the Great, from the Adriatic to the Indus. For Rome the meaning was clear. Just as there had been a time when the Mediterranean could no longer contain both Rome and Carthage, now there would not be room for both Rome and Antiochus.

It was suspected in Rome that Hannibal had been in touch with Antiochus. This would of course have been a breach of the peace treaty by which Carthage was bound not to take part in any hostilities without Rome's consent, especially not when they appeared to be directed against Rome herself. Rome had another reason to be angry with Hannibal, for his skill in reorganizing the finances of Carthage had made the Roman plans miscarry; they had hoped that the war indemnity that Carthage had to pay would cripple her, and they were disappointed. Two thousand years later, the same mistake was made by Prussia after her war with France.

A Roman commission was sent to Carthage in 195 BC, alleging that Hannibal was helping an enemy of Rome. Hannibal's position in Carthage was insecure, for he had made enemies of all those whose peculations he had stopped. With his keen sense of appreciation that the Roman commissioners could not fail to demand his surrender, and the probability that the Carthaginian Senate would agree, he withdrew himself from their grasp by a characteristic series of tricks. Pretending to be going out for a short ride, he went to his house near Thapsus. His fortune had already been embarked on a ship, and he sailed for Cercina, an island off the coast. There he was recognized by the crews of some Carthaginian ships, which was unwelcome to him as the news of his presence there could not fail to reach Carthage. In order to forestall them, Hannibal suggested to the ships' captains that they should bring their sails ashore, to provide shelter from the sun, which

Relief of a Phoenician merchant ship, showing details of its rigging and sails. By persuading the ships' captains at Cercina to bring their sails ashore to provide shelter from the sun, Hannibal was able to get away to a good start when fleeing from Carthage

they did. What they had not realized was that by so doing, they had delayed the time of their departure next day. Meanwhile, Hannibal got clean away during the night, with too much start to be intercepted. The Roman commissioners were naturally furious, and Hannibal's enemies in the Carthaginian Senate placated them by declaring him to be an outlaw, confiscating his property (such as he had left behind him), and razing his house to the ground. So was Hannibal honoured in his own country.

HANNIBAL'S LAST YEARS

HANNIBAL LANDED at Tyre, the original mother city of Carthage, now in Antiochus's hands, and was given a great reception before going on to Antioch. Antiochus, however, had gone to Ephesus; Hannibal followed him there and was welcomed by the king to whom he explained his plan for opposing Rome. It involved entrusting to Hannibal an army of ten thousand infantry and one thousand cavalry and a fleet of one hundred ships, with which he would land in Italy while Antiochus attacked Greece. The plan was divulged to the Romans by Carthage itself, for it was alleged that a man from Tyre had been found trying to get in touch with Hannibal's friends. The Romans therefore sent a mission to Ephesus to interview Antiochus and discover his intentions.

This was probably the famous occasion when the second interview between Hannibal and Scipio took place, as related by Livy and Plutarch. Scipio asked Hannibal who he thought was the greatest general in history. 'Alexander the Great', replied Hannibal. 'Whom do you put next?' inquired Scipio. 'Pyrrhus', replied Hannibal. 'Whom do you put next?' continued Scipio. 'Myself', said Hannibal. Scipio laughed and continued, 'What would you have said if you had beaten me?' 'I should have regarded myself as the greatest general of all', replied Hannibal. Scipio appreciated the compliment.

Ephesus was also the scene of an episode related by Cicero. The philosopher Phormio gave a lecture on the duties of army commanders which Hannibal attended, and when he was asked what he thought of it, he replied 'I have seen many old fools in my life, but this one beats them all.'

One member of the Roman commission, Publius Villius, made a point of repeatedly interviewing Hannibal in person, to discover what his intentions were. The result of this was to discredit Hannibal in the eyes of Antiochus, and Hannibal was never given the men and ships for which he had asked to carry the war into Italy. Rome sent an ultimatum to Antiochus to evacuate all the Greek cities which he held, and on his refusal declared war; the Syrian War had begun, 191 B.C. Antiochus now had to defend the mainland of Asia Minor, but he also sent a derisorily small force to Greece, where it took up a position at Thermopylae. The Roman Consul Manlius Acilius Glabro landed an army in Greece and routed Antiochus's troops in their historic position; this was the battle in which Marcus Porcius Cato, the Censor, distinguished himself by leading a column round the pass of the Thermopylae and attacking the enemy's rear.

The measures which it was most important for Antiochus to take were to keep the Dardanelles and to preserve sea-power in the Aegean, so that the Roman army could not cross to Asia Minor. To help Antiochus, Hannibal went to Tyre to collect a fleet from the Phoenicians and bring it to Ephesus, so that, combined with Antiochus's fleet, they would be able to defeat the Romans at sea. But Hannibal's ships encountered a fleet of Rhodians, who were allied to Rome. In the ensuing battle, fought in the Bay of Adalia, the Rhodians won; Hannibal had to break off the engagement and retire, with the result that he was unable to bring his ships into the Aegean. There, Antiochus's fleet was decisively defeated by the Romans at the battle of Myonessus, and there was now nothing to prevent their army from crossing the Dardanelles into Asia Minor.

The Roman army was now commanded by the Consul Lucius Cornelius Scipio, Scipio's brother, whom Scipio himself accompanied in the rank of Pro-Consul, in reality in command. Antiochus withdrew his army to Ephesus and asked Scipio what the Roman terms were. They were simple: evacuation by Antiochus of Asia Minor south of the Halys river, and retreat to the south of the Taurus mountains. So much Antiochus could not concede.

The two sides came to battle at Magnesia, on the Hermus river, north-east of Smyrna, in 189 B.C. The Scipios' army contained forty thousand men, including a contingent from Pergamum. Antiochus had seventy thousand infantry and twelve thousand cavalry with eighteen Indian elephants, some scythed war-chariots, and dromedaries. It is said that when the battle array of Antiochus's army was shown to Hannibal, and his opinion was asked about it, he said cynically, 'Yes, it will be enough for the Romans, however greedy they may be.' The Duke of Wellington was more open when he said

298

of the disposition of Blücher's army at Ligny, 'He will get damnably mauled.'

Hannibal was right. According to Livy, fifty-four thousand of Antiochus's army were left on the field, while the Roman losses were under four hundred. Antiochus again inquired what the Roman terms were. Scipio replied that they were the same as before. Antiochus then retreated south of the Taurus mountains.

Following the defeat of Antiochus, Hannibal appeared in a new role— as an expert in town-planning. Both Strabo and Plutarch relate that, after he left Antiochus, Hannibal went to Armenia where he persuaded King Artaxias of the advantages of siting a town in a particular stretch of countryside, and that the king requested Hannibal to superintend its construction; under the name of Artaxiata it became the capital of Armenia.

Hannibal had suspected that the peace treaty between Rome and Antiochus contained another clause providing for the surrender of his own person, and therefore took steps to avoid this fate; having embarked his treasure on a ship, he sailed to Crete. In Rome, now dominant over the eastern as well as the western Mediterranean, Lucius Cornelius Scipio was awarded the title of Asiaticus.

In Crete, Hannibal ran a danger of a different kind, for the Cretans knew that he had come with a great sum of money. Hannibal countered any desire which the Cretans might have had of helping themselves to it by filling a number of narrow-necked jars with lead and covering this with a shallow layer of gold pieces at the top. He had these heavy jars deposited in the temple of Artemis, where the Cretans jealously mounted guard over them. His real treasure Hannibal hid in some hollow bronze statues which he left lying about in his garden.

One more chance was given to Hannibal of fighting, if not Rome at least an ally of Rome. Eumenes, king of Pergamum, was at war with Prusias, king of Bithynia, to whom Hannibal (with his treasure safely brought from Crete) offered his services. Prusias's army was defeated on land, and hostilities were continued at sea. Hannibal advised Prusias to collect poisonous snakes, put them into earthenware jars, and throw them into the enemy's ships. The ribald laughter of the Pergamum sailors at these tactics, fighting with pots instead of with swords, can be imagined. But when these missiles crashed on board the Pergamum ships, which were soon crawling with snakes, the laugh was on the other side of their faces, and, as Trogus Pompeius related, 'they conceded the victory'. An early example of biological warfare.

Asia Minor had now become a Roman sphere of influence, and Rome intervened between Pergamum and Bithynia to stop this little war. In Rome, Prusias's ambassadors let out the fact that Hannibal had been helping them, and the Roman Senate gave orders for his surrender. This time there was no escape, for Hannibal was cornered 'like a bird that had grown too old to fly and had lost its tail feathers', as Plutarch put it.

The date was 183 BC, and Hannibal was sixty-four years old. He eluded the Romans once more, by taking poison, saying as he did so, 'Let us now put an end to the great anxiety of the Romans, who have thought it too lengthy, and too heavy a task, to wait for the death of a hated old man.'

Coin of Prusias I of Bithynia, who gave refuge to Hannibal and provided him with his last opportunity to fight against Rome's ally, Pergamum

So died Hannibal, denounced by his own country for which he had done so much. Within a year, Scipio Africanus also died, and in comparable circumstances, for he was accused in Rome of having negotiated the peace treaty with Carthage to his own advantage, and of embezzling public money. Summoned before the tribunal, he came with the documents which proved the perfect propriety of his conduct, but he spurned to show them. Instead, he left Rome and retired to a country house near Linterno, where he gave instructions that his tomb-stone was to bear the inscription, 'My ungrateful country shall not have my bones.'

In the same year 183 BC which saw the deaths of the greatest Carthaginian and the greatest Roman general, there also died the greatest Greek general of the day, Philopoemen. He had commanded the forces of the Achaean League, but in the course of an expedition

300

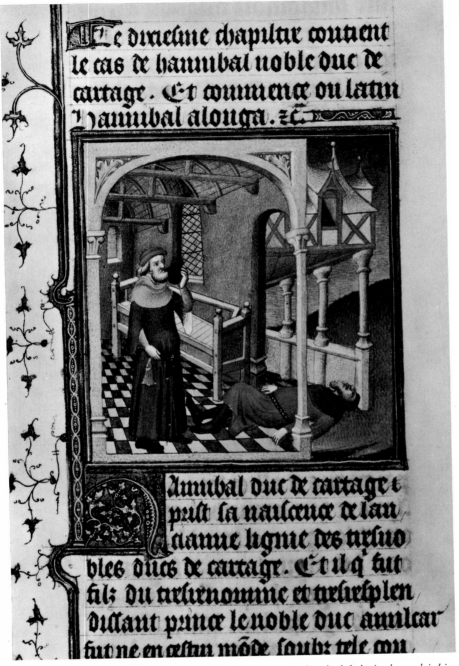

Hannibal's death in 183 BC, from a medieval manuscript. On the left he is shown drinking poison, 'to put an end to the great anxiety of the Romans', and on the right he can be seen lying dead

against the Messenians who had turned against the League he was taken prisoner and made to drink poison. His remains were returned to Megalopolis, his birthplace, and at his funeral the urn containing his ashes was carried by his fellow townsman, another general, Polybius.

AFTERMATH: THE THIRD PUNIC WAR

THE PEACE TREATY imposed by Rome on Carthage after the battle of Zama was, and was intended to be, a permanent cold war. By hard work and profitable trade, Carthage performed an economic miracle and remade a life for itself, but was perpetually harassed by Rome's protected ally Massinissa whose great ambition it was to include the dominions of Carthage under his own and to become the sole master of north Africa.

Under this constant provocation and encroachment, Carthage could do nothing except complain to Rome, for one of the clauses of the peace treaty was that Carthage could not engage in war, let alone fight an ally of Rome, without Rome's consent which would clearly never be forthcoming.

As was to be expected, Rome supported Masinissa's actions every time. Eventually, a Roman mission was sent to Carthage under Marcus Porcius Cato. He considered that Carthage was so prosperous that not only did he grant no redress against Masinissa, but when he returned to Rome he denounced Carthage as a persistent danger. As he concluded his speech he took from under his toga a splendid bunch of figs which he had brought back from Carthage, and, exclaiming that these figs grew within three days' journey by sea from Rome, he ended with his famous phrase: 'Ceterum censeo Carthaginam delendam esse' ('In other words, I consider that Carthage must be destroyed').

The provocations and encroachments by Masinissa continued, and, unable to endure them any longer or to get redress from Rome, Carthage took to arms. Rome declared war, 149 BC. Carthage sent an embassy to Rome, promising to give any satisfaction that might be required. The Senate replied that the Carthaginians would preserve their freedom, their laws, and their territory, if they sent three hundred youths, chosen from among the most noble families, as hostages. Carthage complied.

Scarcely had the hostages arrived when the Consuls, Marcus Manilius and Lucius Marcius Censorinus landed at Utica with an army of

Ruins of the Punic acropolis at Carthage, destroyed by the Romans in 146 BC. A Roman colony was subsequently established on the site by Augustus; it was captured in AD 439 by the Vandals, in 533 by Belisarius, and in 698 by the Arabs; little remains

eighty thousand men, giving to understand that the object of the expedition was to oppose Masinissa. Then, having burnt the Carthaginian fleet in the harbour of Carthage, they ordered all its inhabitants to retire to villages not less than ten miles from the coast. When the Carthaginians protested that the Roman Senate had promised that Carthage would preserve its freedom, the Consuls replied that the promise covered the *civitas,* the people of Carthage, but not the *urbs,* the city. The Romans were always eloquent in their denunciation of what they called 'Punic faith', but they were not backward themselves in such practices.

sympathy which are not extended to Scipio. The same can be said of Arthur and the Anglo-Saxons, Harold and William the Conqueror, Napoleon and Wellington. Admiration is like belief; as Shelley so eloquently showed, it is not a matter of volition, but of temperament, and therefore of taste.

SELECT BIBLIOGRAPHY

See the classical texts of Polybius, Livy, Silius Italicus, Ammianus Marcellinus, Cornelius Nepos, Plutarch, Strabo, Appian, etc.

F. W. WALBANK, *A Historical Commentary on Polybius*, Oxford University Press, 1957; contains comments on Livy, Appian, and other classical authors

T. H. DODGE, *Hannibal*, Boston and New York, Houghton Mifflin, 1891

GAVIN DE BEER, *Alps and Elephants*, London, Geoffrey Blès, 1955, and New York, Dutton, 1959; revised and enlarged edition *Hannibal's March*, London, Sidgwick & Jackson, 1967; contains detailed argument and references

On the Mediterranean and its Peoples

CECIL TORR, *Ancient Ships*, Cambridge U.P., 1894, and New York, Argonaut, 1964

ERNLE BRADFORD, *Ulysses Found*, London, Hodder & Stoughton, 1963, and Sphere, 1967; New York, Harcourt, 1964

GAVIN DE BEER, *Genetics and Prehistory*, Cambridge U.P., 1965; on Ligurians and Gauls

GAVIN DE BEER, 'Who were the Etruscans?', *Reflections of a Darwinian*, London, Nelson, 1962

CHARLES LENTHÉRIC, *La Provence maritime*, Paris, Plon, 1880

P. BOSCH-GIMPERA, 'Réflexions sur le problème des Étrusques', *Mélanges d'archéologie et d'histoire offerts à André Piganiol*, Paris, S.E.V.P.E.N., 1966

A. PIGANIOL, 'Les Étrusques. Peuple d'orient', *Cahiers d'histoire mondiale*, I, 1953, Paris, Librairie des Méridiens

Also the following volumes from the series 'Ancient Peoples and Places', London, Thames & Hudson, and New York, Praeger:

ANTONIO ARRIBAS, *The Iberians*   DONALD HARDEN, *The Phoenicians*

RAYMOND BLOCH, *The Etruscans*   A. H. MCDONALD, *Republican Rome*

L. BERNABÒ BREA, *Sicily*   A. G. WOODHEAD, *The Greeks in the West*

MARGARET GUIDO, *Sardinia*

On Elephants

SIR WILLIAM GOWERS, 'African Elephants and Ancient Authors', *African Affairs*, London, July 1948

H. H. SCULLARD, 'Hannibal's Elephants', *Numismatic Chronicle*, 8, 1948

SIR WILLIAM GOWERS and H. H. SCULLARD, 'Hannibal's Elephants Again', *Numismatic Chronicle*, 10, 1950

C. DAVIES SHERBORNE, 'The Elephant before A.D.', *Annals & Magazine of Natural History*, ser. 10, 15, 1935

FERNAND DE VISSCHER, 'Une histoire d'éléphants', *Antiquité Classique*, Brussels, 29, 1960

On the Hannibalic War in Italy

ERNESTO BIGNAMI, *L'esame di Storia Romana,* Milan, Bignami, 1955

GIANCARLO SUSINI, 'Ricerche sulla Battaglia del Trasimeno', *Annuario XI dell' Accademia Etrusca di Cortona,* 1960, Florence, Leo S. Olschki

'Studi Annibalici', *Annuario XII dell' Accademia Etrusca di Cortona,* 1964, Florence, Leo S. Olschki. Its sixteen papers include the following:

GILBERT CH. PICARD, 'Carthage au temps d'Hannibal'

VINCENZO TUSA, 'La questione Fenicio-Punica in Sicilia'

GIOVANNI VITUCCI, 'Un nuovo episodio della seconda guerra Punica?'

NEVIO DEGRASSI, 'La zona archeologica di Canne della Battaglia'

FERNANDA BERTOCCHI, 'Recenti scavi ai sepolcreti di Canne'

LUCIANO LAURENZI, 'Perche Annibale no assediò Roma'

GIANCARLO SUSINI, 'L'archeologia della guerra annibalica'

PIETRO ROMANELLI, 'Roma e i Libi durante le guerre Puniche'

FRANCESCO ROSATI, 'La monetazione Annibalica'

A. D. FITTON BROWN, 'La stratégie romaine, 218–216 a.C.'

GILBERT CH. PICARD, 'Le portrait d'Hannibal: hypothèse nouvelle'

ANTONINO DI VITA, 'Le stele puniche dal recinto di Zeus Meilichios a Selinunte'

UMBERTO CIOTTI, 'La Battaglia al Lago Plestino'

On the Oracle at Delphi

H. W. PARKE, *Greek Oracles*, London, Hutchinson, 1967, and New York, Hillary House, 1967

On the Iconography of Hannibal

GILBERT CH. PICARD, 'Le portrait d'Hannibal' in 'Studi Annibalici' *supra*

E. S. G. ROBINSON, 'Punic Coins and their Bearing on the Roman Republican Series', *Essays in Roman Coinage presented to Harold Mattingly,* ed. R. A. G. Carson and C. H. V. Sutherland, Oxford University Press, 1956

On Writing

JACQUETTA HAWKES and SIR LEONARD WOOLLEY, *Prehistory and the Beginnings of Civilization,* London, Allen & Unwin, 1963, and New York, Harper and Row, 1963

LIST AND SOURCES OF ILLUSTRATIONS

Unless otherwise specified the photographs reproduced were supplied by the author or taken from the Thames and Hudson archives. The maps and plans were drawn by S. Schotten

I THE STAGE AND THE PLAYERS

9 North entrance to the Palace of Minos at Knossos, Crete. Photo Max Hirmer

11 The triumphal monument of Augustus at La Turbie near Monaco, built in 6 BC to commemorate the Roman victory over the Ligurian tribes who lived along the Riviera and in the Western Alps. The names of the tribes were recorded by Pliny before the monument was ruined.

12 The eruption of Santorin in 1925. The eruption of this volcano, 110 km. north of Crete, in the fifteenth century BC is believed to have annihilated Minoan sea-power and to have been the origin of the story of Atlantis

13 Tablets written in Minoan Linear A and Linear B scripts, respectively in the Heraklion Museum and the British Museum, London. Michael Ventris showed Linear B to be Greek; by applying to script A some of the phonetic values of script B, Professor Cyrus H. Gordon demonstrated that the language of script A was probably North Semitic. Photos Peter Clayton; courtesy, Trustees of the British Museum

15 The Lion Gate of Mycenae. After the collapse of the Minoan empire sea-power in the Mediterranean devolved on the Mycenaean Greeks, but they held it for only a few centuries before they were destroyed by the Dorians. The seas were then open to the Phoenicians. Photo Max Hirmer

16 Remains of the Temple of Zeus at Acragas (Agrigentum), Sicily, with the giant figure of Atlas. Acragas was founded by the Greeks from Gela in the seventh century BC; it was praised by Pindar above all cities, and was renowned as the birthplace of the philosopher Empedocles. Photo Edwin Smith

17 The island of Ischia, first called Pithecussae, opposite the Bay of Naples. Founded by Greeks from Chalcis, it was among the earliest Greek settlements in the West. A cup discovered there bears possibly the earliest known inscription in Greek. Photo Italian State Tourist Office

18 Coin struck to commemorate the alliance between Crotona and Sybaris: (obverse) the tripod of Crotona; (reverse) the bull of Sybaris. Crotona's army under the athlete Milo de-stroyed Sybaris completely (510 BC) but it was refounded later. British Museum, London. Photo John Webb

19 The entrance to the Old Harbour of Marseilles, the inlet where c. 600 BC Phoenician Greeks founded the settlement of Massalia. Engraving from J. F. Albanis Beaumont, *Select views of the Antiquities and Harbours in the South of France*, 1797
Reverse of a drachma from Massalia, c. 350 BC, depicting a lion and bearing the inscription MASSA. British Museum, London. Photo John Webb

20 The Temple of Apollo at Delphi at the foot of Mount Parnassus. Photo Rosmarie Pierer

21 River boats carrying timber from the forests of Lebanon. Assyrian relief in gypsum, from the palace of Sargon II (722–705 BC) at Khorsabad, Iraq. Louvre, Paris; photo courtesy of the museum

22 Ivory plaque from Nimrud, eighth to seventh century BC, showing a priestess wearing the horns and disk of the Egyptian goddess Hathor, while the wings surrounding her body are an attribute of the Phoenician Ashtoreth. Iraq Museum, Baghdad. Photo courtesy British School of Archaeology in Iraq and Professor Sir Max Mallowan

Two necklaces and pendants from Tharros, Sardinia, of gold, coloured glass beads, cornelian, agate, and amber, examples of Phoenician manufacture of ornaments, sixth century BC. British Museum, London. Photo courtesy Trustees of the British Museum

23 Gold belt end, seventh to sixth century BC, with Phoenician embossed and granulated decorative motifs, from Aliseda, Spain. Museo Arqueologico Nacional, Madrid; photo courtesy of the museum

24 Pendant glass heads from Carthage, sixth to fourth century BC. Louvre, Paris; photos courtesy of the museum

25 Obelisks in the enclosure behind the temple at Byblos in Phoenicia. Photo Arthaud

26 The alphabet from the tenth century BC. All 22 Phoenician letters were consonants, but some of them (*alpha, epsilon, eta, iota, omicron*) became vowels in Greek, which added two more vowels (*upsilon, omega*) and three con-

sonants (*chi*, *phi*, *psi*). The Phoenician alphabet had three sibilants (*samekh*, *tsade*, *shin*). After Harden

27 Fragment of a Punic inscription, fourth to third century BC, from Carthage. The text concerns regulations by 'overseers of payments' for sacrifices, for all kinds of which there were tariffs to be paid to the priests. British Museum, London; photo courtesy of the Trustees of the British Museum

28 Tyre, mother city of Carthage, originally built on an island. Photo Institut Français d' Archéologie, Beirut

Repoussé bronze band showing tribute being shipped from Tyre; from the Assyrian gates of Balawat built by Shalmaneser III (858–825 BC) to commemorate his victories. British Museum, London; photo courtesy Trustees of the British Museum

29 Reverse of a shekel of Sidon, showing the fortified city from the sea with warships before the walls; obverse of a coin of Adramalek of Byblos, showing a warship manned by armed soldiers. Both mid-fifth century BC. British Museum, London. Photos John Webb

30, 31 Map of the Mediterranean, showing the spread of Greek and Phoenician influence throughout the ancient world

32 Coloured limestone sarcophagus from Amathus, Cyprus, seventh century BC, showing a procession with a royal chariot preceded by an advance guard of horsemen. The Metropolitan Museum of Art, New York, Cesnola Collection; photo courtesy of the museum

Fragment of a terracotta statuette of a woman, from Idalion, Cyprus, showing Syriac and Asiatic influences. Louvre, Paris. Photo M. Chuzeville

34 Site of the Phoenician settlement of Gades (modern Cadiz), showing the change of coastline since ancient times (after Harden)

Punic tombs excavated at Punta de la Vaca, Gades (Cadiz) in 1912. Photo Mas

35 Askos, or small jug, in the shape of the head of a Negro, from Lilybaeum (Marsala), Sicily, fourth to third century BC. Photo Leonard von Matt
Staircase at the entrance of the Punic town on the island of Motya, sixth century BC

36 Remains of the citadel of the Punic settlement of Soluntum, on the north coast of Sicily, near Palermo. Photo Publifoto, Palermo

37 The Bay of Carthage with the sands known as the 'Plage d'Amilcar'. Photo Roger-Viollet

38 The ancient Punic harbour at Carthage. Photo Roger-Viollet

39 Plan of the inner city of Carthage (after Harden)

40 Stele of Baalyaton, from Umm el Amad near

Tyre, fourth or early third century BC. Ny Carlsberg Glyptotek, Copenhagen; photo courtesy of the museum

Stele of Baal Hammon, from Lilybaeum (Marsala), Sicily. Museo Nazionale, Palermo; photo courtesy of the museum

41 The precinct of the goddess Tanit at Salammbô, Carthage. Photo Musée Alaoui, Bardo, Tunis

Funerary urns from the Precinct of Tanit, Carthage, eighth to fourth century BC. Ashmolean Museum, Oxford; photos courtesy of the museum

42 Limestone stele with inlaid slab recording seventeen generations of priests of Tanit, from Carthage, fourth century BC. Museo di Antichità, Turin

Limestone obelisk showing a priest holding an infant for sacrifice, from the Precinct of Tanit at Salammbô, Carthage, fourth century BC. Musée Alaoui, Bardo, Tunis; photo courtesy of the museum

43 Bronze figurine of an Etruscan peasant ploughing with yoked oxen, sixth century BC, found near Arezzo. Museo di Villa Giulia, Rome. Photo Gabinetto Fotografico Nazionale, Rome

44 Detail of one of the bands of the bronze *situla* or pail from the Etruscan necropolis of La Certosa near Bologna, sixth to fifth century BC. Museo Civico, Bologna; photo courtesy of the museum

45 Map of Italy and Sicily, showing principal Etruscan settlements and spheres of Etruscan, Greek and Phoenician influence; seventh to sixth century BC (after Bloch)

46 Etruscan bronze model of a liver, third century BC, found near Piacenza. Museo Civico, Piacenza; photo courtesy of the museum

Etruscan engraved bronze mirror, fourth century BC, from Vulci. Museo Gregoriano, Vatican. Photo Archivio Fotografico dei Gallerie e Musei Vaticani

47 Ivory writing tablet from Marsiglia d'Albegna, *c.* 700 BC. Museo Archeologico, Florence; photo courtesy of the museum

48 Detail of an Etruscan stele from Felsina (Bologna), third century BC, showing a well-armed horseman attacking a naked warrior, presumed to be a Gaul. Museo Civico, Bologna; photo courtesy of the museum

50 Reconstruction (model) of a dwelling-hut of the Villanovan period (eighth century BC), characteristic of the Early Iron Age in Etruria. Photo Fototeca Unione, Rome

51 Fragment from the *Ara pietatis* in Rome, showing the banquet of the Vestal Virgins, first century AD. Museo dei Conservatori, Rome; photo courtesy of the museum

52 Reverse of a bronze coin of Antoninus Pius,

c. 150 AD, showing Mars and Rhea Silva; reverse of a Roman Republican denarius showing Romulus and Remus suckled by the she-wolf, and the shepherd Faustulus. British Museum, London. Photos John Webb

55 Stone funerary stele of Avele Feluske, *c*. 650 BC, bearing one of the earliest known Etruscan inscriptions. Museo Archeologico, Florence; photo courtesy of the museum

The opening into the river Tiber of the *Cloaca Maxima*, built in the reign of Tarquin the Elder (616–578 BC) to drain the Forum in Rome

56 Terracotta statuette of Aeneas and Anchises from Veii, fifth century BC. Museo di Villa Giulia, Rome
Coin of Antoninus Pius (138–161 AD) showing Aeneas escaping from Troy carrying his father Anchises and leading his son Ascanius. British Museum, London. Photo John Webb

57 Roman mosaic (detail) at Low Ham, Somerset, showing Venus (upper panel) and Dido and Aeneas embracing. Somerset County Museum, Taunton. Photo courtesy of the Warburg Institute, University of London

58 Roman Republican bronze coin bearing the double-headed profile of Janus; reverse of a sestertius of Nero showing the Temple of Janus with its doors closed. British Museum, London. Photos John Webb

Relief on the altar of the Temple of Neptune in Rome, *c*. 40 BC. Photo Alinari

61 Fresco found in 1853 in the Via Graziosa, Rome (one of several illustrating episodes from Homer's *Odyssey*): Odysseus in the land of the Laestrygones. First to second century AD. Vatican Library. Photo Archivio Fotografico dei Gallerie e Musei Vaticani

62 Base of the monument dedicated at Delphi by Gelon of Syracuse after his victory at the battle of Himera, 480 BC. Photo Antonio Giuliano
Votive stele representing the 'Mourning Athena'. Acropolis Museum, Athens. Photo Max Hirmer

63 Silver decadrachm of Syracuse, the so-called 'demareteion', 480–479 BC. The original demareteion pieces were said to have been struck by Gelon's wife Demarete from the gold crown sent to her by the Carthaginians as a thank-offering for her good offices after their defeat at Panormus. British Museum, London. Photo John Webb

64 The unfinished Greek Temple at Segesta, late fifth century BC. Photo Italian State Tourist Office

67 One of the Dioscuri, from the left pedestal of the Arch of Diocletian in Rome, third century AD. The Dioscuri, Castor and Pollux, sons of Jupiter, were the legendary protectors and saviours of Rome. They were believed to have intervened in the Battle of Lake Regillus and

to have appeared in the Forum in Rome on the same day to announce the victory. Photo German Archaeological Institute, Rome

68 View of Lake Albanus at the foot of Monte Cavo. Photo Italian State Tourist Office

69 Head of the Apollo of Veii, terracotta, sixth century BC. Photo Anderson

70 Bronze figurine of a Gaulish warrior, late third century BC, found near Rome. Staatliche Museen, Berlin

71 Bronze figurine of a Gaulish prisoner, third century AD, from Gaul. British Museum, London

Part of the painted Tomb of the Warrior from Paestum, fourth century BC. Museo Nazionale, Naples. Photo Mansell-Brogi

72 Reconstruction (model) of the Temple of Fortuna at Praeneste (Palestrina), second to first century BC. The temple was seriously damaged and almost ruined during the Sullan Civil War (88 BC). Museo Archeologico, Praeneste. Photo Fototeca Unione, Rome

75 Campanian landscape with part of the aqueduct built by the Emperor Claudius in AD 52. Photo Mansell-Anderson

76 Bust of Pyrrhus (*c*. 318–272 BC), king of Epirus, found at Herculaneum. Museo Nazionale, Naples. Photo Mansell-Anderson

77 Seated statue of a goddess of Tarentum (Taranto), possibly representing Persephone; fifth century BC. Staatliche Museen, Berlin

II THE RIVALS: CARTHAGE AND ROME

79 Part of a relief from the Temple of Fortuna at Praeneste depicting a Roman bireme with armed legionaries, first century BC. Musei e Gallerie Vaticani

80 Punic text invoking Ashtoreth on a gold tablet from the Etruscan temple at Pyrgi (Santa Severa); sixth century BC

81 Etruscan bronze helmet captured by the fleet of Hiero I of Syracuse off Cumae in 474 BC. British Museum, London; photo courtesy Trustees of the British Museum

82 Bronze coin of the Mamertini of Messana (Messina), third century BC. British Museum, London. Photo John Webb

83 Bust of Hiero II of Syracuse (269–216 BC). Museo Capitolino, Rome. Photo Mansell-Alinari

The great altar of Hiero II at Syracuse in the form of a stadium. Photo Mansell-Anderson

84 Roman warship showing the inventions of grappling irons and gangplanks for boarding enemy ships. From J. C. de Folard, *Histoire de Polybe*, 1827–30

Triumphal column of Caius Duilius in the Forum, Rome, decorated with prows of ships captured from the Carthaginians. From E. Hennebert, *Histoire d'Annibal*, vol. I, 1870–91

87 The cliffs of Mount Eryx in western Sicily. Photo Leonard von Matt
Entrance to the harbour of Carthagena, the principal Carthaginian base in Spain. Photo Mas

92, 93 Map of the western Mediterranean to illustrate the approximate route of Hannibal's march (218 BC) from Spain to Italy, and the campaign against Rome in the early part of the Second Punic War

96 Presumed portrait busts of Hannibal: (1) marble head in the Ny Carlsberg Glyptotek, Copenhagen; (2) bronze head from Volubilis, Morocco, now in Rabat Museum. Both after G. C. Picard, 'Le portrait d'Hannibal', in *Annuario XII dell'Accademia Etrusca di Cortona*, 1964

97 Obverse of a Punic silver double shekel struck at Carthagena, *c.* 220 BC, showing a beardless head of Melqart which is generally accepted as a portrait of Hannibal. British Museum, London. Photo John Webb

99 Punic brass armour, decorated breast and back-plates with shoulder braces and belt, from a tomb at Ksour-es-Sad, Tunisia, third century BC. Musée Alaoui, Bardo, Tunis; photo courtesy of the museum
Hoplites, heavy infantry, depicted on the Chigi vase found at Veii. Protocorinthian, mid-seventh century BC. Museo di Villa Giulia, Rome. Photo Gabinetto Fotografico Nazionale

100 Reverse of a Punic coin minted at Carthagena, *c.* 220 BC, depicting a palm tree and a Numidian horse, both symbolic of north Africa. British Museum, London. Photo John Webb

101 Reverse of a tetradrachm of Seleucus I of Syria, minted at Pergamum *c.* 280 BC, depicting an Indian elephant; reverse of a decadrachm of Alexander the Great, minted at Babylon to commemorate his conquest of the Punjab (326 BC), depicting Alexander on horseback attacking King Porus on an Indian elephant. Both British Museum, London. Photos John Webb

102 Terracotta figure of an Indian war elephant of Antiochus I of Syria (280–261 BC) crushing a Galatian warrior. Louvre, Paris. Photo Giraudon

103 Painted dish from Capena, in Campania, of Etruscan style, third century BC. It shows an Indian elephant carrying a driver (*mahout*) and a castle (*howdah*) containing two Macedonian warriors, followed by a baby elephant. Museo di Villa Giulia, Rome. Photo Gabinetto Nazionale Fotografico

Silver phalera (military decoration) showing an Indian elephant bearing a driver with goad

in hand and a castle with two soldiers. Hermitage, Leningrad

104 Reverse of a tetradrachm of Antiochus III of Syria showing an Indian elephant, minted at Ecbatana *c.* 205–200 BC. British Museum, London. Photo John Webb

105 Roman mosaic of the Imperial period at Ostia, showing an African elephant. Museo delle Corporazioni, Ostia

106 Reverses of Carthaginian silver coins from Hannibal's time, showing African elephants. British Museum, London. Photos John Webb

107 Roman cast bronze bar (*aes signatum*), weight approx. 5 lb, depicting (obverse) a sow, and (reverse) an Indian elephant. British Museum, London. Photo John Webb

110 Saguntum (Sagunto): general view of the site of the ancient city captured by the Carthaginians under Hannibal in 219 BC; the fall of the city precipitated the outbreak of the Second Punic War. Photo Mas

112 The siege of Saguntum, illuminated miniature from *Les Histoires Romaines de Jean Mansel*, 1454–60. Bibliothèque de l'Arsenal, Paris

117 Bronze statuette of a Roman legionary, second century AD. British Museum, London; photo courtesy Trustees of the British Museum

Inscribed funerary stele of Favonius Facilis, a Roman centurion of the XXth legion in Britain, second century AD. Colchester and Essex Museum; photo courtesy of the museum

III OVER THE ALPS AND FAR AWAY

119 View from Montdauphin looking north across the upper basin of the river Durance towards the Col du Mont-Genèvre, which may have been Hannibal's intended pass

121 The foothills of the Pyrenees at their eastern extremity near Banyuls. Photo Photothèque Française, Paris

123 Ruins of the ancient Greek settlement of Emporiae (Ampurias). It is now known as Castellón de Ampurias. Photo Spanish National Tourist Office

125 The river Rhône looking from Fourques towards Arles

The river Rhône at Avignon. Photo French Government Tourist Office

128, 129 Hannibal's crossing of the Rhône, engraving from J. C. de Folard, *Histoire de Polybe*, 1727–30

133 Stele found at Kleitor in Arcadia, said to represent the Greek general and historian Polybius (202–120 BC). Formerly in Berlin. Photo Alinari

IV HANNIBAL ROUTS THE ROMANS

COLOUR PLATES

I *facing page 32*
Ivory plaque inlaid with glass pastes and partly covered with gold foil, eighth century BC, from Nimrud. The Negroid features and curly close-cropped hair of the boy are evidence of Phoenician influence. British Museum, London; courtesy, Sir Max Mallowan and the Trustees of the British Museum. Photo Eileen Tweedy

II *facing page 33*
Phoenician glass scent bottle, fifth to fourth century BC, from Cyprus. The Metropolitan Museum of Art, New York; photo courtesy of the museum

III *facing page 48*
Inscribed stele beneath the black marble pavement known as the *Lapis Niger* in the Forum, Rome; the inscription, still not fully understood, dates from *c.* 500 BC. Photo Peter Clayton

IV *facing page 49*
Aeneas received by King Latinus on the Latin shore, from a manuscript copy of Virgil's *Aeneid* of the fourth century AD (*Codex Vaticanus Latinus* 3225). Biblioteca Apostolica Vaticana

V *facing page 80*
Terracotta figure of a man and his wife, from the lid of an Etruscan sarcophagus from Caere, *c.* 500 BC. Museo di Villa Giulia, Rome. Photo Georgina Masson.

VI *facing page 81*
Handle of an Etruscan bronze cista depicting two armed warriors carrying the body of a dead comrade, probably fourth century BC, from Praeneste. Museo di Villa Giulia, Rome. Photo Aleandro Anchora

VII *facing page 88*
Punto Milazzo on the north coast of Sicily. Photo Ciganovic

VIII *facing page 89*
Reverse of a gold stater of Ptolemy I of Egypt (266–283 BC) depicting a quadriga of elephants drawing a chariot; diameter of coin 1.5 cm. British Museum, London. Photo Peter Clayton

IX *facing page 184*
Jacques-Louis David, *Napoleon crossing the St Bernard Pass* (1800). Versailles, Château. Photo Bulloz

X *facing page 185*
The source of the river Po on the north flank of Monte Viso. Photo Ciganovic

XI *facing page 200*
Fragment of a wall-painting from a tomb on the Esquiline, Rome, third or early second century BC. The picture is divided into four bands, in the first of which only a fragment of a leg and a foot remains. In the second two sentinels can be seen, with the two leaders whose names are given: M. Fannius and Q. Fabius. Of Q. Fabius only part of the arms and legs remains; in one hand he holds a spear. The same figures, with their names clearly visible, also appear in the third band: M. Fannius is followed by a trumpeter and Q. Fabius by four soldiers. In the fourth band part of a battle scene is shown. The events depicted may refer to the victory of Q. Fabius Rullianus over the Samnites at the battle of Sentinum in 295 BC; his great-grandson Q. Fabius Maximus Cunctator was to achieve fame in the war against Hannibal. Capitoline Museum, Rome. Photo Scala

XII *facing page 201*
The river Vulturnus near Venafrum. Photo Pedone

XIII *facing page 264*
The death of Archimedes, Roman mosaic, probably third century AD. Städelches Kunstinstitut, Frankfurt on Main. Photo Kurt Haase

XIV *facing page 265*
Monument to a Numidian prince near Dugga, Tunisia, third or second century BC. Photo Bury Peerless

XV *facing page 280*
Cap Bon, the point on the north coast of Africa nearest to Sicily. Photo Bury Peerless

XVI *facing page 281*
Stele and other remains on the site of Punic Carthage. Photo Bury Peerless

Page numbers in italics refer to illustrations

DATE DUE

OCT 8 '71			
FEB 3 '73			
NO 24 '93			